Understanding Religious Conversion

Understanding Religious Conversion

Lewis R. Rambo

Yale University Press

New Haven and London

Designed by Deborah Dutton.
Set in Palatino type by The Composing Room of Michigan, Inc., Grand Rapids, Michigan.
Printed in the United States of America

Library of Congress Cataloging-in-Publication Data

Rambo, Lewis R. (Lewis Ray), 1943–
    Understanding religious conversion / Lewis R. Rambo.
        p.   cm.
    Includes bibliographical references and index.
    ISBN 0-300-05283-9 (cloth)
            0-300-06515-9 (pbk.)
    1. Conversion.   I. Title.
BL639.R35   1993
291.4'2—dc20   92-39404
                                                            CIP

A catalogue record for this book is available from the British Library.

The paper in this book meets the guidelines for permanence and durability of the Committee on Production Guidelines for Book Longevity of the Council on Library Resources.

10 9 8 7 6 5 4

To
    Anna Catherine Rambo
     Beloved daughter
    Roy M. Carlisle
    Corina Chan
    Warren Lee
     Extraordinary friends

Contents

Figures

Preface

This book is both a scholarly enterprise and a personal journey into questions of how faith is possible in the modern world. What are the factors that make conversion viable for people? How do we explain different kinds of conversion? How (or perhaps why) do we evaluate the quality of a conversion? These and other questions haunt and provoke me in the quest to understand the phenomenon of religious conversion.

The process of researching and writing the book has been an adventure. My investigations of conversion began more than a decade ago, starting with extensive reading in psychological literature. It was not long before I came to feel that psychology alone was not sufficient to interpret the nature of religious change in either individuals or groups, and I turned to the work of sociologists, particularly to explore the nature of "cults" and "New Religious Movements." As I read more deeply in the sociological literature, its limitations also became apparent when I began to consider the importance of cultural issues. Forays into cultural anthropology unveiled an exciting discipline that promised new insights into the conversion process. Subsequently I discovered missiology, a field of scholarship initiated by missionaries working in cross-cultural settings that confront them daily with the complexities of interwoven religious, cultural, and societal issues affecting and effecting change. (Ironically, missiologists, concerned primarily with the religious or spiritual dimensions of conversion, are frequently critical of secular academics, whom they see, not unjustly, as tending to minimize religious factors.)

While delving into these fields of study, I also conducted numerous interviews with converts from a wide variety of backgrounds: men and women who had embraced the Unification Church, Jews who had become Christians and Christians who had become Jews, Japanese secularists who had adopted Christianity, and Chinese people with little or no religious background (because of official government discouragement) who had become Christians. I traveled extensively: to Japan and Korea to compare and contrast the experience and perceptions of conversion in those countries, and to Israel for extended study as a Lady Davis Fellow and Visiting Professor of Comparative Religions at Jerusalem's Hebrew University. I had the opportunity to exchange views with such noted scholars as Janet Aviad, Steven Kaplan, and Nehemiah Levtzion and to interview converts between Judaism and Christianity (in both directions) as well as secular Jews who had adopted Orthodox Judaism.[1]

The subject of conversion has occupied (perhaps preoccupied) much of my personal and professional life. Awareness about my perspectives and perceptions became clearer as I did this research, so let me say at the outset that I subscribe to the view that all scholarship is ultimately a projection of one's own personal predicaments.[2]

What is authentic conversion to me? As will be apparent, my own approach to that question is unavoidably influenced by my sectarian past, but I see "genuine" conversion as a total transformation of the person by the power of God. While this transformation occurs through the mediation of social, cultural, personal, and religious forces (as I show in this book), I believe that conversion needs to be radical, striking to the root of the human predicament. For me, that root is a vortex of vulnerability.[3] Given my acceptance that human beings are capable of infinite self-deception and that our proclivities are often anti-God, we require change that is foundational and pervasive. Every aspect of human existence (as I have been taught to see it) is corrupted by perversity and the influences of the "world," which generally point us in the direction of evil. I believe that conversion requires the intervention of God to deliver me from the captivity that I perceive ensnaring me.

I was reared in the Church of Christ, a religious movement founded in the nineteenth century with the goal of restoring "New Testament Christianity." My life revolved around this religious sect until about five years ago, and my consciousness was shaped by that experience in profound ways. My mother took my younger brother and me to church every Sunday morning,

Sunday night, and Wednesday night. Twice a year we attended a "gospel meeting" (the Church of Christ equivalent of revivals), the goal of which was to save our souls. This conservative denomination has very precise notions of religious change. We were taught that salvation was possible only by hearing the gospel, believing in Jesus Christ as the Son of God, adopting a self-judgment of evil and confessing our pervasive and pernicious sins, affirming our faith in Jesus as our personal Savior, and being baptized by total immersion.

I found that the Church of Christ stressed knowledge of the Bible and obedience to God's will: "correct" knowledge and "right" behavior were essential. Emotional issues like joy and peace and blessedness were regarded as secondary or irrelevant alongside knowledge and action (yet knowledge and action, I see now, are motivated by fear, self-loathing, and insecurity—emotional issues if ever there were any).

During these formative experiences, I had friends in our small-town community of Comanche, Texas, who were Southern Baptists or Methodists. I was taught that they were "lost" because they proclaimed an "easy" gospel of merely believing in Jesus and inviting him into their hearts in order to be eternally saved. We Church of Christ folk were, by contrast, serious and intense and fearful. The only thing that seemed eternal to us was the threat of damnation, not salvation. Still, we believed that we had THE TRUTH and could prove it by quoting verbatim (not just citing the passage reference, mind you) specific chapters and verses from the Bible.

It seemed then—and still does—that it was necessary for Church of Christ believers to work very hard at salvation; we dismissed the Baptist notion of "eternal security" as mere wishful thinking. The easy consolation and emotional gratifications of other denominations were deemed deceptive and seductive. For years I debated and discussed this difference with friends. How could the Church of Christ have "the Truth" and yet derive such little joy from it, while Baptists could enjoy such intense emotional experiences?

I was and am fascinated by the fact that in a town of only four thousand inhabitants it was possible for individuals to have such divergent perspectives on the nature of salvation. Those differences shaped us and ultimately separated us. I have come to believe that, whatever may be "true" theologically, the singular home-church community of faith has a definitive influence on a person's experience of conversion. There are many different experiences of salvation and no one way is mandatory. Stated starkly, conversion is what a faith group says it is.

My approach to conversion is also shaped by my current orientation to the human sciences. I strive to transmit, appropriate, and critique psychology, anthropology, and sociology. My particular appropriation of the human sciences follows several specific themes or motifs, focusing on empathy, personal experience, and the complexity of the human predicament.

Empathy, the authentic desire and ability to get inside another person's skin, is a capacity I strive to foster in my work. I advocate seeing the world from the perspective of the "other." Lived experience is another crucial theme for me. I affirm the importance of each person and group's journey, history, and ethos. Anton Boisen spoke of the "living human document."[4] We need to see our lives, both individual and collective, as important sources of information, insight, experience, and (dare I say?) revelation.

As I read the literature, spoke with acknowledged experts, attended conferences and seminars, and shared reflections with numerous people, I began to believe that the published material on conversion resembled a metropolitan train yard crowded with separate tracks that ran parallel to each other, where each individual train had its own assigned track and never crossed over to another. I began to suspect that only a few scholars of conversion were aware that the subject was traversed by more than one track, and that there could even be more than one train on each track.

Much that has been written in the human sciences about religion and conversion seems to be flawed by reductionism. The secular assumptions that pervade the human sciences result in an often derogatory tone by those purporting to "study" religious phenomena. Little wonder that many (though not all) religious people see the "psychology of religion," the "sociology of religion," and the "anthropology of religion" as subversive at best, completely erroneous at worst. Work published in the human sciences is regarded first with suspicion, then, if at all, as interesting or useful only to professionals in the field of religion.

I hope that religious people may see this book as helpful and interesting because it respects the religious perspective while also incorporating the importance of personal, social, and cultural issues. I also hope that the book will expand the horizons of religious interpretation of conversion. On the other hand, I trust that scholars in the human sciences will find it valuable from an academic standpoint, demonstrating in a new way the crucial role of multiple religious factors in conversion.

Acknowledgments

One of my best friends, Warren Lee, often reminds me that the central virtues in life are gratitude, humility, and hope. Upon completion of this book I felt gratitude and humility in overwhelming measure. As I attempt to thank adequately all those who have played direct and indirect roles in its creation, faces from my past and present rush through my mind's eye. I hope that anyone who is inadvertently left out will forgive me for the oversight.

Abilene Christian University offered me my first taste of the wider world. Under the tutelage of Professors LeMoine G. Lewis (of blessed memory), Anthony L. Ash, James Culp, Everett Ferguson, and Dale Hesser, among many others, I came to understand that the life of the mind and the life of faith are rich partners. In more recent years, Carley Dodd, David Lewis, Jack Reese, and Charles Siebert have befriended me. Encompassing all those years, James and Francis Fulbright have given me constant love.

At Yale University Divinity School James E. Dittes, Paul Holmer, Abraham J. Malherbe, and Sidney Ahlstrom, among others, made my years there an intellectual delight. At University of Chicago Divinity School Don S. Browning, Donald Capps (now at Princeton Theological Seminary), Peter Homans, and Martin E. Marty were superlative mentors and guides. Fellow students, especially Gary Alexander, Lucy Bregman, Tom Green (of blessed memory), Richard Hutch, Robert Moore, Greg Schneiders, and Judith Van-Herik, among others, provided a constant source of friendship and new ideas.

After completing my Ph.D. at the University of Chicago I taught psychology at Trinity College in Deerfield, Illinois, for three years. Under the dynamic leadership of Dean J. Edward Hakes, the school flourished. I thank Clark Barshinger, Mark DenBroeder, Kirk Farnsworth, and Mark Noll for being such delightful colleagues. I also thank Trinity for inviting me to deliver the Staley Lectures in 1979. I gave the Staley Lectures at Abilene Christian University in 1980 as well, which offered me an opportunity to present a very early version of this book. I appreciate the encouragement given to me by the Staley Foundation.

For the past fourteen years I have enjoyed the privilege of teaching at San Francisco Theological Seminary in San Anselmo and the Graduate Theological Union in Berkeley, California. Both institutions have treated me graciously. I am especially indebted to the faculty, students, staff, and board of SFTS for their intellectual curiosity, profound faith, passion for social justice, and affirmation of pluralism. The Seminary has provided me with faculty resource funds and sabbatical leaves that have made it possible to devote extended periods to research and writing. Presidents Arnold Come, Bob Barr, and Randy Taylor and Deans Surgit Singh, Browne Barr, Walter Davis, Don Buteyn, and Lewis Mudge have been constant sources of encouragement. Ted Stein has been an especially wonderful friend and colleague. Sandra Brown, Jana Childers, Robert Coote, Walt Davis, Roy Fairchild, David Glick, Elizabeth Liebert, James Noel, Christopher Ocker, Steve Ott, Howard Rice, and Herman Waetjen are among the colleagues who have made my life such a banquet. Staff members Loel Millar, Pat Lista-Mei, and Mary Poletti have "saved" me with their gift for organization and detail.

The Graduate Theological Union in Berkeley is an amazing center for scholarship. I thank Robert Barr, Judith Berling, Rosemary Chinnici, Valerie DeMarinis, Clare Fischer, Donald Gelpi, Daniel Matt, Timothy Lull, Ben Silva-Netto, Archie Smith, Charles Taylor, Claude Welch, and all the students who have enriched my understanding of faith and scholarship. I especially want to acknowledge the research funds provided by the GTU, the Lily Endowment, and the Luce Foundation. The Center for the Study of New Religious Movements provided a unique entrée to the fascinating world of "alternative religions."

The members of the Church of Christ in San Rafael, California, have been sources of faith and nurture. It was a distinct honor to serve them as their minister from 1978 to 1985.

This book is the fruition of conversations, readings, debates, conferences, and a host of other activities provided by the community of scholars who have devoted themselves to the study of conversion. I cannot repay the debt I owe them. The bibliography lists some but not all of these students of religious change. I have also acknowledged intellectual debts in my notes and bibliography. Any failure to attribute sources properly is due to oversight. I owe a debt as well to the individuals and groups who have given of themselves through various interviews and meetings. Many people come to mind as I write these words. Those who have especially encouraged this project include James Beckford, Walter Conn, H. Newton Malony, Lamin Sanneh, Alan Segal, Araceli Suzara, and Guy E. Swanson.

My trips to Israel during sabbaticals in the fall of 1985 and 1986 allowed me to interact with a group of remarkable people. Yaakov Ariel, Na'im Ateek, Benjamin Beit-Hallahmi, Steve Kaplan, Nehemiah Levtzion, Ruby Little, Joseph Shulam, and Gedaliahu G. Stroumsa were especially helpful. In 1986 I was a Lady Davis Fellow at the Hebrew University of Jerusalem, and I offer my sincere gratitude for the generosity and kindness of the staff of the Lady Davis Fellowship Trust. I am also grateful to the Ecumenical Institute for Advanced Research at Tantur. Landrum Boling, the Kenneth Bailey family, and the staff provided a home away from home that was especially nurturing.

In the fall of 1985, I spent time in Japan and Korea. Tomoko Hoshino was a splendid friend and host, whose extensive contacts and expert translation made the trip very rewarding. In Korea, Chang Bok Chung of the Presbyterian Theological Seminary, Byong-Suh Kim of Ewha University, and former SFTS/GTU student Jong-Hyon Chun all provided hospitality and guidance.

Whatever literary merits this book possesses can be attributed to four San Francisco Bay Area free-lance editors who worked with me over the past three years: Dorothy Wall, Elizabeth L. Morgan, Lawrence A. Reh, and Corina Chan. In addition to their editorial acumen, their constant patience, encouragement, and insight enabled me to complete the project. Thank you so much for living with me in the writing trenches.

No one deserves more thanks for the completion of this book than Roy Carlisle. He, more than any other person, has kept pushing me. His encouragement, advice, and unending support have sustained me in this undertaking.

In addition, my daughter, Anna C. Rambo, and my precious friends Warren Lee and Corina Chan have provided me with affection, consolation, affirmation, and faith. My parents, Harold J. and Gwendolyn Rambo, and my brother, James R. Rambo, continue to manifest love beyond measure. To Hsifei Helen Chen I offer my deepest gratitude for what we shared and profound grief for the loss of what might have been.

Finally, I wish to thank my editors, Charles Grench and Otto Bohlmann, and Yale University Press for their interest and support. Their endeavors have made it possible for this long journey to come full circle.

Introduction

How and why do people convert? In the past twenty years there has been an amazing resurgence of religious vitality, both in the United States and in many other parts of the world. A scant quarter-century ago most social scientists, and indeed many theologians, predicted the secularization of society and pronounced the death of God. Those predictions and pronouncements were clearly wrong.

Forces of religious vitality have not been destroyed; they have merely been regrouping.[1] The power of religion is reasserting itself in many parts of the world, both as a personal and as a public phenomenon. There has been the resurgence of Islam in the Middle East and other areas, the reinvigoration of Christianity by the charismatics and the liberation theologians, the new springtime of Buddhism in the land of its origins. In the United States and Western Europe, cults and New Religious Movements have attracted thousands of young men and women. These developments have stimulated scholars to re-examine the nature of the conversion process.

My choice of the word *process* over *event* is a deliberate distinction resulting from my personal interpretation that, contrary to popular mythology, conversion is very rarely an overnight, all-in-an-instant, wholesale transformation that is now and forever. I do not, however, exclude the possibility of sudden conversion; a deliberately inclusive overview is doomed from the outset if any possible experience is declared beyond the pale. Similarly, the popular polarization of "religious" (read "institutional") change versus "spiritual" ("personal") change is, I believe, belied by the actual experience of most people. We are all inherently connected through the sociocultural world, and perceived spiritual realities are generally shared, not unique. All conversions (even Saul's on the road to Damascus) are mediated through people, institutions, communities, and groups.

We humans are fragile beings. Confronting the realities of our lives triggers not only fears but also hopes, doubts, and dreams. Religious conversion is one of humanity's ways of approaching its self-conscious predicament, of solving or resolving the mystery of human origins, meaning, and destiny.[2]

Through conversion an individual may gain some sense of ultimate worth, and may participate in a community of faith that connects him or her to both a rich past and an ordered and exciting present which generates a vision of the future that mobilizes energy and inspires confidence. Affiliating with a group and subscribing to a philosophy may offer nurture, guidance, a focus for loyalty, and a framework for action. Involvement in mythic, ritual, and symbolic systems gives life order and meaning. Sharing those systems with like-minded people makes it possible to connect with other human beings on deeper intellectual and emotional levels.

In this book the word *conversion* will mean several things—not necessarily in any particular order of priority, not in any weighted system of valuation, and certainly not all at one time. It will mean simple change from the absence of a faith system to a faith commitment, from religious affiliation with one faith system to another, or from one orientation to another within a single faith system. It will mean a change of one's personal orientation toward life, from the haphazards of superstition to the providence of a deity; from a reliance on rote and ritual to a deeper conviction of God's presence; from belief in a threatening, punitive, judgmental deity to one that is loving, supportive, and desirous of the maximum good. It will mean a spiritual transformation of life, from seeing evil or illusion in everything connected with "this" world to seeing all creation as a manifestation of God's power and beneficence; from denial of the self in this life in order to gain a holy hereafter; from seeking personal gratification to a determination that the rule of God is what fulfills human beings; from a life geared to one's personal welfare above all else to a concern for shared and equal justice for all. It will mean a radical shifting of gears that can take the spiritually lackadaisical to a new level of intensive concern, commitment, and involvement.

Such a universe of possible meanings for a single word to carry! The central meaning of conversion, of course, is change. The first question that confronts a student of conversion is the issue debated by Alice and Humpty Dumpty in *Through the Looking Glass*—whether a word must have a given, specific, reliable definition or whether it can mean whatever one chooses it to mean. History and experience have taught that Alice's righteous indignation did not make her any more "right," and that Humpty Dumpty's openness to varieties of meaning was at least realistic, although precarious.

In the Judeo-Christian Scriptures, the Hebrew and Greek words generally equated with *conversion* are words that literally mean *to turn* or *return*. The precise meaning of the turning or returning is contextually determined. Likewise, in this book *conversion* means turning from and to new religious groups, ways of life, systems of belief, and modes of relating to a deity or the nature of reality. The focus, but not exclusive preoccupation, will be on how and why people change religious group membership, including (though not limited to) the "born-again" experiences of certain evangelical or conservative Christian groups and the qualitative "intensification" experiences of other groups. The varieties of change, one might expect, are to a great degree shaped by the expectations of particular groups and/or religious traditions.

So it is with conversion. Varied use of the word by many people in many situations leads one to believe that it means just what a given individual or group wants it to mean, neither more nor less. It is this laissez-faire character of the word (and by extension, the experience itself, for the word only stands in for the experience) that has distanced scholars from each other over centuries of concern for the phenomenon of conversion. This built-in ambiguity makes it hazardous indeed for anyone to undertake a survey of the subject, to try applying an interconnected model that might define patterns and reveal relationships among the various scattered bits of material, pieces of research, shards of anecdotal experience, slivers of theory, and crumbs of inductive or deductive commentary available to the researcher.

I believe that such a broad survey approach is necessary and appropriate in an increasingly pluralistic religious environment. More specialized, normative definitions of conversion are the preserve of particular spiritual communities. These narrow definitions tend to multiply and become idiosyncratic as the number of considered groups (and even individuals) grows larger and the sense of urgency to pin down the meaning of conversion becomes stronger. Such attempts at definition are elusive and ultimately too specialized to have general value in a study like this.

The goal of the book is to explore—and beyond that to suggest a few possible interconnections among—the complex, multifaceted experiences culminating in conversion, making use of scholarly perspectives from a number of disciplines, chiefly psychology, sociology, anthropology, and theology. Each theory and model offered by these various disciplines should ideally take into account a religious system's own model of conversion, appreciate the metaphors and images of the anticipated transformation, and delineate the methods used by the given religious community to realize its goals. Any assessment of a particular theory or model of conversion must carefully examine the strengths and limitations of the researcher's assumptions, the primary images shaping interpretation, and the research methods influencing perception of conversion. Most studies of conversion to date have been too narrow in orientation, employing theories too restrictive in disciplinary perspective and assumptions too deeply rooted in religious traditions.[3]

There is a hunger within every human being for the kind of meaningfulness associated with new life, new love, new beginnings. Religious conversion offers that hope and provides that reality to millions of people. The precise contours of conversion will differ from person to person and from group to group, but the innate needs for explanation and renewal are universal, and the appeal of the possibility for transformation is pervasive.

Models and Methods

Chapter 1

Conversion is a process of religious change that takes place in a dynamic force field of people, events, ideologies, institutions, expectations, and orientations. In this book we will see that (a) conversion is a process over time, not a single event; (b) conversion is contextual and thereby influences and is influenced by a matrix of relationships, expectations, and situations; and (c) factors in the conversion process are multiple, interactive, and cumulative. There is no one cause of conversion, no one process, and no one simple consequence of that process.[1]

Definitions

Definitions of conversion abound.[2] Within Judaism and Christianity, for instance, conversion indicates a radical call to reject evil and embrace a relationship with God through faith. Some scholars in the human sciences limit conversion to sudden, radical alterations in people's beliefs, behaviors, and affiliations. Others, such as A. D. Nock, make sharp distinctions between Christian and Jewish conversion and the form of conversion in the ancient pagan world, suggesting that Jewish and Christian conversion is radical, complete, and decisive, while pagan religious change is merely an "adhesion," or an add-on, to a person's life.[3]

In addition to the proliferation of contradictory definitions, there is the problem of *who* defines genuine conversion. Often the convert sees the conversion as sincere and profound, whereas the advocate or the missionary (the agent of the new religious option) sees it as less than adequate. Such a problem is a classic issue in missions. Western missionaries seek to find the "pure" convert, while the converts themselves assimilate the faith in the categories relevant to them, not to the dictates of the advocate.

The best way to deal with the problem of definition is to perceive that distinctions are usually based on ideal types, and that few people or situations are as pure or simple as these definitions imply. Establishing pure types of conversion may be useful conceptually and academically, but we must question how useful these categories are in the actual world of what people *experience* as conversion. Rigidity of conceptualization can only hinder the quality of research in this area of scholarship.[4]

An important distinction needs to be made between the normative and the descriptive approaches to definitions of conversion. According to the normative approach, a genuine conversion is formulated according to the theological convictions of a particular tradition. The tradition is specific in elaborating what is expected or required for conversion to be valid. In Jewish conversion, for example, the potential adherent must agree to obey the laws of Judaism, submit to total immersion in water, participate in the life and destiny of the Jewish people, and (if male) undergo circumcision.[5] In many conservative Christian traditions, conversion is defined as a confession of sin (that is, a sense that one's past life has been contrary to the will of God), a submission to the will of God, affirmation of genuine belief that Jesus Christ is the Son of God and Savior of the world, and an invitation to Christ to come into the person's heart. Many churches also require baptism.

Descriptive approaches to conversion, on the other hand, seek to delineate the contours of the phenomenon, with little concern for what the ideology of the group says is happening. The descriptive approach observes the nature of the process. This book will be primarily descriptive rather than normative; in other words, it will explore the varieties of conversion rather than a specific theological perspective. What actually happens in conversion processes? What behaviors are changed? What beliefs are changed? What sorts of experiences are elicited in the process? By focusing on a descriptive approach, we can treat conversion as a dynamic, multifaceted process of transformation. For some, that change is abrupt and radical; for others, it is gradual and very subtle in its effects upon a person's life.

It is imperative for scholars of conversion to recognize it as a variable phenomenon subject to the structural, ideological, theological, and personal demands of both advocates and potential converts. Debates about whether conversion is sudden or gradual, total or partial, active or passive, internal or external, are useful only if we accept that conversion can occur anywhere between these poles, which have been constructed both by scholars of conversion and converts themselves. As I remarked earlier, conversion is a process, not a specific event. Perhaps the word *converting* better captures the phenomenology of the process. But, for readability, I employ the noun form *conversion*, although it implies a static phenomenon. We should bear in mind that conversion is *actively constructed* by a religious group and by the wishes, expectations, and aspirations of the convert or potential convert.

For the purposes of this book, I suggest that conversion is what a group or person *says* it is. The process of conversion is a product of the interactions among the convert's aspirations, needs, and orientations, the nature of the group into which she or he is being converted, and the particular social matrix in which these processes are taking place.

Holistic Model

The holistic model of conversion I propose is an exploratory orientation enabling a student of conversion phenomena to confront a wide range of questions and issues. This model is not yet a complete theory; it is a beginning framework only, based on an extensive survey of the literature, numerous interviews with converts, and participant-observation research.

No model can encompass the whole of reality, but I submit that the study of conversion must include, at the very least, the following four components: cultural, social, personal, and religious systems.[6] For conversion to be understood in all its richness and complexity, the disciplines of anthropology, sociology, psychology, and religious studies must all be taken into account. Considerations of politics, economics, biology, and so forth, should also be noted, but I shall focus mainly on the first four components, which I believe to be the most crucial to an understanding of conversion.

These components (cultural, social, personal, and religious) are of varying weight in each particular conversion. In some instances, the social mechanisms of group control may be so powerful and effective that they are able to overpower considerations of culture, person, and religion. In other situations, it may be that the religious sphere is the dominant force, over-shadowing the others. It is essential, however, that all four dimensions be given serious consideration, bearing in mind the variable relevance and potency of each element. In the past, scholars have tended to give undue weight to their own discipline's point of view, even when open to the influence of other factors. Thus, the psychologist tends to focus primarily on the isolated individual who is converting; the sociologist tends to see conversion as the result of forces shaped and mobilized by social institutions and mechanisms; and the religious person emphasizes the dominant influence of God and minimizes the impact of other factors. Anthropologists have been the least likely to be limited by one narrow perspective. As a holistic human science, anthropology may serve as a model to those of us immersed in our more parochial disciplines, which demand loyalty to one point of view or empha-size only a particular dimension.

In examining the cultural, social, personal, and religious components, we need to consider the following questions: What relative weight should be accorded each component, given the particular conversion under consider-ation? In what ways do these four components interact with one another? What significance does the convert attribute to these elements? What signifi-cance does the observer give to each component? (If these assessments are different, we must explore the divergence.) Which theoretical orientation should one employ *within* anthropology, sociology, psychology, and religious studies or theology? What are the methods used in the studies under consid-eration? What are the goals of the scholar (for instance, advocacy, rejection, or trivialization of the phenomenon of conversion)?

Culture

Culture constructs the intellectual, moral, and spiritual atmosphere of life. The myths, rituals, and symbols of a culture provide guidelines for living, which are often unconsciously adopted and taken for granted. An individual's core sense of reality is rooted in language, which is the central vehicle for the transmission of cultural perceptions and values. Anthropologists explore and delineate culture. They consider culture a manifestation of human creativity and a powerful force in the shaping and renewal of individuals, groups, and societies. They study phenomena such as rites of passage, rituals, myths, and symbols, which weave the meaningful fabric of a culture. Anthropologists also examine a culture's symbols and methods for religious change, the cultural impact of conversion, the way culture impedes or facilitates religious change, and stages of development of new religious orientations in a particular culture.

Society

Sociologists examine the social and institutional aspects of traditions in which conversion takes place. They consider social conditions at the time of conversion, important relationships and institutions of potential converts, and characteristics and processes of the religious group to which people convert. Sociologists focus also on the interaction between individuals and their environmental matrix, and on the relationships between individuals and the expectations of the group in which they are involved.

Person

Changes in an individual's thoughts, feelings, and actions are the domain of psychology. Psychology considers transformation of the self, consciousness, and experience, in both objective and subjective aspects. The classic psychological study of conversion is William James's *Varieties of Religious Experience.*[7] Following the model of James and other early figures, the typical psychological study of conversion stresses the way in which conversion is often preceded by anguish, turmoil, despair, conflict, guilt, and other such difficulties. Psychological theorists approach conversion from various theoretical perspectives: psychoanalytic, behaviorist, humanistic, transpersonal, social, and cognitive psychology.

Psychoanalysts focus on internal emotional dynamics, especially as they reflect on the relationship between parent and child. Behaviorists emphasize a person's behavior and judge the degree of congruence between this behavior and the rewards and punishments of the immediate social environment. Humanistic and transpersonal psychologists stress the way in which conversion gives the person a richer self-realization, accentuating the beneficial consequences resulting from conversion. Finally, social and cognitive psychologists examine the impact of interpersonal and intellectual influences on individuals and groups. Whatever the psychological interpretations of conversion, those that focus exclusively on the individual are limited. Conversion can be seen as personal, but not as individualistic.

Religion

Religion is the sacred—the encounter with the holy that, according to many religions, constitutes both the source and goal of a conversion. Religious people affirm that the purpose of conversion is to bring people into relationship with the divine and provide them a new sense of meaning and purpose. Theologians consider this dimension absolutely essential to the whole process of human transformation; other factors are subordinate to it.

Scholars of religion focus on transcendence, inquiring into the religious expectations, experiences, and worldviews of converts. Recently scholars have argued that conversion is a progressive, interactive process that has consequences in the community. Conversion is usually not a single event but an evolving process in which many aspects of a person's life may be affected.

However scholars may choose to delineate its causes, nature, and consequences, conversion is essentially theological and spiritual. Other forces are operative, but the meaning, the significance, and the goal are religious and/or spiritual *to the convert*. Phenomenologically speaking, interpretations that deny the religious dimension fail to appreciate the convert's experience, and attempt to put this experience into interpretative frameworks that are inappropriate, even hostile, to the phenomenon. Some psychological and sociological explanations of conversion are reductionist, and converts are rightly disconcerted when their experience is discounted, if not rejected, by the researcher. Nevertheless, there is value to the researcher in *bracketing* the theological dimensions in order to uncover the social and personal dynamics of conversion. Good scholarship should start with rich description of the phenomenon, and with respect for its integrity. On the other hand, some religious scholars have a tendency to spiritualize the study of conversion by relegating everything that is not spiritual to the realm of the demonic or the irrelevant.

Exploring the role of religion is methodologically difficult. How can we understand, predict, and control that which is generally invisible to the outsider, mysterious and sacred to the insider, and more often than not subject to debate within the tradition itself? Additionally, we scholars may be reluctant to give serious consideration to the religious factor because it might challenge us to modify our own worldview, and confront us with the possibility that we are limited creatures who may be dependent upon a deity expecting moral responsibility and obedience.[8]

If we are to be phenomenologically true to the experiences and the phenomena of conversion, we must take the religious sphere seriously. We need not capitulate to religious or theological points of view, but we do need to find ways of integrating religion into our analysis; otherwise our examinations of conversion will remain one-dimensional. We may begin by taking into account the religious ideology that shapes the conversion process, the religious imagery that influences the consciousness of the convert, and the religious institutions that are often the matrix in which conversion takes place. Taking religion seriously does not require *belief*, but it does imply *respect* for the fact that conversion is a *religious* process involving an elaborate array of forces, ideas, institutions, rituals, myths, and symbols.[9]

History

Consideration of the historical dimensions of conversion may also be valuable. Historians collect and integrate the concrete details of conversions.

Attention to historical particulars may complement theoretical models, providing a substantive and detailed data base of information about conversion, and may also help to trace the nature of conversion over time. Psychology and sociology are generally synchronic rather than longitudinal disciplines, focusing on a particular time without reference to antecedents. Diachronic approaches like history are concerned with change over time. Historians have demonstrated conclusively that conversion (even within a specific tradition) may be different in different times and places. William Bulliet[10] and Ramsay MacMullen,[11] among others, have argued persuasively that converts may have different motives at different times in a particular historical context. For instance, those who are the first converts to a new movement are likely to be different in motivation and demographic profile from those who convert when a movement is already successful. Bulliet shows that the first converts to Islam were different from those who followed over a long period of time. In other words, conversion is usually phenomenologically different depending on whether it is an innovative movement or a powerful movement already accorded respect and authority in a society. These observations are not designed to question the validity of particular conversions, but serve to illustrate the different contours of the process in different times and places in history.

Some scholars believe that the form and structure of conversion are universal, but that its consequences are different in different locations and times. Jerald C. Brauer observes that conversion among Puritans in England triggered dissent from the political system, whereas conversion in New England was a requirement for legal status.[12] The former was revolutionary, while the latter garnered acceptance and encouraged conformity. Some historians argue, and I tend to agree, that the conversion process is different under different historical circumstances.

Types of Conversion

One way to understand better the nature of conversion is to describe various types of conversion. An "ideal type" is an intellectual construction that is designed to help understand the range and varying characteristics of many kinds of conversion. In this case, my typology portrays the nature of conversion in terms of *how far someone has to go socially and culturally in order to be considered a convert.*[13]

Apostasy, or *defection,* is the repudiation of a religious tradition or its beliefs by previous members. This change does not involve acceptance of a new religious perspective but often indicates adoption of a nonreligious system of values. Deprogramming, an intensive method sometimes used to remove people from religious movements viewed as cults, may be seen as a form of forced deconversion, or apostasy. Apostasy is included in this typology because the dynamics of loss of faith or of leaving a group constitute an important form of change, both individually and collectively, in the contemporary setting.

Intensification is the revitalized commitment to a faith with which the convert has had previous affiliation, formal or informal. It occurs when nominal members of a religious institution make their commitment a central focus in their lives, or when people deepen their involvement in a community of faith through profound religious experience and/or life transitions like marriage, childbirth, and approaching death.

Affiliation is the movement of an individual or group from no or minimal religious commitment to full involvement with an institution or community of faith. Affiliation has recently become a controversial notion, with allegations of manipulative recruitment strategies often leveled against some New Religious Movements (such as the Unification Church, Hare Krishna, and so forth) and Christian fundamentalist groups. Many converts to New Religious Movements have little or no religious background, so that few countervailing forces act against the desire to affiliate.

Institutional transition involves the change of an individual or group from one community to another within a major tradition. An example is conversion from the Baptist to the Presbyterian church in American Protestantism. This process, which sociologists call "denominational switching," can involve simple affiliation with a church because of convenience (such as geographical proximity) or significant religious change based upon profound religious experience.

Tradition transition refers to the movement of an individual or a group from one major religious tradition to another. Moving from one worldview, ritual system, symbolic universe, and life-style to another is a complex process that often takes place in a context of cross-cultural contact and conflict. Such movement has occurred throughout history, especially in the eighteenth, nineteenth, and twentieth centuries, when massive numbers of people were involved in this type of conversion because of European colonial expansion. Christianity and Islam are religions that have initiated and benefited from massive tradition transition.

Conversion Motifs

Another approach to the varieties of conversion processes is delineated by John Lofland and Norman Skonovd. They propose the notion of conversion motifs, by which they mean defining experiences that make each type of conversion distinctive. This notion of motifs combines the convert's subjective experience with the scholar's more objective, "scientific" view. Lofland and Skonovd argue that differing perceptions and descriptions of conversion are not merely the result of various theoretical orientations but are, in fact, descriptions of qualities that make conversion experiences substantially different.[14]

They identify six motifs: intellectual, mystical, experimental, affectional, revivalist, and coercive. To assess the dimensions of each motif, one examines the degree of social pressure on the potential convert, the temporal duration of the conversion process, the level of affective arousal, the affective content, and the belief-participation sequence.

In *intellectual* conversion, the person seeks knowledge about religious or spiritual issues via books, television, articles, lectures, and other media that do not involve significant social contact. The person actively seeks out and explores alternatives. Belief generally occurs prior to active participation in religious rituals and organizations.

Mystical conversion is considered by some to be the prototypical conversion, as in the case of Saul of Tarsus. Mystical conversion is generally a sudden and traumatic burst of insight, induced by visions, voices, or other paranormal experiences.

The third motif, *experimental* conversion, has emerged as a major avenue of conversion in the twentieth century because of greater religious freedom and a multiplicity of available religious experiences. Experimental conversion involves active exploration of religious options. The potential convert has a "show me" mentality, essentially saying, "I'll pursue this possibility and see what spiritual benefits it may provide to me." Many groups encourage this mode by welcoming a quasi-scientific stance. Potential converts are urged to take nothing on faith but to try the theology, ritual, and organization for themselves and discover if the system is true (that is, beneficial or supportive) for them.

The fourth motif is the *affectional*. First identified by John Lofland and Rodney Stark in their essay "Becoming a World-Saver," this motif stresses interpersonal bonds as an important factor in the conversion process.[15] Central to it is the direct, personal experience of being loved, nurtured, and affirmed by a group and its leaders.

Revivalism is the fifth motif Lofland and Skonovd discuss. Although less prominent in the twentieth century than in the nineteenth, this type of conversion uses crowd conformity to induce behavior. Individuals are emotionally aroused and new behaviors and beliefs are promoted by the pressures exerted. For instance, revival meetings feature emotionally powerful music and preaching. In addition to the group experience, individuals are sometimes sought out by family members and friends to exert direct influence on the potential convert.[16]

The sixth conversion motif is the *coercive*. Because specific conditions need to be present in order for such conversion to occur, Lofland and Skonovd believe that this type of conversion is relatively rare. Brainwashing, coercive persuasion, thought reform, and programming are other labels for such a process. A conversion is more or less coercive according to the level of intense pressure exerted on the person to participate, conform, and confess. Deprivation of food and sleep may render the person unable to resist the pressure to surrender to the group's ideology and submissive life-style. Fear and, some allege, physical torture and other forms of psychological terror are deployed to gain control over the person's life.

Lofland and Skonovd's motifs are important contributions, identifying the different experiences, themes, and goals of various types of conversion. They are correct to note that much of the theorizing about conversion has been complicated by the fact that some scholars talk about conversion as if it were a single, universal process. In fact, there is a range of types of conversion, and no one type is normative.

Stage Model

Given the multiplicity of approaches that I have briefly introduced, one may very well feel a sense of theoretical or informational overload at this point. With apologies to the originator of the fable in which ten blind persons went to "see" an elephant, I believe that what has been described thus far is very much like sighted people entering through separate doors into a dark room—one barely large enough to contain the elephant—and each trying to describe the beast discovered with only a penlight to see by. Our endeavor here must be to try to find the electrical switch on the wall that will illuminate the whole animal, so that all these accurate, helpful, but fragmentary efforts at explanation may be integrated.

More light and more distance may both be helpful, and a heuristic model which maintains that conversion takes place in stages may provide a framework for integrating research within the various disciplines, offering a deeper, more complex understanding of the multilayered processes involved in conversion. A stage model is appropriate in that conversion is a process of change over time, generally exhibiting a sequence of processes, although

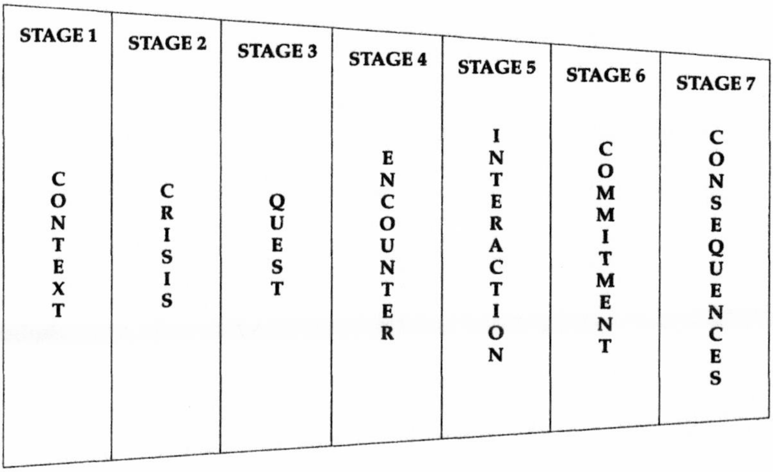

STAGE 1	STAGE 2	STAGE 3	STAGE 4	STAGE 5	STAGE 6	STAGE 7
CONTEXT	CRISIS	QUEST	ENCOUNTER	INTERACTION	COMMITMENT	CONSEQUENCES

Figure 1 *A sequential stage model.*

there is sometimes a spiraling effect—a going back and forth between stages. A stage may be seen as a particular element or period during that process of change. Each stage has a cluster of themes, patterns, and processes that characterize it. Determining how and to what extent the existing literature on conversion fits into this framework will enable us to view the research in a broader context, and will reveal areas in which further research is needed.

The model I am proposing is not only multidimensional and historical but also *process oriented;* that is to say, conversion is approached as a series of elements that are interactive and cumulative over time. No single process or stage model articulated thus far has been satisfactory to everyone, but the work of Lofland and Stark, and the missiological model of Alan R. Tippett, provide useful heuristic models.[17] I propose an adaptation of their stage models as a strategy for organizing complex data, not as a universal or invariant tool. Scientific understanding of conversion is merely a human attempt to comprehend a phenomenon that is an encounter between a mysterious God and an individual of vast potential, perversity, and extraordinary complexity.

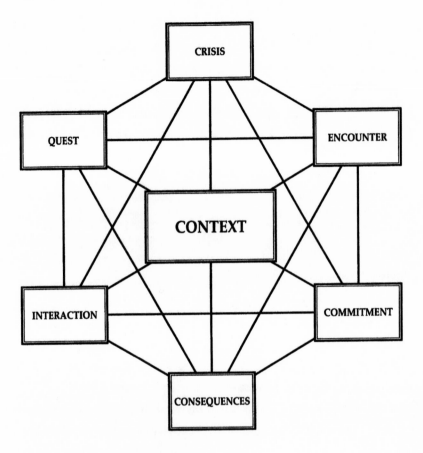

Figure 2 *A systemic stage model.*

Methodology

Observation may seem obvious as the first and foremost methodological guideline, but I am frequently amazed at studies that display all too little careful, objective, and systematic observation, conducted with noticeable effort by the researcher to maintain a distance from personal bias, so that new perception, new vision is possible.

Second, *description* of the phenomenon is necessary. Clifford Geertz advocates "thick description," description that is rich, complex, and complete.[18]

Third, *empathy* is required; that is, an attempt to see and feel the world from the point of view of the person or group being studied. Empathy is never perfect, but it is always a worthy goal. Acknowledging the researcher's own points of view as much as possible and bracketing those biases can free the scholar to engage the experiences, thoughts, feelings, and actions of the convert, promoting an ability to see and feel the world in a manner close to (but never identical with) that of the convert.

Fourth, *understanding* is central to the process of studying conversion holistically. Understanding is grasping the worldview, experience, and cognitive systems of the people we are studying, utilizing *their* orientation as much as possible to view their life situation, an effort that will itself deepen the capacity for empathy.

Fifth, *interpretation* can take place once the previous stages have been completed with integrity. Interpretation makes the process and content of conversion more fully understandable in terms of the scholar's frame of reference. It is important that the scholar recognize, be alert to, a deliberate shift of perspective here from that of the convert to the scholar's own point of view, a view that may be valuable but is not intrinsically superior to the one being analyzed.

Sixth, *explanation* is the systematic application of another frame of reference that is even more removed from the experiential world of the convert. Explanation is a form of interpretation that utilizes theories derived from various disciplines and applies them to the phenomenon. Ideally, explanation is tentative, respectful, and subtle. Interpretation and explanation are closely related, but interpretation is more integral to humanistic points of view and explanation is more typical of the social sciences. The social sciences tend to be more analytical, critical, and reductionist than the humanistic models of religious studies, history, and theology. Explanatory models tend to be more secular and less interested in the dimension of human meaning and of spiritual depth.

Context

Chapter 2

Conversion takes place within a dynamic context.[1] This context encompasses a vast panorama of conflicting, confluent, and dialectical factors that both facilitate and repress the process of conversion. When seen from a broad perspective, conversion is part of a human drama that spans historical eras and both shapes and is shaped by geographical expansion and contraction. Context embraces an overall matrix in which the force field of people, events, experiences, and institutions operate on conversion.

Context is more than a first stage that is passed through; rather, it is the total environment in which conversion transpires. Context continues its influence throughout the other conversion stages. The obverse is also true: conversions, whether due to unusual power or cumulative force, may have a reciprocal impact upon context. Context shapes the nature, structure, and process of conversion. John Gration puts it this way: "In a very true sense every conversion is in context, a context that is multifaceted, embracing the political, social, economic and religious domain in which a person is living at the time of his or her conversion. Thus whatever the meaning of conversion, it never takes place outside a cultural context."[2]

Gration asserts only the external context. But conversion is a process influenced not only by objective, external forces but also by subjective, internal motivations, experiences, and aspirations. To deny either is to truncate our understanding of conversion.

Context is the integration of both the superstructure and the infrastructure of conversion, and it includes social, cultural, religious, and personal dimensions. Contextual factors shape avenues of communication, the range of religious options available, and people's mobility, flexibility, resources, and opportunities. These forces have a direct impact on who converts and how conversion happens. People can often be induced, encouraged, prevented, or

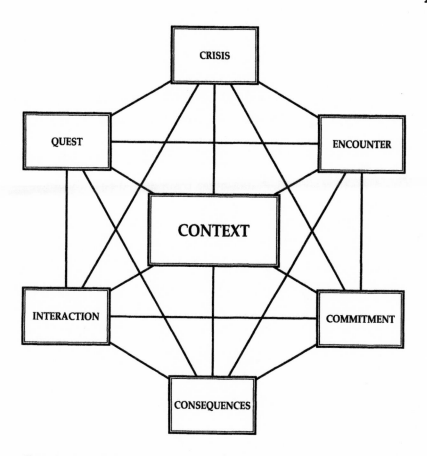

Figure 3 *Stage 1: Context.*

forced to either accept or reject conversion on the basis of factors external to the individual. These considerations are rarely delineated in studies of conversion, but I believe it is imperative for students of the topic to be more systematic in detailing the context so that these patterns, themes, and issues can be made more explicit.

Macrocontext: "The Big Picture"

To understand context better, it is useful to distinguish between *macrocontext* and *microcontext*. Macrocontext refers to the total environment, including such elements as political systems, religious organizations, relevant ecological considerations, transnational corporations, and economic systems. These forces can either facilitate or obstruct conversion, and may have individual impacts as well as broad, societal ones. In the United States and Great Britain, for instance, the macrocontext combines industrialization, extensive mass communication, and the shrinking of Christianity's traditional spheres of influence. Such a situation allows people an enormous, sometimes overwhelming, range of options. Pluralism can create alienation and confusion; in consequence, individuals may eagerly choose a new religious option to lessen anxiety, find meaning, or gain a sense of belonging.

Microcontext: The Local Setting

Microcontext is the more immediate world of a person's family, friends, ethnic group, religious community, and neighborhood. These immediate influences play an important role in the creation of a sense of identity and belonging and in shaping a person's thoughts, feelings, and actions. Microcontext and macrocontext interact in various ways; some elements of the microcontext affirm and foster the larger context (as when a religious organization reinforces patriotic values), while other elements oppose and seek to alter the macrocontext (as when a group challenges prevailing political values). The microcontext can, with enormous effort, neutralize the influence of the macrocontext. For instance, some religious groups deliberately isolate themselves from the wider world, protecting (or controlling) their members' communication and interaction with the outside world in order to encourage an intense focus on individual and group relationship with the divine.

Contours of Context

The range of issues to be considered when examining context include: What is the precise nature of the macrocontext and microcontext? How do the two interrelate? Do they facilitate and nurture one another? Do they hinder and undermine one another? To what degree is there integration and coordi-nation within these domains?

To answer these questions we must examine specific aspects of the con-tours of context. First, we shall examine general issues regarding the cultural, social, personal, and religious dimensions of context. Second, we shall sur-vey particular mechanisms of context, such as enculturation, paths of dis-semination, forces of resistance and rejection, enclaves of receptivity, dynam-ics of congruence and confluence, types of conversion, and models for conversion. The goal of this chapter is to portray the panorama of forces and agents that configure context, facilitating and/or impeding the process of conversion. As I mentioned in the introduction, I realize that it is artificial to isolate rigidly culture, society, persons, and religion from one another. These features of human existence are inextricably and intimately intertwined. I make these distinctions only for the sake of exposition.

Culture and Context

Anthony F. C. Wallace's important essay "Revitalization Movements" is central to an understanding of cultural aspects in the context of conversion.[3] Wallace sees culture as a dynamic entity constantly in process. The essence of his view is that culture contains internal mechanisms that enable it to renew itself when there is entropy or crisis. A culture, like all organisms, has a life history. When a culture begins to collapse, a process occurs in which the core myths, rituals, and symbols are broken down and reconstituted in such a manner as to give people a revitalized vision of themselves and new strategies by which to enhance and maintain life.

This process, which Wallace calls "mazeway reformulation," takes place when an individual has a vision and/or a conversion experience in which the old way is modified so as to be more adaptive to the current situation. The new vision is communicated to disciples, who in turn communicate the mes-sage to the wider culture. In the process of communication, the message is further adapted to the environment and, when successful, spawns a movement to transform the culture and society according to the new vision. This process of renewal takes place because cultural myths, rituals, and symbols have a life of their own and are deeply embedded within the individual psyche. During severe crisis these myths, rituals, and symbols may emerge within an individual in the form of dreams, visions, or other experiences which give that person a feeling of revitalization. Hence individuals and groups experience a process of change that gives them a new set of rules, visions, and values.

Wallace believes that this dynamic process of cultural renewal is illustrated in the founders of three great world religions: Christianity, Islam, and Buddhism. The founders experienced profound transformations that led to the creation of revitalization movements. The founders' conversions or transformations provided models for their disciples and guidelines for the creation of new communities.

Wallace's theory of revitalization movements is built primarily upon a case study of a man named Handsome Lake (Ganiodaiio), a chief in the League of the Iroquois. In 1799, Handsome Lake was, at the age of 54, a very sick man. His wife and child were dead, and he had become an alcoholic. He was destitute, depressed, and near death. On 8 August 1799, Handsome Lake began to experience a series of visions. Eight hours of trance was mistaken for death, and preparations were made for his burial. However, he came out of the trance and reported his visions to the people. Profoundly stirred by this series of visions, Handsome Lake reformed not only his own life but also the lives of many other individuals and eventually the whole Iroquois nation.[4]

This kind of revitalization process that is operative in mass movements usually springs from the experience of individual lives. A pivotal moment for Eldridge Cleaver, which he describes in his book *Soul on Fire*, provides a good example.[5] A leader of the Black Panthers, Cleaver fled the United States because of legal difficulties; finally, he and his family settled in France.[6] After several expatriate years, Cleaver began to feel that he was useless to the Black Power movement and was no longer able to have an influence on political and social change. One evening, having sent his family to their house in Paris, he was sitting alone on the balcony of their apartment near Cannes, staring down at the Mediterranean with a pistol on his lap. Cleaver recalls:

> I . . . began thinking of putting an end to it all by committing sui-
> cide. I really began to think about that. I was sitting up on my bal-
> cony, one night, on the thirteenth floor—just sitting there. It was a
> beautiful Mediterranean night—sky, stars, moon hanging there in a
> sable void. I was brooding, downcast, at the end of my rope. I looked
> up at the moon and saw certain shadows . . . and the shadows be-
> came a man in the moon, and I saw a profile of myself (a profile that
> we had used on posters for the Black Panther Party—something I had
> seen a thousand times). I was already upset and this scared me.
> When I saw that image, I started trembling. It was a shaking that
> came from deep inside, and it had a threat about it that this mood was
> getting worse, that I could possibly disintegrate on the scene and fall
> apart. As I stared at this image, it changed, and I saw my former
> heroes paraded before my eyes. Here were Fidel Castro, Mao Tse-
> tung, Karl Marx, Frederick Engels, passing in review, each one ap-
> pearing for a moment of time, and then dropping out of sight, like
> fallen heroes. Finally, at the end of the procession, in dazzling, shim-
> mering light, the image of Jesus Christ appeared. That was the last
> straw.
>
> I just crumbled and started crying. I fell to my knees, grabbing
> hold of the banister; and in the midst of this shaking and crying the
> Lord's Prayer and the 23rd Psalm came into my mind.[7]

Later that evening Cleaver began to feel a return of peace, hope, renewal. That experience was the beginning of his conversion process. Cleaver was often asked what Jesus looked like in his vision; his response was that Jesus looked like the traditional portrait that hung in his grandmother's kitchen. Cleaver's experience is a vivid example of the renewing power of cultural symbols. Even symbols that a person may have directly and explicitly rejected can remain a powerful part of his or her psyche. Cleaver's childhood image of

Jesus, imprinted on his unconscious, re-emerged at a crucial time as a symbol of healing and transformation.

Wallace's theory is useful in understanding larger social movements of renewal and revitalization, such as those outlined in William G. McLoughlin's *Revivals, Awakenings, and Reforms,* as well as in understanding the power of cultural symbols in the conversion of individuals. (John Weir Perry, a Jungian theorist, believes dynamics similar to those at work in the transformation of culture also operate in the conversion of individuals, but on a more intimate and personal scale.)[8]

Similar forces are described in Clifford Geertz's theory of "primordial revolutions."[9] Geertz believes that most cultures tend toward innovation, but that innovation has its limits. When those limits are reached, it is necessary for the core symbols to be reasserted so that the society and culture can return to these constitutive and formative symbols. In some cases the return is a reinterpretation or reconceptualization of core symbols, while in other cases it is an attempt to reassert core symbols in a literalistic, fundamentalist mode. Thus modernization may be a powerful force in all nations, but there are limits to the degree to which the original cultural system can be modified or rejected. When these limits are violated, the society may experience an explosive return to the core and thus an often violent rejection of the process and agents of modernization. The resurgence of fundamentalist Islam is a dramatic illustration of this theory.

Social Milieu and Context

Social context is extraordinarily complex, but at least three factors need to be examined closely: communications, transportation patterns, and increasing secularization.

Transportation and Communication

Conversion becomes possible in locations made accessible by transportation, trade, and communication routes, especially in locations penetrated by military or commercial powers that bring with them novel religious beliefs, behaviors, and life-styles. Forces of world military, economic, or political exploration, domination, and exploitation have historically provided opportunities for the missionary to make contact with indigenous populations in thousands of places.

During the fifteenth century C.E., for example, the opening of the so-called New World, made possible by an extraordinary burst of exploration by the Portuguese and Spanish (and later the French, Dutch, and English), allowed the missionary enterprise of Christianity to spread to what is now North, Central, and South America, all of Africa, parts of Japan, Korea, China, the Philippines, and many other places. Roman Catholic missions followed the Spanish, French, and Portuguese explorers and colonizers, and Protestant missions followed the Dutch, German, and English.[10]

It is important to note that it is the macrocontext that makes such access and interaction possible. The power of governments or other forces to either halt or prevent contact can reduce or eliminate the possibility of conversion, at least temporarily. For example, even though the Jesuits arrived in Japan in the early sixteenth century, the Japanese soon expelled the Portuguese and ruthlessly persecuted Japanese Christians. The Chinese were also able to control, to some extent, access by Christian missionaries to their people. Early missionaries were limited to Beijing, Macao, and Canton. Only later, when Europeans and Americans pursued both military and diplomatic initiatives as well as private trade, were missionaries able to reach other areas.[11]

Today, several countries have made proselytizing illegal. India, Israel, and most Muslim and Communist countries do not allow any activities that are missionary in intention. Many Muslim nations, such as the Sudan, have a prohibition against leaving Islam. In some countries apostasy (renunciation of the state religion) is prohibited by law, and the punishment is execution.[12] One need hardly point out that it would be difficult to convert (and to solicit conversion) in a country in which execution was the price. Muslim nations rarely use such a law, but their societies do have an attitude toward conversion that is very different from that of secular societies.

In the United States, on the other hand, the general atmosphere allows (even encourages) the individual to determine choices in his or her own personal life, including choice of religion. One's family may pose constraints, but the relative freedom to move into new religions and to shop the "religious supermarket" seems to foster an atmosphere of religious mobility and personal choice as well.

Secularization

A second major social force that influences the conversion process is secularization. For the past one hundred years scholars of religion, especially sociologists, have suggested that religion is diminishing in its influence, both as institution and as experience.[13] Religion, particularly in the West, is no longer the sole arbiter of morality, shaper of education, or controller of political legitimacy. In many countries, religion no longer has the power, prestige, and influence it once had. This was especially true in the antireligious societies of former Communist states; the role of religion in their future is now in great flux as the prohibitions fall and exposure to the secular influences of the West increases.

Peter L. Berger believes that a major source of secularization is the rampant pluralism dominant in contemporary culture. With the growth of urbanization, mass communication and technology, and the rationalization of many spheres of life, a unified religious worldview seems less plausible, and religion is thus relegated to the private realm. The public world is ruled by politics and economics; the private world is governed by whatever beliefs the individual uses to shape the personal life of family and inner experience.

Secularization is, at its core, a process in which religious institutions, ideas, and people lose their power and prestige. Most secularization theory is based on the European experience of the dominance of the Roman Catholic Church for more than one thousand years. Education, politics, ideology, economics, and of course spirituality were all molded by the imperial church. While its fortunes varied over time, its massive presence and influence were inescapable. But with European expansion, the Protestant Reformation, industrialization, and the development of modern science, the influence of the Roman Catholic Church diminished.

The debate over secularization is extremely complex. On one extreme is Andrew M. Greeley, who rejects the whole notion as a fiction.[14] Greeley argues that religion continues to be important to a large percentage of people. On the other extreme is Bryan Wilson,[15] who claims that secularization has indeed become pervasive, and that although religion is still important to millions of people, its importance is as a personal choice with no significance for the larger social reality. Religion is, in effect, a form of personal entertainment or leisure-time activity. David Martin, in contrast to both Greeley and Wilson, probes historical and political forces in a region-by-region assessment of the nature and consequences of secularization.[16]

My own work has been influenced most by Peter L. Berger.[17] For Berger, the most important aspect of secularization is pluralism. Because of modern communication and transportation systems, people are aware of the many options available in the world. Unlike the past domination of Europe by one universal church that controlled ideology and destiny, people today are keenly aware of other religious and political traditions. Berger believes that people's knowledge of other religious options (and their viability for other people) undermines the "taken for granted" reality that is possible when there *is* only one "reality."

Berger's perspective is relevant to conversion for several reasons. First, in the modern world pluralistic options mean that people can choose a religion other than the one they were given as a birthright. Millions of people travel extensively, and millions more know about other possibilities because of newspapers, magazines, books, radio, and television. Berger presents an astute assessment of the contemporary religious scene in *The Heretical Imperative*.[18] He asserts that three religious options or strategies are currently available: deductive, reductive, and inductive. Deductive religiosity is based on some authority, such as the Bible or a religious leader, that provides a "legitimate" interpretation of life and God. Followers acknowledge the revelation derived from these authorities and follow their dictates explicitly. In the deductive orientation, conversion is regulated by norms that delineate specific requirements for change in belief, behavior, and feeling.

Reduction is the strategy utilized by people who feel that *contemporary philosophical and theological orientation is epistemologically superior to all other orientations*. Thus traditional religious ideas and beliefs are translated into today's idiom and used for meaning-building and interpretation. Reductive orientations tend to interpret religious conversion as being motivated by nonreligious needs such as the need for compliance, status enhancement, or guilt reduction. Thus conversion is seen as a coping mechanism in religious garb.

Induction is the third option. It is Berger's view that if one has profound respect for human experience and religious tradition, the emerging dialectic will provide a relevant and plausible worldview, system of living, and community of faith. Inductive perspectives encourage a phenomenological approach to conversion, allowing for diversity and complexity. I agree with Berger that the inductive approach is the most comprehensive and appropriate to the contemporary situation.

Personal Dimensions of Context

Typically, psychologists do not address the context of religious conversion because their emphasis is on the individual. Until recently, they have tended to ignore or discount cultural and social variables. Yet we cannot talk adequately about a person's psyche without contextualizing that psyche. Someone growing up in a small, remote town lives in a world different from that of a person in an urban environment with its supermarket of social, moral, and religious options. A Buddhist in India and a Christian in the United States will have different sets of symbols, rituals, and myths with which to express and experience religious life.

Context not only provides the sociocultural matrix that shapes a person's myths, rituals, symbols, and beliefs; it also has a powerful impact in terms of

access, mobility, and the opportunity for coming into contact with new religious influences. Increased mobility in the modern world, for example,
makes it easier for the advocate (the missionary) to move into new areas to
propagate religious ideology. Increased mobility also enables the potential
convert to more readily leave behind old patterns of social relationships that
may feel constricting, and to find new options.

Psychiatrist Robert Jay Lifton recognizes the role of the macrocontext in
the creation of psychological reality.[19] Lifton argues that due to erosion of
cultural tradition, high rates of mobility, instantaneous communication networks, and increased secularization in the modern world, the self is no longer
clearly defined and has become progressively more fragile. He develops the
concept of the "protean" personality to describe a self that is malleable by its
sociocultural situation. Because our cultural context fosters a great deal of
change, he suggests, people within this context experience much fluctuation
of identity and self-definition.

The fragility of the self that Lifton describes can be a powerful motivation
for conversion to a conservative religion, whether it be fundamentalist Christianity, Orthodox Judaism, fundamentalist Islam, or the Unification Church.
Conversion to a religion that offers clear answers and belief systems can
provide relief from the overwhelming multiplicity of options and cacophony
of voices pulling the individual in different directions. It can provide a coherent center from which to conduct one's life in a world where that center
has been lost. This providing of focus can be viewed either negatively, as a
constriction of options, or positively, as a stable creative center or unchanging
core that can enrich and expand one's life.

Psychological theorist Philip Cushman also examines contextual factors
influencing individual conversion. Citing such elements of modern life as the
negative effects of laissez-faire child-rearing practices, increased mobility,
social change, and the erosion of a unified culture, he constructs a view of the
self as narcissistic, empty, and hungry for confirmation.[20] The drive to find
nurture and fill the inner void, Cushman feels, renders people vulnerable to
charismatic leaders, dogmatic belief systems, and rigidly controlled life-

styles. Although Lifton developed his ideas of the protean personality in the 1960s and Cushman developed his ideas in the 1980s, both writers recognize the importance of contextual factors and provide similar approaches to the psychology of conversion. It is imperative that psychologists undertake systematic research and theory in this vein, making explicit the links between personality and the larger sociocultural environment.[21]

Religious Sphere of Context

The quest for the sacred and the experience of the holy, the yearning for transcendence, and the human desire for interaction with the supernatural pervade human history. The religious sphere, like the cultural, social, and personal spheres, is a vital and complex dimension of the dynamic force field in which conversion takes place. Religion is a crucial force in a macrocontextual approach to the process of conversion. Powerful religious motivations energize conversion experiences throughout the world and during all periods of history. The power of religious experiences, leaders, and institutions are fundamentally important to an adequate understanding of conversion.

Buddhism spread over all of Asia through the power of religious experience inspired by the Buddha himself, his disciples, and the institutions they created.[22] Christianity spread throughout the Roman Empire, and later to other parts of the world, because followers believed profoundly in the revelation of God through Jesus of Nazareth.[23] The doctrines, rituals, and churches that developed were designed to impart the good news of salvation and to sustain disciples in the face of external opposition and internal erosion. The spread of Islam is compelled by Mohammed's revelation of Holy God calling people to new life and a new structure of society.[24] In all these movements, the experience of the holy, the transcendent, and the vision of a community of worship and solidarity propelled both leaders and followers.

Sociologists James T. Duke and Barry L. Johnson have recently developed a macrosociological theory of religious change.[25] They assert that religious

Decline	established religion loses influence, new religions originate, evolve, and challenge the established religion
Dominance	growing religion establishes itself as majority religion — either through displacement of dominant religion or through ascendance over competition
Sustained growth	new majority religion consolidates gains and increases influence
Transition	majority religion peaks in influence and begins to decline
Reform	declining majority religion attempts to regain its losses through revitalizing members and proselytizing new members

Figure 4 *Cycle of religious transformation.*

change is generally cyclical, rather than linear, in character. Duke and Johnson built their theory on the data provided in David B. Barrett's *World Christian Encyclopedia.*[26] They argue that religions follow a cycle of development, rise to dominance, steady growth, peak in growth and dominance, and then gradual decline. Some religions are able to deploy forces to reform and stave off decline. Others decline slowly at first, and then later the momentum accelerates until membership drops dramatically. Decline in the dominant religion is often accompanied by the development of new religious movements that proceed to gain majority status.

Duke and Johnson's perspective is important to the study of conversion because it enables us to understand conversion within the broader context of the religious and sociocultural matrix. Conversion patterns differ in each of the stages outlined by Duke and Johnson. A religion in decline would devote less energy to the recruitment of new members and also would suffer more apostasy. Although Duke and Johnson make no mention of it, I would speculate that religious parents would have more difficulty retaining their children within the faith when their religion is losing its influence. Religions that are gaining power and sustaining growth would be vigorous in their proselytizing. A religion on the rise is also more attractive to potential members. In a transitional phase fewer and fewer people would be converting. Proselytizing, if undertaken at all, would be motivated by the need to protect the institutional status quo, not by genuine religious vitality. The early phases of decline would be marked by a reduction in the rates of conversion, and these rates would drop off more and more rapidly with time. The number of apostates would increase. Groups seeking to reform themselves would try vigorously to convert new people and intensify the depth of commitment of current members in order to stave off decline.

Conversion takes place (1) when a person or group is connected to relationships in a religious community; (2) when rituals are enacted that foster experience and action consonant with religious mandates and goals; (3) when the rhetoric or system of interpretation of life is transformed into a religious frame of reference; and (4) when a person's role or sense of place and purpose is enacted and guided by religious sensibilities and structures.

The nature of conversion is, to a large degree, formed out of the *religious matrix*. In other words, the ideas, images, methods, and metaphors of a religious tradition give shape to the nature of the conversion experience. It should also be mentioned that the religious matrix is important when we consider contact between religious systems. Some religious traditions, especially indigenous traditions and folk traditions, are much more eclectic and open to outsiders. Judaism, Christianity, and Islam are more exclusive; they demand rejection of all other religious paths and require total allegiance from their followers. Such a difference obviously has an impact on the nature of religious contact and the nature of the religious conversion that takes place. A. D. Nock was one of the first to note that the prophetic religions (Judaism, Christianity, and Islam) generally require total repudiation of all other religions and complete, exclusive allegiance to their own systems. Hence, conversion to any of these religions will often entail explicit abandonment of past religious commitments in order to embrace the new religion fully. As we shall see later in the book, such religious requirements will make a difference in patterns of religious change in different environments.[27]

Contextual Influences on Conversion

Now that we have seen the broad contours of the context of conversion, I want to focus on some specific processes that are crucial features of the ever-shifting interplay of forces within the context. These processes blend the cultural, social, personal, and religious elements into powerful shapers of conversion.

Resistance and Rejection

Forces within the context may facilitate conversion, or act powerfully to prevent it. Indeed, I would argue that resistance is the normal or typical reaction of both individuals and societies to conversion attempts. Yet most conversion studies, perhaps this one included, emphasize conversion and make little mention of resistance. From a careful reading of the literature it is clear that in fact most people say no to conversion. Even when one reads reports of thousands of people who converted in a particular setting, little notice is paid to all the people who refused. Kraft's study of the remarkable growth of Christianity among the Higi people in northeastern Nigeria adjacent to the Cameroon Republic stresses the conversion of thousands. As a matter of fact, the huge majority of people rejected the new option. Kraft tells us that in 1958 there were 242 Christians, in 1962 there were 2,131 Christians, and in 1976 approximately 10,000. Needless to say, that is a rapid growth rate in less than twenty years. But the population of the Higi people was estimated by Kraft himself to be between one hundred and fifty thousand and two hundred thousand! Hence, more than 90 percent of the people said no to Christianity.[28]

In some settings rejection, resistance, and repudiation are blatantly obvious. China and Japan are two prime examples. Even though thousands of Christian missionaries have spent their lives in China and Japan, and millions of dollars have gone to build schools, hospitals, churches, and orphanages, the response has been slight. In Japan, Christians comprise less than 1 percent of the population. Chinese Christians are a tiny fraction of 1 percent. Chinese and Japanese cultures are sophisticated, complex, and resilient. Their cultures are so coherent, powerful, and adaptable that they have resisted or assimilated outside threats for thousands of years.

Enclaves

Contexts are rarely homogeneous. Generally speaking, most societies and cultures have some measure of ethnic, cultural, and social variety. Scattered throughout the world are groups able to live relatively distinct and independent lives, despite being surrounded by an environment that may be hostile to their values. These enclaves often maintain linguistic, dietary, and ritual distance from the surrounding milieu. In the Western world, Jews are a good example. Other examples include the Amish, the Hutterites, and Black Muslims. These groups serve as reminders that despite a macrocontext often hostile to religious orientations, with sufficient energy and effort groups can separate themselves from the wider culture and develop independent spheres of existence. These enclaves can serve either as environments in which particular types of conversion are expected, nourished, and flourish, or as contextual factors that serve as powerful resources for resistance to the conversion attempts of proselytizers.

Enclaves can be formed along racial or ethnic lines, according to religious beliefs, political beliefs, and other varieties of identity, or even by strongly held philosophical beliefs. Robert Balch and David Taylor argue that a major factor in the conversion of people to a cult centered on unidentified flying objects is what they call the "cultic milieu." To outsiders, conversion to a group that proclaims salvation via a flying saucer would be utterly ridiculous. Balch and Taylor report, however, that all converts to a flying-saucer cult that

they studied were people who had for years engaged in metaphysical spec-
ulation, occult practices, and various other forms of spiritual seeking. Balch
and Taylor describe the existence of thousands of people, hundreds of book-
stores, numerous organizations and groups, and hundreds of teachers who
foster and cater to a large subculture within the United States that believes in
spheres of existence beyond ordinary perception. Hence, converts to a UFO
cult are not changed radically in their beliefs. There is continuity between the
new option and beliefs they have held for a long time.[29]

Paths of Conversion

One way in which context influences conversion is by shaping the conversion process along pre-existing social, cultural, ethnic, or political lines.
Alan Tippett, studying the people in Oceania, found that acceptance and/or
rejection of conversion often followed lines of social cleavages already existing in the society. In addition, Tippett reports that patterns of denominational
conversion followed friendship and kinship networks of a particular tribe in
the South Pacific Islands. Hence, who converted to particular churches in
particular ways was determined to a large extent by family and social patterns
established before the missionaries arrived. The form of conversion varied
according to the denominational norms, and, unfortunately, denominational
conflicts were often established within the matrix of differing tribal groups.[30]

Congruence

Congruence—the degree to which elements of a new religion mesh with
existing macro- and microcontextual factors—is another important determinant of whether conversion will occur. Kraft's study of the Higi people in
Nigeria provides a good example. He describes how the congruence of
various cultural factors facilitated the Higi conversion to Christianity. Even
though Muslims lived in the same vicinity, the Higi did not consider conversion to Islam because the Muslims in that area were the Fulani people, traditional enemies of the Higi. In fact, the Fulani were warriors who had pre-

viously captured fellow Africans and sold them into slavery; hence there was a proclivity to reject Islam because of its association with the Fulani. On the other hand, within Higi culture there was a powerful tendency to have special respect for white people. The Higi had a saying, "Fear God, fear the White Man." Since the Christian missionaries were white, they were received with great respect. Moreover, their God was a figure who corresponded to a figure in Higi myth, Hyelatamwe. According to local traditions Hyelatamwe had departed because his son had been killed. The people were eager to hear from the Christians where their God had gone. Needless to say, the Christian message about God and Jesus resonated profoundly with Higi tribal religious stories.

These very important points of congruence were reinforced by other events of the time. Some of the Higi people suffered from leprosy and had been sent to a leprosarium located eighty miles away in Garkinda. The family and friends who remained in their villages considered the lepers dead, never to be seen again. While at the leprosarium the people came into contact with other lepers who were Christians and discussed with them the assets and liabilities of Christianity. In the 1950s, sulfa drugs were developed and most of the lepers were cured or were able to control their disease with the drugs. When they returned to their homes, family and friends felt the dead had been made alive. The healed lepers testified to the power of God and to their newfound faith in Jesus Christ. Thus, convergence between various factors in the context helped to foster and elicit conversion among the Higi.[31]

Types of Conversion in Context

Another way to understand the significance of context is to examine it in relation to each of the types of conversion, since context plays an important role in what type of conversion will transpire. *Tradition transition* generally takes place when there is contact between two different cultures. The most common example would be the missionary setting, in which a foreign religion is imported. The way contact is made varies. For example, a missionary may be allowed contact with the indigenous people because he or she is a representative of a powerful government that is colonizing the area. In other cases, contact is possible because the potential convert's society is already open to the contributions of outsiders, or because the society may simply be too weak to prevent contact.[32]

Institutional transition occurs in a context in which it is possible to move to new religious options within an existing tradition. Movement from the Methodist Church to the Roman Catholic Church is, from a sociological point of view, relatively easy in an urban environment in which various denominational options are readily available and in which there are few constraints for a person who chooses to leave one denomination and become involved in another.[33]

Affiliation involves joining a group that requires very high levels of commitment, and it generally happens when there is little or no commitment to a previous group. An example would be a young person who becomes involved in the Hare Krishna movement or the Unification Church.[34] The context allowing such mobility must be one that encourages religious pluralism, or at least does not deter it significantly, leaving a group free to proselytize actively.

Intensification takes place within a tradition, and thus the context that is especially important is the milieu of the movement itself. The mode of intensification is determined primarily by the ideology of the group and its methods for intensification. Currently, a popular form of intensification in Europe and North America is the *cursillos* movement, designed as a retreat for men and women who are already Christians but who desire to deepen their appreciation of and commitment to their faith.[35]

Apostasy and *defection*, at least in the context of the United States and Western Europe, are very common when there are few or no material or social rewards for participation in religious organizations. In fact, many theologians would argue that in the United States and much of Europe education provides training in secular modes of interpretation that ideologically discourage a religious construction of reality.[36]

Context and Normative Conversion

One way in which context influences the conversion process is by providing metaphors, images, expectations, and patterns for conversion. Thus, certain models of conversion are perceived to be the normative form through which people must pass in order to be valid converts. The metaphors and expectations offered by a particular model of conversion can have a powerful shaping influence on the consciousness and experience of individuals.[37] Olive Stone reports on a people in a remote village on an island (fictitiously named River Island) in the Atlantic for whom (in 1943, at the time of her field research) "membership in the church is achieved solely through conversion, and conversion is signaled by a vision."[38] River Island's 746 inhabitants, with the exception of 7 percent, were members of the church. Stone's detailed analysis of the visions is not important here. Rather, it is crucial to note that the requirement of a vision to verify the conversion experience actually elicited and shaped the production of such a vision. It is not my intent to question the validity of the visions but to stress the way in which the context's requirement for conversion influenced the actual experience of the conversion process. There was, of course, variation in the details of the visions, but the vision experience itself, when mandatory as a proof of genuine conversion, was universally reported.

Bill J. Leonard's account of his own Southern Baptist experience is another excellent example of the roles social and cultural conditioning may play in the conversion process.[39] Leonard grew up in a culture that deemed a particular form of conversion to be the only "true" conversion experience. To be saved one had to have a conscious experience of conversion. Required elements included a sense of sin, a "coming forward" to the "anxious bench," praying the sinner's prayer to acknowledge one's sinfulness, and inviting Jesus to come into the heart of the convert.

Hypotheses Emerging from Context

To encourage discussion and focus attention on specific issues, and to stimulate further research, let me propose some hypotheses about the dynamics of conversion.

1. Indigenous cultures that are stable, resilient, and effective will have few people receptive to conversion.

1.2. A strong culture will reward conformity and punish deviance.

1.2.1. Benefits go to those who perform according to expectations.

1.2.2. Punishments will be exacted from deviants and outsiders who violate the culture in any way.

1.3. Those who do convert in a hostile setting are marginal members of the society.

1.3.1. Marginality may have many sources.

1.3.2. Marginal people are, in some way, disconnected from the sources of power and support of the traditional culture. The more marginal, the more likely they are to convert.

1.3.3. Marginality can be cultivated via many methods.

2. Indigenous cultures that are in crisis will have more potential converts than stable societies.

2.1. The duration, intensity, and extent of the crisis influences the degree of receptivity.

2.2. During a severe crisis, the deficiencies of a culture become obvious to many people, thus stimulating interest in new alternatives.

2.3. During a cultural crisis, an important factor affecting conversion patterns is whether the crisis was created externally or internally.

2.4. In a colonial setting, the perceived strength of the colonial power is a crucial variable.

2.5. In a cultural crisis, it is possible that the most talented, creative people will take the lead in conversion because they may perceive advantages to themselves and to the group as a whole.

3. The more consonant the cultural systems—in the context of cultural contact—the more likely it is that conversion will transpire. The more dissonant, the less likely it is that conversion will occur.

3.1. The relative degree of consonance and dissonance will determine the rate of conversion.

3.1.1. Consonance of core values and symbols will facilitate conversion.

3.1.2. Consonance of values and symbols high in the hierarchy of values and symbols will facilitate conversion.

4. In a situation of cultural pluralism, there will be differential responses to conversion based on cultural and social factors.

5. Except in cases of coercion, converts choose a new option on the basis of perceived advantages to themselves.

6. Converts selectively adopt and adapt the new religion to meet their needs.

7. Contact between advocates and potential converts is a dynamic process.

7.1. The relative power of the advocate and the recipient influences the interaction.

7.2. The circumstances of the contact shape the interaction.

7.3. Characteristics of the advocate and the recipient, vis-à-vis their own cultures (especially marginality or centrality), influence the interaction.

We have now seen that context comprises a dynamic force field of people, institutions, ideologies, expectations, and global settings in which people confront the human predicament. Individuals, groups, communities, ethnic groups, and nations are situated within and shaped by various superstructures and infrastructures that influence the content and form of the drama of conversion and resistance. Congruence and conflict come together in fascinating ways to either inhibit or promote the onset of the crisis stage.

Crisis

One of the problems facing the student of conversion is to understand the sequence of events that constitute the conversion process. Some form of crisis usually precedes conversion; that is acknowledged by most scholars of conversion. The crisis may be religious, political, psychological, or cultural in origin. Where scholars disagree is on whether the disorientation precedes contact with a proselytizer or comes afterward. Luther P. Gerlach and Virginia H. Hine, for instance, found that the conversion process began for their subjects when they had contact with an advocate who sought to persuade them to see the world and themselves in a new light.[1] That is no doubt one valid conception of the process. However, an equally valid assumption, I suggest, is that many (indeed, most) converts are active agents in their conversion process. The sequence of my chapters reflects this latter view: context, crisis, quest, encounter, interaction, commitment, and consequences. For the other perspective the stages would be re-sequenced: context, encounter, crisis, quest (or a response that resists or repudiates the new option), interaction, commitment, and consequences.

Two basic issues are at stake in a discussion of the crisis stage. The first is the importance of contextual issues, and the second is the degree of activity or passivity of the convert. Let me illustrate the first with reference to Christianity. In the United States, Western Europe, and other places (such as the Philippines) where Christianity is the dominant religion, Christianity is an integral part of the culture. It is not unusual for people to seek out Christianity when they desire "salvation." But conversion to Christianity is fundamentally different in sociocultural settings where Christianity is not the dominant religion or, in more extreme situations, is not even known.

When missionaries try to convert people who know nothing about Christianity, the process is very different from situations where Christianity is

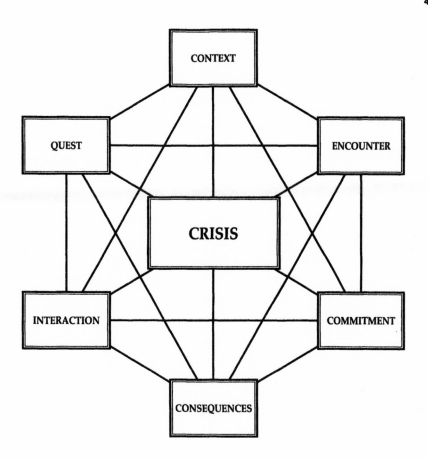

Figure 5 *Stage 2: Crisis.*

taken for granted. The advocate knows and controls the processes of conversion, and the potential convert is by definition more passive because of his or her lack of knowledge and power. Except in very rare circumstances, however, the potential convert does retain some power, expressed primarily in the way he or she responds to and assimilates the new faith. The power to say no is the ultimate control.

Scholars of conversion have long been divided as to whether the convert is active or passive. The truth is that this is not an either/or but rather a both/and factor, with a multitude of variations along the spectrum. As with many of the issues vexing conversion studies, resolution can be found in acknowledging both possibilities and seeking richer understanding based on a continuum.[2]

Nature of Crisis

The crisis stage must be assessed carefully.[3] What is the nature of the crisis that stimulates or facilitates conversion? Are all crises equally important to the process? What is the intensity, duration, and scope of the crisis? Is the real issue the severity of the crisis rather than the precise nature of the crisis? As in the matter of a convert's degree of activity or passivity, crisis should be seen as existing along a continuum rather than as an absolute either/or state. There are many different types of disorientation and crisis. Much of the literature in the human sciences has emphasized social disintegration, political oppression, or a dramatic event as the instigator of crisis. But crisis can also be brought on by something less dramatic, such as the response of a person to powerful preaching that convicts him or her of sin, starting a process of self-exploration and a search for salvation.

Two basic types of crisis are important to the conversion process: crises that call into question one's fundamental orientation to life, and crises that in and of themselves are rather mild but are the proverbial straw that breaks the camel's back. It is easy to see that death, suffering, and other painful experiences can challenge one's interpretation of life, calling everything into question, but other events that appear to be rather insignificant may also eventually serve as triggers—crises in retrospect. Cumulative events and processes are often crucial to conversion. Someone could well argue that merely hearing childrens' voices say "Take up and read" is trivial, but for Augustine those words were the culmination of a process that had enormous significance for his religious journey.[4]

The flexibility, resilience, and creativity of the *context* of crisis also need to be considered. Some cultures, societies, persons, and religions are able to withstand a severe crisis and adapt to it in a productive manner. Others are

Intensity:	Mild	Severe
Duration:	Brief	Prolonged
Scope:	Limited	Extensive
Source:	Internal	External
Old/New:	Continuity	Discontinuity

Figure 6 *Contours of crisis.*

more vulnerable to outside influence. We recall that, as a general rule, most scholars of conversion agree that few conversions take place in areas with well-organized, literate religions supported by the economic, political, and cultural powers of the region. Christianity gains few converts from Islam. In fact, few converts are made from any of the so-called world religions. The most "fertile" field of conversion in the missionary setting has tended to be among the so-called animists, such as the various tribal groups in Africa, South America, and India. Folk religion is less resilient in the face of the world religions—especially Christianity and Islam. Animists rarely have extensive organizations and ideologies that are linked with anyone beyond their village. Lacking these internal structures and external resources, they are more easily disconnected from indigenous modes of thought and action.

The Relative Importance of Crises

Debates have long raged about the importance of tension or crisis as an instigator of conversion. Among the first social scientists to note the importance of crisis in the conversion process were John Lofland and Rodney Stark.[5] They describe this crisis as a "felt discrepancy between some imaginary ideal state of affairs and the circumstances in which these people saw themselves caught up."[6] Observing participants in a cult in an urban area, they found that some sort of tension in the people's lives triggered a religious quest.

Some researchers have confirmed the Lofland and Stark findings, while others reject the necessity of tension or crisis as an instigator of conversion.[7] One of the most statistically sophisticated studies of the role of stress is the work of Max Heirich.[8] He compared Roman Catholic charismatics and a control group of noncharismatic Roman Catholics in terms of several factors related to stress. Both groups experienced various forms of stress and crisis. Heirich reports, however, that the only statistically significant finding was that charismatic converts "were less likely than others to deny stress rather than more likely to report some stress." He concludes that "stress . . . is insufficient to account for what is going on." In other words, converts are aware of stress and have no need to deny its role in their lives. Clearly, stress, tension, or crisis alone is not enough to explain conversion, although a catalyst of some sort is often an initiator of the conversion process. The precise nature of the crisis will vary from person to person and from situation to situation.

Catalysts for Crisis

Mystical Experiences

In the more than fifty interviews I have conducted and the countless books and articles I have read, conversions are often stimulated by an extraordinary, and in some cases mystical, experience. The nature of the experience varies, but for most people a mystical experience, especially an unexpected one, is profoundly disturbing. The paradigmatic example is the experience of Saul of Tarsus. The biblical accounts describe the catalyst of his conversion as a mystical experience triggered by divine intervention. As recorded by Luke in his narrative of the early church, the Acts of the Apostles, Saul was the chief architect of the opposition to the new sectarian, messianic movement in Judaism. While on a mission to persecute the followers of Jesus in the city of Damascus in Syria, he had an experience that transformed his life. As reported by Luke, Saul was confronted by the resurrected Jesus. Blinded, he was sent to Damascus and ministered to by Ananias, a follower of Jesus.[9] Whatever the precise nature of the experience, it is clear that Saul's life was profoundly altered. The mystical experience convinced him that his commitment to persecution was untenable. He felt compelled to change allegiance. Saul the persecutor of Christians became Paul, the leading proclaimer of Christianity.

Several years ago I interviewed a woman who told me that the beginning of her conversion process was a shattering experience. One day while she was taking a bath, the radio fell into the water. She said that she was lifted bodily out of the tub and onto the floor. She believed that God had literally taken her out of the water and saved her life. This experience triggered an intensive interest in the Bible—for weeks she did little else but read the Scriptures to try to make sense of her miraculous experience. Later she came into contact with people from a conservative church and converted, but the beginning of her conversion process was a crisis triggered by a dramatic life-or-death experience.

Near-Death Experiences

During the past two decades many books and articles have recounted what has come to be called the near-death experience.[10] These experiences, usually after an almost fatal accident or during surgery, tend to be similar. The person experiences his or her spirit separating from the body. Often the person will feel as if he or she is traveling through a long tunnel. At the end of the tunnel are a bright light and a gathering of friends and family. Usually the person feels joy and delight in the experience and is sometimes not eager to return to physical life. Thus far, little direct research has been conducted on the specific relationship between conversion and the near-death experience. However, a person who has had such an experience sometimes comes to believe that there is another reality beyond the scope of our ordinary senses. The experience can be a catalyst for change in one's "normal" perspective on life, and for a profound spiritual awakening.

Illness and Healing

Severe illness or recovery from severe illness is often another catalyst for conversion.[11] One convert, this time to the Sikh religion, reported that he had experienced a general sense of tiredness and lack of physical well-being. He began yoga classes and soon felt better. Some time later he had to have abdominal surgery, which caused adhesions in his intestines that were quite painful. He told his yoga teacher about the problem, and his yogi urged him to begin a more serious practice of yoga and a change of diet. His symptoms disappeared, and his general physical state improved considerably. From this experience of improved health, he began to see that there was more to yoga than merely physical exercise. He then began to explore the spiritual foundation of the physical practice of yoga.

Is That All There Is?

It is not uncommon for the crisis to be less dramatic than the experiences we have just considered. For some people the "opening" is made by a vague and growing sense of dissatisfaction with life as it is. One feels that the ordinary way of doing things and of thinking about things is not as comprehensive and compelling as it should be. Perhaps the person has achieved all of his or her goals and then asks the question, Is that all there is? Perhaps getting a promotion, having a family, or achieving a central goal proves to be less fulfilling than expected. One may feel that life does not have the meaning and purpose it should have. Such a perception may stimulate a search for new options or a quest to rediscover roots in the tradition in which one was raised.

Desire for Transcendence

Rather than thinking in terms of crisis, it might be helpful to think in terms of the desire for transcendence. Some would argue, especially from a theological point of view, that human beings are motivated to seek beyond themselves for meaning and purpose. Many people desire to experience God in a way that will enrich and expand their lives. Social scientists rarely admit such positive motivations for conversion, tending to see them as rationalizations for "deeper" motivations (often pathological) that are being masked by religious ideas. Whatever the case, some people do convert even though no overt crisis seems to exist. They simply desire more. For whatever reasons, that "more" is defined in terms of religion, and thus they pursue transcendence.

Altered States of Consciousness

For many people, the beginning of a new vision came through the use of drugs. During the 1960s in particular, drugs became catalysts for seeing reality in a different way. Once it became clear that very serious dangers often accompanied the use of drugs, many people began to seek nondrug alternatives that would provide the same altered states of consciousness. James Downton's study of converts to the Divine Light Mission noted that most of the people who became followers of the Guru Maharaj Ji had previously used drugs, and wanted to attain a "higher state of consciousness" that would be less dangerous and more sustainable over time than the euphoria produced by the use of drugs.[12]

Protean Selfhood

Another way of understanding the nature of crisis is to appreciate the way in which the very cultural fabric of the modern world makes a search for meaning and for a more stable sense of self mandatory. Robert Jay Lifton's classic essay "Protean Man" articulates this point of view. Given the various alternatives open to contemporary people, Lifton suggests, it is inevitable that, for some, selfhood takes on a form of permanent malleability. Since no one cultural model exists, such people may continually seek new ways of being. Religious conversion offers both a new experience of transformation and a refuge from constant change. Hence, some people are interested in religious conversion because they want to try something new, and in the case of certain forms of conversion, they seek a core or center that will provide stability in the midst of chaos.

Pathology

Much of the psychological literature that explores motivation for conversion is psychoanalytic in orientation and proceeds from the view that crisis implies a debility, a breakdown. From this perspective, the motivation to convert derives from a deficiency generated out of fear, loneliness, or desperation, and the conversion itself is seen as an adaptive mechanism that attempts to resolve psychological conflict.

Research by humanistic and transpersonal psychologists offers an alternative perspective, suggesting that a desire for fulfillment can be just as strong a motive as deficiency. According to this orientation, some people are spiritual questors, always growing, learning, developing, maturing. Rather than being viewed as passive victims of aggressive advocates, these people are characterized as actively searching for new options, new stimulation, new ideas, new depths of involvement.

The psychoanalysts, then, because their subjects are primarily people who are "emotionally ill" (or drawn from clinical cases), see the primary motivation for conversion to be a search for emotional resolution. The humanists, because they presume their subjects to be, on the whole, psychologically "healthy" people, view conversion as a quest for intellectual, spiritual, and emotional transformation and growth.

One of the few comparative studies in this area that attempts to move beyond this dichotomy by examining a more diverse sample of converts was conducted by Chana Ullman.[13] Ullman studied ten converts to Orthodox Judaism, ten Roman Catholic converts, ten Hare Krishnas, ten Bahai, and a group of thirty people who served as a matched control group. Ullman's research compared and contrasted factors such as the amount of trauma or family conflict in the converts' lives during childhood and adolescence, their degree of interest in religious and existential questions, and their degree of involvement with religious groups. Although Ullman initially theorized that the major motivation for conversion was the need for cognitive meaning, she found, in fact, that the major issues motivating the forty converts (in comparison to the control group) were emotional, involving problematic relationships with their father, unhappy childhoods, and a past history of disrupted, distorted personal relationships.

Joel Allison also conducted a comparative study of converts.[14] He selected twenty male students at a Protestant seminary. Within this group, he compared seven students who had had intense religious conversions with seven who had had mild conversions and six who had had no conversion experience at all. Allison found that those who converted, almost without exception, had absent, weak, or alcoholic fathers. Those who did not convert came from intact families. He theorized that conversion for these young men was adaptive and growth producing, in that they were able to move away from dependence upon and enmeshment with the mother by identifying with strong father figures, namely God and Jesus. Allison's study is one of the few psychoanalytic studies that view the adaptive element of conversion as positive. Ullman's and Allison's studies point to the need for further comprehensive, comparative research projects in adult populations to provide us with a more accurate picture of the nature of religious change.

Apostasy

Another catalyst for crisis and conversion is leaving a religious tradition. Whatever the cause for the disruption, many people who leave a particular religious orientation are thrown into a crisis that triggers their quest for new religious experiences, institutions, teachings, and communities.

This is perhaps another way of saying that some forms of conversion also require an apostasy.[15] Some conversions require explicit and enacted rejection of past affiliations, but all conversions implicitly require a leaving-behind or a reinterpretation of some past way of life and set of beliefs. Of course the break is not always a significant split, but by definition a person moves from one orientation to another in conversion, which requires some degree of personal change.

Apostasy inevitably elicits grief over lost relationships, ideas, beliefs, rituals, and connections with friends and family.[16] The harshness with which some new converts denigrate their past can be understood when we realize that strong ties are being severed or realigned in a new religious orientation. Apostasy makes a person sad because many aspects of the past are difficult to give up: the certainty, the rhythm of the ritual cycle, the force of leadership, the interconnections with many people, and the symbolic richness of a tradition. These issues of loss are not dealt with well in the modern world. We are simply told to let go of the past, as if there were some electronic switch that one can flip, jettisoning years of experience with a single gesture. Such attitudes do not acknowledge the powerful pull of the past—even if that past is perceived to be evil and destructive. The past is powerful because that is the world in which we dwelt for years, and it lives on in our minds and hearts. There is no easy escape from the past, no easy transition to the future. Conversion is painful for many because it uproots converts from their past and throws them into a new future. However exciting the new option may be, the convert may not want to give up past relationships and modes of living that are still in many ways a part of his or her core identity. Denigration, then, is one tool for making the change more palatable or amenable.

Externally Stimulated Crises

It is clear that some crises are caused by external forces, most notably when colonial powers disrupt and in some cases destroy the existing sociocultural reality of indigenous peoples. Faced with overwhelming outside power, the very fabric of a culture may be rent asunder. Of course most cultures, even the most fragile, are resilient to some degree, but rarely are they able to resist the force of outsiders completely.

Subjects of colonial expansion, especially "smaller," less powerful people—like the indigenous peoples of sub-Saharan Africa and North, Central, and South America—were unable to stave off the influence of the Portuguese, Spanish, and later the Dutch, English, French, and Germans. The enormous power of the Europeans succeeded in undermining the infrastructure of the indigenous peoples.

Another important form of externally triggered crisis is the activity of missionaries or advocates. As I mentioned in the first part of this chapter, the sequence of stages in conversion is influenced, to some degree, by contextual factors. The presence of an advocate may trigger dissatisfaction in a potential convert that had not previously been clearly felt. As we shall see later, the persuasion process is designed in part to foster a sense of dissatisfaction with the contemporary situation and thus to stimulate the search for a new alternative.

In any case, a crisis, from whatever quarter it springs, will more than likely stimulate activity to relieve the discomfort, resolve the discord, remove the sense of tension. For many, this activity can be identified as a quest.

Quest

Chapter 4

Human beings continually engage in the process of world construction and reconstruction in order to generate meaning and purpose, to maintain psychic equilibrium, and to assure continuity. Recently, social scientists like James Richardson have begun to view people as active agents in the creation of meaning and the selection of religious options.[1] One word (of many possible words) that embodies this process of building meaning, whatever its impetus, is *quest*.

The notion of quest begins with the assumption that people seek to maximize meaning and purpose in life, to erase ignorance, and to resolve inconsistency. Under abnormal or crisis conditions this search becomes compelling; people actively look for resources that offer growth and development to "fill the void," solve the problem, or enrich life. Quest is an ongoing process, but one that will greatly intensify during times of crisis. Three sets of factors may be helpful in exploring the quest stage: response style, structural availability, and motivational structures.

Response Style

Response style differentiates the person who reacts actively from one who responds passively to conversion.[2] The working assumption in this book, that converts are often active agents in their own conversion, is shared by many contemporary researchers. Roger A. Straus, for example, has done extensive field work among Scientologists, from which he argues that converts are seekers who actively construct and manage their own conversions.[3] Straus suggests that sometimes religious seekers are engaged in "creative bumbling." Their path to transformation is not always clear and direct, but they are able to seek out beliefs, groups, and organizations that serve their perceived needs.

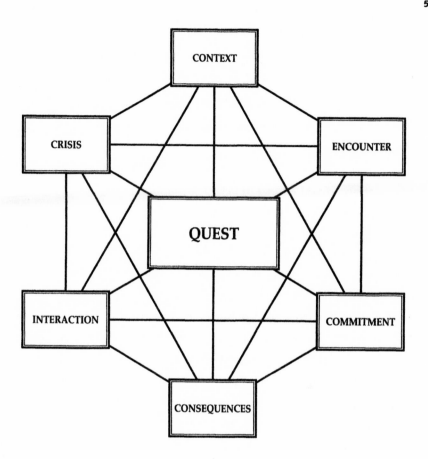

Figure 7 *Stage 3: Quest.*

A dramatic example of active agency is the conversion of Ambedkar to Buddhism.[4] B. R. Ambedkar (1881–1956) was one of the first so-called Untouchables in India to receive advanced education in England. Upon his return to India he became convinced that Hinduism, because of its rigid caste system, was a source of much suffering to his people. For several years he self-consciously searched for a religion that would foster the well-being of his people. He examined Islam and Christianity, two obvious options in India at that time. After careful consideration of the issues, however, he chose Buddhism. Buddhism was of Indian origin, after all, and Ambedkar concludes it was the religion best suited to serve the needs of his people. After extensive preparation he led an estimated two million Untouchables to convert to Buddhism on 14 October 1956.

Another example of active agency occurred in the Indian state of Kerala. The Hill Arrian people heard that there were Christian missionaries from England in the area. According to K. G. Daniel's research, the people approached the Church Missionary Society's Henry Baker, Jr., five times before he finally relented and agreed to preach to them and help found a school.[5] Whatever their motives, the Hill Arrian people were apparently eager to have a missionary come to their village and provide knowledge of Christianity.

Augustine, surely one of the most famous converts to Christianity, was engaged in a protracted religious quest, which took him from North Africa to Italy. His search for spiritual fulfillment motivated him to explore various religious and philosophical traditions, and some argue that he experienced a series of conversions before he finally embraced the Roman Catholic Church.[6]

These are only a few examples of converts who have themselves been active agents. While some converts are undoubtedly passive recipients, it is important to highlight the active quality of many, if not most, conversions. For too long, converts have been viewed as primarily passive. This debate has been particularly harsh between adherents to the so-called anticult movement and those who are either outright advocates of the New Religious Movements or who do not see these movements as employing brainwashing or coercive persuasion. The anticult movement consists primarily of ex-members, their parents and friends, and therapists who have counseled people who have left New Religious Movements. The anticultists interpret recruitment to these movements as fraudulent conversion because the advocates of the cult use manipulative and deceptive strategies to seduce people into involvement. Margaret Singer, considered by some to be the dominant foe of cults, argues that they use "the systematic manipulation of social and psychological influence."[7] Recruits to cults, she believes, are not rational and autonomous religious questors but vulnerable victims. Other scholars of the

Active	Receptive	Rejecting	Apathetic	Passive

Active questing	a person looking for new options because of dissatisfaction with the old ways and/or a desire for innovation and/or a search for fulfillment and growth
Receptive	a person is "ready" for new options for a variety of reasons
Rejecting	someone consciously rejects the new option
Apathetic	someone has no interest in a new religious option
Passive	someone is so weak and fragile that he or she is easily manipulated by external influences

Figure 8 *Modes of response.*

New Religious Movements focus their research on those who are current members, and they generally see recruits as people who join through their own free will because of their quest for meaning and purpose.

This conflict has been dramatized in dozens of court cases during the past decade, as anticultists have sued New Religious Movements on such grounds as false imprisonment and fraud.[8] The argument tends to focus on whether or not a person who joins is a passive victim or an active questor. Because of the adversarial model of justice in the United States, the empirical reality and complexity of the conversion process is generally lost when examined in courts of law. The reality is that some people are passive and others are active, and many people are active at certain times and passive at other times. Of course a fundamental philosophical debate underlies the issue—namely, What is the ultimate nature of humans, and are they capable of intentional action for goals or merely directed by external and internal forces over which they have no control? We cannot resolve this debate, but we may observe that people can be situated in a number of ways along the response-style continuum.

Structural Availability

Another important issue influencing the quest stage is what sociologists call "structural availability,"[9] that is, the freedom of a person or persons to move from previous emotional, intellectual, and religious institutions, commitments, and obligations into new options. The various networks that shape our lives—family, job, friendship, religious organizations, and so forth—are often very powerful in discouraging or even preventing change and development, however desirable that change may be to the individual. Despite the internal responsiveness of a person, he or she may, for various reasons, find the new option inappropriate, unachievable, or unavailable.

For example, a practical concern may be the amount of discretionary time a person has available. If a religious group requires communal living or full-time education and proselytizing, joining such a group would simply not seem practicable for many middle-class, married, employed people. People who could respond to such a group would be those who are generally single or unemployed, or who for some other reason have enough free time and energy to pursue the new option. These structural variations in people's lives are specifically taken into account by some groups that are self-consciously seeking new members. The Church of Jesus Christ of Latter-Day Saints, for instance, seeks out complete families. Their proselytizing strategies include Mormon families reaching out to non-Mormon families to establish friendships by way of invitations to dinner, accompaniment to church meetings, and explicit teaching of Latter-Day Saints doctrine in the advocate's home.[10]

We should bear in mind too that some people are motivated to convert precisely because the conversion can serve as an effective weapon against undesired family ties. In other words, some Jews who convert to Christianity may be symbolically repudiating their blood families, knowing conversion to Christianity is an offense to most Jews. The same could be said of someone with a Southern Baptist background converting to Roman Catholicism, or vice versa.

Of course, the way in which these issues are conceptualized for the individual within a tradition is shaped primarily by the ideology of the group being joined. Some religious groups insist on repudiation of all past associations that do not support and reinforce the new option. For instance, some fundamentalist groups demand that people who become members repudiate with zeal their Roman Catholic or Jewish background.

Emotional Availability

In addition to general structural availability, we need to consider emotional dimensions. Previously existing and/or profound attachments generally limit any active personal quest for new attachments and hinder the success of proselytizing. Marc Galanter's research, for instance, has shown that some people who go through the indoctrination program of the Unification Church (or Moonies) will come out believing in the doctrine and organization, and even perhaps in Sun Myung Moon's messiahship, but will choose to leave the church because they have important emotional connections in the outside world.[11] They may have a spouse, strong family ties, and/or other emotional ties that prevent them from pursuing their interest in the church.

Intellectual Availability

Intellectual availability is another crucial variable influencing whether and how a person engages in religious quest or responds to advocates. The cognitive framework of a movement or option must be somewhat compatible with a person's previous orientation or there will be no attraction. It is rare for someone to be converted to an option that embraces an intellectual framework radically different from the person's previous viewpoint. In most of the conversions I have studied, both the form and content of the new option were appealing to a person because they offered some significant continuity or connection with that person's previous orientation. For example, James Downton's research on conversion to the Divine Light Mission demonstrated that most of the converts were deeply involved in the drug culture. The experience of altered states of consciousness and the ideology of openness to such experiences facilitated conversion to a religious organization that encouraged the experiences.[12]

Robert Balch and David Taylor discovered that people who converted readily to an unidentified flying object cult usually came from a "cultic milieu" in which belief in such things was very common. Thus conversion was an extension of previously held beliefs and involvements.[13] For some persons, conversion is in the nature of a return to previously held beliefs.

David F. Gordon's study of "Jesus People" describes the converts to this particular version of fundamentalist Christianity as finding a compromise between their countercultural views and their family background in fundamentalist Christianity.[14] The point is not that intellectual changes made by converts are insignificant, but that there is generally more continuity than is commonly acknowledged.

Religious Availability

Religious availability means that a person's religious beliefs, practices, and life-style are to some degree compatible with the new option. Sociological studies that examine patterns of movement within religious groups often find evidence of a continuity with the previous orientation. Steven M. Tipton's *Getting Saved from the Sixties* systematically investigates the nature of conversion processes to such diverse groups as charismatic Christianity, Zen Buddhism, and the human-potential movement known as "est."[15] Tipton found that involvement in these groups, while superficially deviant, made sense when probing the life histories of the converts and the sociocultural context in which the conversions took place. The moral values and modes of living and working in these new religious groups were extensions of the orientations to life that the converts had previously held.

A person's religious background influences that individual's conversion process in other ways as well. For instance, Yeakley's studies have shown that someone with a mixed religious background is more likely to change orientation than a person who has a family that is uniform in its religious involvement.[16] There are two ways of looking at this finding. One is to say that mixed families are more tolerant of new options, and thus an atmosphere is created in which people are free to explore new options. Another interpretation is that a mixed family tradition has less holding power over its members than a monolithic family tradition, and there is simply not as much resistance to religious change in a family that is already heterogenous. It is my view that the conversion process is an interplay of forces of attraction, resistance, and repulsion. A person deeply attached to a family that is uniformly committed to a certain religious orientation is less likely to convert to a new option, unless there are compelling forces to counteract the power of the family system.

Motivational Structures

Another way of examining the degree of a person's active quest for religious change or passive vulnerability to religious advocates is to assess motivational structures. There are many theories of motivation in this complicated area of modern psychology. Some theories attempt to identify one overriding motivational factor for conversion, such as conflict resolution, relief of guilt, or compliance with family pressure, but it is probably more accurate to recognize that people are motivated to convert by a wide variety of factors, which can change over time. Seymour Epstein offers a model of motivation that is consistent with this view, in that it synthesizes and integrates many possibilities.[17] Epstein postulates four basic motivations for human beings: the need to experience pleasure and avoid pain; the need for a conceptual system; the need to enhance self-esteem; and the need to establish and maintain relationships. The force of each of these motivations, Epstein suggests, will vary among different people as well as within an individual at different times and in different circumstances. A religious movement that emphasizes community life and offers warm fellowship, for instance, will appeal to someone who is searching for relationships. The person who has a need to understand more deeply the self and the world may be motivated to convert because a religious movement provides a coherent, compelling conceptual system.

I would add to Epstein's model two motivational factors that are rarely discussed in the literature on conversion: power and transcendence. James Beckford argues for the importance of the role of power in religion in his article "The Restoration of Power to the Sociology of Religion."[18] He suggests that the focus on religion's function as a generator of meaning and identity, which was prominent in the late 1960s and early 1970s, overlooked the fact that power is an explicit component in religious experience, ideology, and institutions. Beckford lists various kinds of power that have recently been advanced as playing a pivotal role in the phenomenology of religion, ranging from the power to heal and the power to be successful, to the power to gain control over one's life and the power over death.

Walter Conn argues (persuasively, I believe) for the centrality of a yearning for transcendence as a primary motivation for conversion.[19] He studied the theories and research of developmental psychologists like Lawrence Kohlberg, Erik H. Erikson, Jean Piaget, Robert Kegan, and James Fowler, believing that their work offers clues to a person's inherent attraction to, or need for, transcendence. Conn feels that the model of a person moving through a series of developmental stages in which he or she strives to mature cognitively, affectively, and morally offers evidence of a primary human yearning for transcendence. Conn suggests that this innate drive to go beyond one's present level of development can be a sufficient motivating factor in conversion, rather than conversion being seen merely as a defensive coping mechanism resulting from such things as an absent father or a non-nurturing mother. Thus Conn sees conversion not as an aberrant process but as one integrated into healthy human growth and quest. There are limitations to developmental theory (one could question, for instance, as Carol Gilligan does,[20] whether the developmental stages are as universal and invariant as is often claimed), but Conn's work does offer a specific theologically and philosophically sophisticated approach to developing a normative theory of conversion.

These motivations operative in the quest stage extend also throughout the encounter and interaction stages as attractions to a new religious orientation, and ultimately into the commitment stage as reasons to solidify one's commitment. It is imperative, however, to recognize that motivations to convert are multiple, complex, interactive, and cumulative. Recognition of this diversity is another step toward a fuller understanding of the conversion process.[21]

The Advocate

Chapter 5

At this very moment, thousands of missionaries are seeking to make converts. More than thirty-seven thousand missionaries of the Church of Jesus Christ of Latter-Day Saints are crisscrossing the streets and roads of cities, villages, and rural areas throughout the world. In 1988 they claimed more than two hundred thousand converts. At least thirty-nine thousand Protestant missionaries from Canada and the United States are seeking converts in the inner city of Singapore, the jungles of Brazil, the villages of Tanzania, and elsewhere. Another nine thousand Roman Catholic missionaries from North America are in diverse places serving and preaching to people. Jewish groups are seeking their "fallen-away" brothers and sisters by calling them to return to Jewish ritual and traditions. Buddhists and Muslims around the world are seeking to persuade people of the truth and value of Buddhism and Islam.[1]

It can be a most remarkable event when an advocate and a potential convert come together and begin to engage in processes that will result, for some people, in conversion. This fascinating and complex encounter is a dynamic process. Why do some people reject the new alternative while others embrace it with enthusiasm? Who are the missionaries? Who are the converts? Are there consistent, identifiable traits these people in each group share? How is it possible to bridge the gulf between cultures, religions, and societies in order to convert people to a new religion?

In the past, scholars of conversion have focused their studies almost exclusively on the convert, but in fact a crucial and dynamic interplay exists between the advocate and the potential convert. Both sides maneuver, strategize, and engage in various tactics during the encounter stage. The advocate assesses the potential target audience and formulates persuasive tactics to

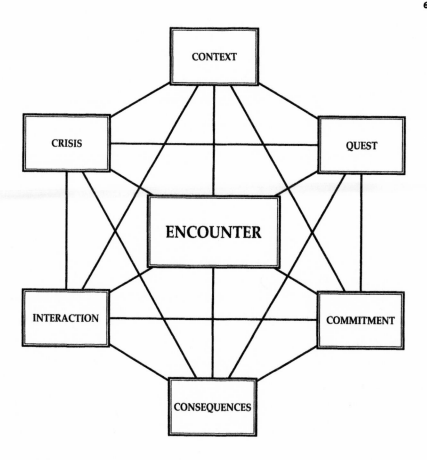

Figure 9 *Stage 4: Encounter.*

bring converts into the religious community. The convert also seeks to enhance his or her own perceived best interests. The ways in which advocate
and potential convert reciprocally meet each other's needs is an area that
scholars have only recently begun to explore. Missiologists have given rich
descriptions of ways in which advocates have been transformed by their
encounters with potential converts and their cultures; the influence is not
unidirectional.[2]

Expansion and Mission

Before focusing on the role of the missionary, or advocate, in the conversion encounter, we need to distinguish between expansion of a religion and deliberate mission.

Expansion refers to the growth of a religious movement through such things as the rate of childbirth or the inclusion of new members without specific and self-conscious conversion by those members. Mission, however, is the intentional effort of a group to proselytize and incorporate new members, which in some cases requires that the new member repudiate old allegiances and affirm an exclusive membership. Christianity and Islam are the only religions that have explicit and specific missionary enterprises, Christianity seems to be more concerned than any other religion with the conversion of "pagans." Social context influences the way in which conversion becomes a more or less explicit goal and concern of theology in an institutionalized church. This concern may be dormant at times and intense at others. For example, when the Catholic Church was the dominant force in Europe there was little need to be concerned with conversion, because most people were already Roman Catholics. Contact with Islam and later with the New World revitalized Catholicism's interest in missionary effort. Outsiders were perceived to be in need of Christianity.[3]

Nature of the Advocate

The nature of advocates (or missionaries) and their activities embraces numerous considerations. Is conversion central to their mission? What is their personal experience of conversion? What do they understand conversion to be? What are their motivations for missionary work? What are the goals of the missionary enterprise as a whole? What does the advocate deem to be the "ideal conversion"? Clearly, there are connections between a missionary's style and ideology and the type of convert who is attracted by the missionary enterprise. In the study of conversion, it is important to make explicit a systematic formulation of the methods and motivations of the advocate.[4]

The work of T. O. Beidelman provides an important contribution to this focus on the advocate.[5] As an anthropologist, Beidelman is interested in missionaries and missionary enterprises as complex organizations that were important to European and American colonial endeavors. He sees the missionary as an "agent of social change" and believes that missionaries and missions should be studied in their own right. For the purposes of this book, his five categories of concern provide a useful framework.

Secular Attributes

The secular attributes of a missionary—the missionary's ethnicity, class, and economic background—will influence many of his or her attitudes and strategies. For example, many Church Missionary Society advocates in the nineteenth century were poor and uneducated by comparison with the foreign-service people of the British Crown. As a result, these missionaries had a different orientation to colonial authority, to say nothing of life-style attitudes and practices such as their rejection of the consumption of alcoholic beverages.

Missionaries are often seen as uncritical supporters of colonial rule; this is not always the case. Foreign missionaries serving in a colony, for example, have frequently served as important advocates for indigenous peoples in the face of the imposition of foreign rule. It is interesting to note that some indigenous peoples regarded the missionaries as "failed" Europeans. In other words, when native people compared the missionaries with the colonial regime, they sometimes found the missionaries an inferior lot in terms of intelligence, life-style, and power. Such considerations sometimes led the natives to reject the missionary (and the message) because they saw that the missionary was not really representative of the people in power. On the other hand, the missionary was often the only European to whom a native had direct access, and in many instances missionaries were rather remarkable people who fought for the welfare of the natives and sought to serve them in an altruistic manner.

The issue of the secular attributes of an advocate is somewhat different in the case of Islam. Until recently there was no such thing as a professional, full-time missionary of Islam. Throughout Muslim history the soldier, trader, and saint have been considered important agents of Islamization and Islamic conversion. Most scholars reject the notion that Islam converted many people by the sword, but it is now agreed that Islamic conquest set the stage for Islamization in that the opposition was defeated, Islamic institutions were created and maintained, and eventually (over hundreds of years) the conversion process of individuals and the society as a whole was accomplished. Thus, the soldier, while not a direct agent of conversion, was a major precursor to conversion, making it possible for the Muslim merchant to travel all over the world and establish Muslim outposts on the frontiers. Islamic traders often established trading posts in remote areas within and beyond the borders of the Muslim empires. Through intermarriage and the establishment of Muslim institutions, the conversion process was initiated.

In some parts of the world, Sufi saints were important agents of Islamic conversion, although their influence was often felt only after their death. On the Indian subcontinent, for example, tombs of Sufi saints became identified as centers of healing and religious power. Richard M. Eaton argues that Islamic conversions did not take place under Islamic governments among the Hindus, but did take place on the frontiers of Islamic kingdoms among those who were either not Hindu or minimally so.[6] In other areas, the Muslim teacher served to introduce people to Arabic and the Koran. As religious functionaries, they often stimulated interest in Islam and thus began the early stages of conversion.

Religious Beliefs

The religious belief system of the missionary is another differentiating factor among advocates. There are many differences, both theologically and organizationally, between the Roman Catholic and Protestant missionary organizations, for example. It is difficult (and risky) to make generalizations about these differences, but some things are relatively consistent. Roman Catholic structures require extremely long periods for native clergy to be educated and deployed. Protestants, on the other hand, can appoint local people as preachers, teachers, and other functionaries after relatively brief periods of training. These differences may influence the rate and pace of conversion in particular areas. Protestants often use large group meetings to foster a revivalist setting. As Beidelman observes, "Revival provides a cheap, speedy mode of dramatic conversion with considerable potential for propagandistic public display. . . . The length and degree of proselytization are closely related to the degree that the convert is incorporated into the new system and also to the rate of relapse into pagan practices."[7]

Theory of Conversion

A third consideration in the nature of the advocate is the missionary's specific theory of conversion, the goals and processes involved in conversion. Do converts have to reject totally their pagan ways and completely embrace the advocate's message? Does the missionary respect the indigenous culture or see it as the work of the devil? What strategies are employed by the missionaries? Do they segregate converts into separate communities or seek to convert the whole community? The advocate's theory of conversion is extremely important in shaping the experience for the convert.

The conversion process advocated by the Mormons, for example, is much more affirmative than that of the Church of Christ. The Mormons' basic message is that God is a loving father who seeks humanity's happiness and well-being. The Mormon religion provides guidelines to enhance family life, spiritual life, and the overall assessment of the quality of life. While sin is discussed, it is seen as merely an impediment to the good life. On the other hand, the Church of Christ conveys a vivid message about human sin. A key experience in conversion is "coming to brokenness," which involves incorporating a keen sense of personal sinfulness and corruption, an individual acknowledgement of responsibility for sin, and an awareness that sin caused

1. Are the requirements general or specific?

2. Are changes mandatory or optional?

3. Are different levels of commitment allowed?

4. Are requirements explicit or implicit?

5. How much time is allowed to conform?

6. Is the convert allowed to negotiate changes?

Figure 10 *Prescriptions and proscriptions.*

the death of Jesus on the cross. Rejection of a wide gamut of sins, prideful attitudes, and "distorted thinking" is required for conversion to be considered valid in the Church of Christ. Such variations in attitudes are obviously determinants of missionary strategy as well as the experience of potential converts.

Career Patterns

The missionary's career trajectory and pattern of professional development may also influence conversion activity. Christian missionaries often feel conflict between an ideal, romantic vision and the administrative realities of the mission station. People frequently choose mission careers with the expectation of interacting with the natives and bringing them the gospel. But in reality, many are placed in positions of leadership in schools, hospitals, and churches, where day-to-day responsibilities leave them little time to interact with the wider community. The Mormon church, however, generally sends young men (required to be at least nineteen years old) to the mission field, for two-year enlistments only. Under such a program a new group of young, energetic, and idealistic missionaries are sent into the field at regular, short intervals. What they lack in knowledge and sophistication they make up for in

vitality and strong motivation to reach new converts. With such a high turn-
over among missionaries, a stronger emphasis may also be placed on developing local leadership and local support for the church. These young, enthu-
siastic lay missionaries return home with exciting tales of conversion,
enhancing the beliefs and morale of the home church while bolstering their
own individual sense of worth to the church.

Inducements to Conversion

Beidelman also discusses what he terms "inducements" that missionaries are able to offer potential converts. During the past two centuries such
inducements have often been the fruits of modern technological society, put-
ting the missionaries in a serious predicament. On the one hand, they may
claim that it is Christianity which brought civilization and advanced technology to the West, but on the other hand, they do not want people to accept the
gospel as a means of gaining material benefits. Beidelman presents this as a
fundamental contradiction. The issue is important to conversion because it
raises the problem of motivation. Do people convert to Christianity because
they are convinced of the truth of its message, or because they see it as a route
to better technology, improved health care, advanced education, or access to
the colonial powers in their area? The truth is usually mixed.

Advocate Motivation

In addition to the five categories outlined by Beidelman, it is important to
ask what motivates a person to *become* a missionary. Motivation for mission
and for conversion is a complicated issue. The stated intentions and goals of
missionaries are not always the best indicators of what actually drives them,
although it is helpful to understand their self-perception.

God's Will

Ruth Rouse explores missionary motivation from a theological point of
view.[8] While recognizing that over the years various concerns have motivated

missionaries, Rouse argues that the fundamental motive is a conviction that God has a purpose for individuals and for the world. People become missionaries because they believe it is God's purpose for their lives. These individuals may sacrifice time, money, energy, and their very lives for the purpose of the mission when they regard the conversion of others to a particular religious tradition as God's will.

The missionaries' view of themselves as being obedient to the will of God cannot be dismissed as mere ideological overlay to other, less altruistic (or at least not theological) reasons. While motivations may not always be as exalted as missionaries claim, what *does* motivate a person to perform extremely difficult work with very little tangible reward? Are these people merely psychologically ill? Are they attempting to control cognitive dissonance? What are their goals, and what is their self-understanding?

One must explore the inner life of missionaries in order to discern their rationale for missionary work. After all, their goals, systems of meaning, and sources of reward are not the ordinary ones of money, power, and fame. "Adventure" may be an attraction to the mission field, but few other rewards would seem to rationalize the degree of sacrifice and hard work required of most missionaries.[9]

Christ's Command

R. Pierce Beaver's work is noteworthy because it has examined the literature of various missionary agencies in North America and England and found that advocate motives shift over time.[10] In the early Puritan setting the dominant concern seemed clearly to be the glory of God. Concern for the souls of lost pagans followed close behind, and compassion for those outside Christianity was crucial. Later, the mandate for mission was perpetuated primarily by the command of Jesus in the Great Commission. Obedience to a command of Jesus was embellished by the notion that the command was given because of the love of God in Christ. Christians were told that they must emulate that love by obedience to the call to mission.

Nationalism

Nationalism has also played a part in the motivation of missionaries. Conversion was a prudent way to deal with American Indians and other "uncivilized" peoples.[11] Sometimes governmental agencies and churches collaborated to pacify native malcontents by "civilizing" them through the work of the missionary school. In the United States, nationalism shaped an attitude that Americans were the major teachers of democracy and had to set a moral example to the world. Civilization, democracy, and Christianization were interwoven in a complex web of motivational rhetoric, a rhetoric so powerful that it was the missionaries of the United States who provided the major personnel, money, and publications to marshal the efforts of the Christian missionary enterprise for the entire world.[12]

Service

One of the strongest motivations for missions is simply a desire to help people. That assistance can take the form of health care, educational advancement, economic expansion, and so forth. In earlier periods of missionary enterprise, advocates often wanted to "civilize" the "heathens" by bringing them European and American clothing, family structures, and other life-style modifications. More pointedly, there has been a consistent concern for development of infrastructures of modernity and technology: improvement of agricultural methods, provision of medical care, the introduction of structured and graded forms of education, and other "benefits" of modern society. Today, a fundamental gulf separates those advocates who believe that the first and central purpose of missions is the presentation of the gospel of Christ and the salvation of souls, and those who say that seeking economic and political justice are most important.[13]

The Advocate's Strategy

Chapter 6

Advocate strategy is important in that the scope, goals, and methods of conversion necessarily shape both the advocate's tactics and the convert's experience. To examine missionary strategy, it is useful to look at four main components: the degree of proselytizing, the strategic style, the mode of contact, and the potential benefits a new religious option offers to the potential convert. First, however, it is important to examine separately the use of force as a missionary strategy.

Force and Conversion

The use of force has been a method of conversion throughout history. Most people prefer not to discuss such issues in this era of ecumenical friendship, but the reality is that all major religions have, at one time or another, used force to make converts. Christians commonly charge that historically Muslims have converted "by the sword." That was sometimes true; however, the use of force has been extensive in the case of Christian missions as well. So great a "Christian" heroic figure as Charlemagne compelled conversion of the Saxons by force of arms between 772 and 804. Using political and military power, he "outlawed pagan practices and mandated baptism for all on pain of death."[1] Such conversions are certainly less than ideal and leave much to be desired in terms of the training and theological knowledge gained by the people targeted. Many Saxons resisted conversion and expressed their discontent through direct and indirect rebellion. "Christianization" in such a context was obviously not immediately effective for most people, but political action of this kind nevertheless set the stage for future generations to be educated in Christian life and thought.

Such forced conversions required subsequent action on many fronts to instill new levels of understanding and reinforce acceptance of Christian faith. Christian priests and leaders directly challenged the power of pagan gods by destroying sacred objects, like the sacred oak at Geismar in Hesse. When no retribution from the gods was forthcoming for these acts, the Christian leadership gained credibility among the pagans as to the power of the Christian God. Even though such dramatic events took place, scholars like Ruth Mazo Karras point out that Christianity did not require total rejection of pagan customs and practices. Indeed, Christianity often consecrated local shrines and turned them into churches. Karras notes that "Monotheistic Christianity also adapted itself to the polytheistic religion of many local deities through the development of the veneration of saints." In addition she states, "Probably the vast majority of Saxons accepted Christianity but simultaneously continued in their old customs." Karras concludes: "Christianity transformed Germanic Europe, not only spiritually but also culturally and politically. The new religion did not only create changes in the cultures it encountered; it also underwent change as it adapted to the understanding and spiritual needs of the new converts. Pagan resistance among the Saxons was stubborn, but gave way within a generation or two. Syncretism, the merging of elements of one religion into another, had more lasting effects."[2]

A major reason for discussing the use of force in the history of Christian conversion is that our stereotype of a radical rejection of the past and an embracing of something totally new is often not corroborated by historical examples of conversion. "Modern" Christians are prone to reject manifestations of Christianity—to say nothing of other religions—in Africa, Latin America, and Asia as being less than ideal because they are "syncretized" with the "pagan" remnants of the past. I would argue that the conversion of Europe exemplifies the same pattern and process of syncretism.[3] Conversion of European peoples did not involve the complete rejection of pagan religious practices; more often than not it brought about a blending of those elements into the new religion.

Degree of Proselytizing

Missionary emphasis and strategy exist on a continuum. When we examine the degree to which a religious organization or movement is seeking to reach out and incorporate new members, we notice that this continuum can range widely. Some religious groups are inclusive and some are exclusive; some have a very sophisticated and extensive missionary strategy and others no interest at all in new converts. Ethnic bodies like the Syrian Orthodox Church have little interest in converts. While I was in Jerusalem, I heard a Syrian Orthodox bishop assert that his church has no interest in converting "outsiders," because "they would have to learn the language and become a part of the culture. Why would anyone want to do that?"

Other groups, like the Southern Baptist Convention, the Church of Jesus Christ of Latter-Day Saints, Churches of Christ, and the Assemblies of God, emphasize activities geared toward the systematic recruitment, training, and retention of new members. Indeed, these churches (as well as many others) see a "mission to the lost" as central to their very being. Not only are professional missionaries deployed by these groups, but members are taught to "share the gospel" at every opportunity. It should come as no surprise that these are the groups that continue to grow numerically in the United States and around the world.

The degree to which an organized religion proselytizes indicates the degree to which it will specifically focus on missionary strategy, deploy advocates to recruit outsiders, and emphasize a theology of conversion. Groups like the Southern Baptists and the Church of Jesus Christ of Latter-Day Saints have an extensive literature on the nature of the missionary enterprise. Indeed, many Christian organizations, from the Roman Catholic Church to the smallest fundamentalist denomination, have amazing literatures on the nature of the missionary process. Strategies, methods, motivations, and other such issues are discussed extensively. Whatever their current stance, it would be safe to say that most Christian groups have found the missionary enterprise important at some time during the last two or three centuries.[4]

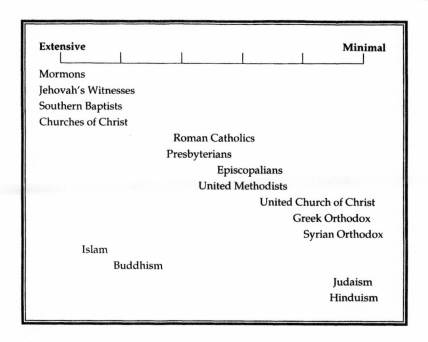

Figure 11 *Degree of missionary activity.*

Strategic Style

In addition to the degree of commitment to proselytizing, one must consider the overall strategic style of proselytizing. Several dimensions are important. For instance, the style can be diffuse or concentrated, or somewhere on a spectrum between the two.[5]

In diffuse (or systems-oriented) strategy the advocate circulates widely within a community and seeks to persuade large numbers of people, especially community leaders, and thus convert a whole community or village. Concentrated (or personalistic) strategy tends to focus upon particular individuals who for one reason or another are marginal to their community. Through intense indoctrination of individuals, an advocate can build a separate community outside, or at least somewhat distanced from, the dominant community. The marginality of prospective converts can be due to (1) their being poor and unattached to the power structure, (2) their having the free-

dom to explore new options because of financial security, or (3) role dislocation (as in the case of the samurai in Japan).[6] Marginal persons are important
in the study of conversion because they are often the earliest converts to a new
movement.[7]

Mode of Contact

A third strategic consideration is the actual mode of contact with people.
Is the contact public or private, personal or impersonal? David A. Snow, Louis
A. Zurcher, and Sheldon Ekland-Olson have explored this issue in a very
helpful manner.[8]

Public but mostly impersonal means of communicating the message include such media as television, radio, mass rallies, and revival meetings.
Face-to-face forms of contact, on the other hand, are more likely to be private
and very personal. They occur through individual missionaries who come to
one's home to offer tracts, invitations to worship or study, and other forms of
contact in which the advocate communicates personally with the potential
convert. Probably the most successful forms of contact are via friendship and
kinship networks, which are obviously the most personal forms. Private
channels of connection also include direct-mail contact. While that avenue is
private it is also, as with television or radio, impersonal or mediated. A
message is presented, but no direct human interchange takes place.

Very few evangelistic organizations rely on only one method of contact.
For instance, Mormons have excellent radio and television programs, a publications network, and even live-theater productions in addition to their
better-known door-to-door missionaries. When people respond to any of
these messages, they are contacted in person by someone from the local
church and/or the missionary stationed nearest them.

It is not possible here to explore all the nuances of missionary strategy,
but it should be emphasized that an advocate can be extremely flexible, innovative, and versatile in choosing modes of proselytizing.[9] Presentation of the
new religious option can vary in both content and form, different audiences

can be targeted, and different personnel can be used to locate, cultivate, persuade, indoctrinate, and ultimately convert people to a new religious option. Missionaries have always sought various means to implement their goals, including schools, entertainment, and technological assistance. Merrill Singer tells of the ingenuity of Orthodox Jews who sought to bring fallen-away Jews back to strict observance. They used music to appeal to young people and were willing to seek out Jewish youth in popular gathering places. Folklore, jokes, music, art, and other means are often used to build bridges to those people the advocate is interested in reaching.[10]

Today probably no group is more energetic in finding new and creative ways of proselytizing than the Church of Jesus Christ of Latter-Day Saints. According to church leaders, every Mormon should consider himself or herself a missionary. Thousands of Mormon families send their children (both young men and women, though the majority are male) into the mission field for two years. The family, the local congregation, and the young person together share the expense. These young people are trained to speak the language of the target population, and they are taught the fundamentals of Mormon doctrine and methods of missionary work. In addition, the church has developed a radio and television production center that produces quality outreach programs as well as brief "commercial" announcements designed to catch people's attention and develop an interest in the church. They report a doubling of their membership, to almost seven million members, since 1971. Flexibility and creativity have made their style of mission outreach possible.[11]

Benefits of Conversion

A fourth strategic consideration is the type and degree of benefit that the religious community, ideology, and/or way of life provides to the potential convert. Five basic categories include: (1) a system of meaning (cognitive); (2) emotional gratifications (affective); (3) techniques for living (volitional); (4) charisma (leadership); and (5) power.

Any specific religious system, of course, may provide all of these benefits or only a few. The combination, emphasis, and relative value of each attraction will vary among religious groups, and even from one observer to another. The proselytizer may portray the new religious option as having all or some of the five attractions, placing emphasis according to an evaluation of the target audience or individual.

Systems of Meaning

Any religious option may offer a more or less comprehensive, coherent, and compelling cognitive framework. Religious beliefs and myths can function as potent intellectual systems that enable people to make sense of the flux of history, their own place in history, and the nature of the world. Understanding the human predicament and the origin and destiny of the world is a powerful incentive for people to convert. As Seymour Epstein has pointed out, finding an appropriate and comfortable cognitive system seems to be a fundamental motivation for human beings.[12]

How is such a meaning system communicated? One clue comes from the work of Susan Harding.[13] An anthropologist, Harding has written a fascinating article in which she examines the vital and persuasive role of language in conversion, thus recognizing the centrality of advocate method to the conversion process. She examines fundamentalist Christian conversion and describes the way rhetoric may be used by the advocate to insinuate himself or herself into the psychology of the potential convert. As the advocate tells the story of the Bible and various Christian beliefs, he or she will usually try to personalize it in a way that draws the potential convert into the Christian narrative and interpretative framework. The metaphors of the death, burial, and resurrection of Jesus Christ, for instance, may be related to a prospect's recent divorce and the need to "resurrect" to a new life. In this way the convert's life history is incorporated into the ideology and narrative presented, so that the group's story becomes the convert's story in a very powerful and emotional way.

Anthropologist Peter Stromberg also discusses the importance in conversion of this congruency of personal life and theological system. [14] He describes what he calls the "impression point," the point at which the religious story connects with a personal aspect of a person's life, and thereby becomes internalized. When the potential convert discovers the relevance of a sermon or story to his or her own life, an integration is achieved so that the theological system makes sense on a peculiarly individual, human level. Religious symbolism then seems to parallel and interpret the convert's life experience. At this point the new symbolic system becomes plausible, meaningful and attractive, and the convert is able to identify with and adopt the system, to enter personally into this new story, to own it.

The work of both Harding and Stromberg represent excellent examples of interdisciplinary approaches to religious change, providing rich and provocative descriptions and explanations of conversion. Their observations are important not only in the encounter stage; the interactions they describe also continue to weave through and influence the interaction and commitment stages as well.

Emotional Gratification

A religious option can also offer a wide range of emotional gratifications, like a sense of belonging or community, relief from guilt, development of new relationships, and—something few studies of conversion mention—excitement and stimulation. Some groups are extraordinary in their utilization of such things as music, theater, art, and architecture, as well as a sense of mission, challenge, or comfort. The myths, rituals, and symbols of religion can infuse life with intensity, drama, and significance, offering many people a deep sense of affective gratification. [15]

A consistent finding in the study of conversion is the importance of establishing early a connection between the potential convert and a member (advocate) of the new group. While contact with a charismatic leader is dramatic and important for some people, the connection between ordinary people who either establish a bond or build upon pre-existing ties is also important. Many scholars have found that the major way to conversion is via friendship and kinship networks.[16] Benjamin Weininger suggests that establishment of an interpersonal connection is a powerful, even critical step in the conversion experience. In fact, for some potential converts, finding someone who loves and cares for them is a potent experience in itself, enabling them to transcend immobilizing conflicts and to utilize the freed energy to build a more productive, more "spiritual" life.[17] Establishing a bond between advocate and potential convert makes transition to deeper involvement attractive and possible.

Techniques for Living

A third category of benefits presented by a religious community is what Jacob Needleman has termed "techniques for living." Based on many interviews with converts, I have found that a major appeal of religious change is a conviction that the new option provides the person with new methods and techniques for religious life, and often for life in general. Methods of prayer, meditation, scripture reading and interpretation, and other practical steps for making life different are very appealing to a potential convert. Many people want to change and grow religiously but do not have the practical tools or "how-to" experience to make that growth possible. A religious option that offers these tools and careful instruction for their use will win over many such people.[18]

Leadership

A fourth attraction is convincing leadership. Leadership may not be crucial in *every* conversion, but it seems to be important in *many* conversions. In its most dramatic form, the leader is a charismatic figure, deemed by the community to be especially gifted. The charismatic leader may be seen as having special access to the divine realm or special abilities of healing, prophecy, or other qualities to which the group ascribes importance. The leader can function in many ways, but more often than not embodies the virtues and powers that are articulated by the religious ideology, or has accomplished particular feats, or has extraordinary powers of discernment and persuasion.[19] Not to be minimized is the leader who appears to be the embodiment of qualities, experiences, and attitudes idealized by followers. "If that one can achieve such things," the reaction goes, "then I may somehow achieve them too by following, watching, and emulating the leader."

In the encounter stage, the charisma or personal attraction of a religious leader or advocate can have a powerful effect on potential converts. Charisma, however, like conversion itself, is an interactional phenomenon in which the needs, expectations, and hopes of both leader and follower are involved. The charismatic leader may offer a potential role model, guidelines for living, and affirmation of the follower's value as a person, while the new convert may fulfill the leader's need for adoration, affirmation, and obedience. Moral questions abound as to whether the effect of a charismatic leader is more to victimize or to empower the follower, and whether such leadership contributes more to evil or good purposes in the long run. Any judgment must be reached within the interactional model suggested; that is, responsibility for charismatic power cannot be seen as residing in the leader alone. The complicity of the follower must be explored as well.

Power

A fifth and perhaps related attraction to conversion involves power.[20] It is possible to argue that all the previous elements involve and invoke power to some degree. Nevertheless, one theme that emerges in many conversions is that the convert feels filled with power, has access to power, or is somehow connected with either an external source of power (God) or an internal sense of power that may be perceived as spiritual or divine. Harold W. Turner reports that in the confrontation with European colonials, "primal" people sometimes sought out Christian missionaries because they believed that religion was key to gaining access to the power of those with superior technology.[21] Whatever the precise definition, power is an important ingredient in many forms of conversion. Either power is perceived as a gift to be won through conversion, or extraordinary power has made the conversion possible, or an ethos of power helped cultivate an openness to the transcendent dimension. Power attracts people and can serve as a validation of ideology and leadership when a sense of power is experienced directly and personally.

All considerations up to this point have been, in a way, prologue to the actual interactive dynamics that begin only when advocate and potential convert engage each other one-on-one. No conversion occurs without encounter.

Encounter between Advocate and Convert

Chapter 7

In every encounter between advocate and potential convert, the real details of their interplay are extraordinarily complex. Encounter might be seen as the vortex of the dynamic force field in which conversion takes place. As a simple linear continuum, the outcome of the encounter can range from total rejection at one end of the spectrum to complete acceptance at the other. Initial reactions to an advocate can change over time; positive reactions can turn negative and vice versa. The advocate also may change over time, altering strategy in response to what is learned through interaction with the potential convert. The potential convert can also be modified and/or adopt new strategies through the interplay.[1]

An interesting finding rarely mentioned in conversion studies is that the majority of target populations reject new religious options.[2] In researching many reports of conversion, I found it striking that a scholar or missionary might enthusiastically report hundreds or even thousands of converts, then in one throwaway sentence note that the *percentage* of converts was less than 10 percent. The truth is that enmeshment with old systems of religion, family, society, and politics seldom encourages movement to a new religious option. Personal and social conditions rarely facilitate change. Hence, what makes any voluntary conversion process possible is a complex confluence of the "right" potential convert coming into contact, under proper circumstances at the proper time, with the "right" advocate and religious option. Trajectories of potential converts and available advocates do not often meet in such a way that the conversion process can germinate, take root, and flourish.

Even the relatively more successful Latter-Day Saints report that only one in one thousand contacts eventually becomes a Mormon.[3] Similarly, a leader in the discipling movement of the Churches of Christ conceded to me that fewer than one in one hundred responds to invitations to Bible talk

sessions—the preliminary step in that church's attempt at building relationships that lead to conversion. Galanter reports that his research indicates only
one person in one hundred responds to invitations to Unification Church
dinners, while even fewer attend workshops and fewer still become members.[4] Indeed, seeking proselytes is extremely difficult and discouraging
work. Evangelistic organizations continually have to build enthusiasm
among members to preserve the momentum required to convert a relatively
few others.[5]

To date, no one theoretical system has, to my knowledge, been able to
choreograph all the salient features and forces operative in the critical encounter stage. But let us briefly survey some interpretations provided by the
social sciences.

Isichei's View of Encounter

Elizabeth Isichei, a historian, examines the response of the Igbo people in
Nigeria to Christianity.[6] She restates an admonition we have also stressed:
"Igbo responses to mission teaching were conditioned by a whole variety of
factors—age, sex, status in the community and the nuances of the individual
personality among them—and . . . no analysis can even begin to mirror this
variety and complexity." Isichei's assumptions are familiar: "The history of
ideas does not occur in a vacuum, and any analysis is misleading if it excludes
at least a mention of the historical determinants of conversions. It is a truism
that most movements of conversion were determined by social factors. This
was true of the Igbo, and it [is] necessary to see the encounter of ideas against
the background of the actual social processes which ultimately determined
the success—if success it can be called—of the missionary enterprise."[7]

Isichei focuses on responses of the Onitsha people, a subgroup of the
Igbo. The initial reaction was welcome. As an isolated people they were
delighted to have allies and new avenues of trade. Their curiosity about for-
eigners made them warm and open. As time went on, however, only the
marginalized of Igbo society actually converted. Isichei states: "As in other

missionary contexts, the missionaries drew their converts mainly from the rejects of Igbo society—those like slaves, or accused witches, who had no prospect of happiness in Igbo society and therefore nothing to lose by attaching themselves to another one."[8] As mainstream people began to see the divisive and revolutionary potential of the new religion, they began to persecute both the missionaries and those who chose to convert. She further explains: "The nineteenth and early twentieth centuries were, for the Igbo, an age of anxiety, a time of dislocating economic and social change, of disturbing confrontation with an alien culture, followed by the prolonged experience of violent conquest. Very few men considered becoming Christians who were happily integrated in their own society unless they felt that society to be threatened. This is a commonplace of mission history, and it is equally true of the Igbo."[9]

Isichei found the patterns of interplay between advocate and convert to be extremely complex. The welcome first offered by the indigenous people shifted, upon further interaction, into suspicion and resistance. Those who did convert were generally the outsiders, "rejects" of tribal society. Their mode of conversion involved a syncretism that mixed old and new in a fashion that was determined by their own values, assumptions, and rituals. Paradoxically, after years of missionary education efforts, there was a secularizing effect introduced by Western ideas and values overall. Because of the erosion of indigenous power and prestige, the traditional religion lost its plausibility for many people. Often only an elderly minority sought to preserve traditional religious myths, rituals, and symbols. Rather than being a dynamic system that responded to realities of communal and environmental life, the traditional religion was frequently preserved in a rigid fashion in order to salvage some remnants of it. Tribal tradition became generally denigrated by youth educated in mission schools.

Isichei, with no little pain for the pathos of the situation, asserts: "The encounter takes place, not in debates between Igbo and missionaries, but in the minds of individual Igbo. Since the missionaries did not accept the reality of the Igbo spiritual world, it was inevitable that only the Igbo, consciously or unconsciously, could construct the dialogue. We have seen it lead to three main paths—those of the syncretist, the secular man, and the disillusioned traditionalist. Each gropes with a sense of dislocation, a sense of loss. To select the metaphor this time from Igbo literature:

Onya na-a apa ya ada ana.

A wound heals, and a scar remains."[10]

Resistance to the Advocate

Norman Etherington provides an extensive case study of the importance of the sociocultural context with regard to resistance and rejection of a new religious option.[11] Responding to the work of Beidelman, he explores the relative importance of missionary motives and strategies versus the indigenous context of potential converts in southeastern Africa. By 1880 nine different Christian missionary societies were active in areas of Natal, Pondoland, and Zululand: Methodists, Roman Catholics, Congregationalists, Lutherans, Anglicans, and Presbyterians from France, Germany, Scotland, Norway, Sweden, and the United States.

Careful analysis of differences among these groups (in terms of missionary personnel, goals, and strategies) brought Etherington to the conclusion that, at least in this particular area, these variations could not account for differential response rates among the indigenous Africans. Indeed, Etherington argues that the forces against the missionaries were so strong that all developed a similar strategy: the missionary station. The missionaries found that the best (perhaps only) way to establish a church was to create an option for those few who did convert to live separately from their communities of origin. The missionary compound with its schools, churches, hospitals, and stores provided converts with an insulated life secure from the wider world they had known. Resistance of local people to the new religion was so strong that the missionaries felt they had no choice but to create these compounds.

For example, the American Board of Commissioners for Foreign Missions sent six missionaries to South Africa in 1835. Their strategy was to convert entire groups of Zulus, develop them into independent Christian communities, and then send Zulus as missionaries to the rest of Africa. These American missionaries went so far as to oppose the activities of colonial authorities and sought to improve the status of black Africans. Nevertheless, they met persistent and powerful resistance from the vast majority of Zulus. After years of frustrated efforts, the missionaries ultimately supported the use of imperial force to break the power and authority of tribal leaders and aid in establishing missionary stations where converts could survive.

Macrosocial Relations

Robert L. Montgomery proposes that the spread of religions is influenced by the relationship between the advocate's society of origin and the potential convert's social context.[12] Montgomery asserts that religion provides important resources for the creation, consolidation, and support of a society's identity. Acceptance of a new religious option is possible when there is a perceived threat to the receptive society, and when that threat arises from a source other than the origin of the new religious option. A new religious option is rejected when there is either no perceived threat or the threat arises from the same sources as the new religion. There are situations in which segments of a particular society are under threat from the dominant group. In some such cases the threatened subgroup may adopt a new religious option that may challenge the dominant group. The subgroup may use the new option as a potent weapon in its conflict with the dominant group.

Montgomery illustrates his theoretical model through the Christianization of Korea. Christianity became a very important force in Korea during the Japanese occupation between 1910 and 1945. Because Japan presented such an overwhelming threat to the identity of the Korean people, Koreans welcomed the Christian message advocated by the European and American missionaries. Likewise, Islam thrived most in regions where the Arab armies were able to liberate people from the oppression of such groups as the Byzantine and Persian empires.

In addition to acceptance and rejection of new religions, mixing occurs. In certain situations in which the foreign was mandated, the indigenous peoples fiercely maintained their distinctive identities and modified the new religion to preserve the values and the identity of the receptive society. Such mixing is evident in many colonial nations where Christianity was foisted on the conquered peoples.

Context as a Catalyst for Conversion

Understanding a potential convert's reaction to a new option has been a topic of extensive discussion and debate among scholars. Robin Horton's "intellectualist theory" is an important contribution, developed to account for the differential response to Christian and Islamic missionaries in sub-Saharan Africa.[13] Horton assumes that human cognition is affected by a group's economic, political, sociocultural, and geographical circumstances, and he endorses the view that converts are creatively active in their responses, not passive. In fact, he sees Islam and Christianity as merely catalytic forces behind developments in the indigenous religious systems of thought that were operative prior to the introduction of Islam and Christianity.

Horton explains the different responses to Christianity and Islam in Africa as the result of the context each tradition encountered. The heart of the intellectualist theory is that African cosmology consists of two tiers, or levels: the microcosm and the macrocosm. The microcosm consists of cults, rituals, and beliefs endemic to the local communities and tribal groups. This microcosm is populated with spirits and forces that are understood to be in control of the world of the local setting. The macrocosm, on the other hand, encompasses the wider world or environment, with a supreme being as the overarching power and origin of the lesser spirits.

The balance of emphasis between the supreme being and the lesser spirits is determined by the degree to which the community is focused on microcosm or macrocosm. An isolated or stationary group having few contacts with the wider world devotes most of its energy to local spirits. A group that communicates, travels, and/or trades with differing peoples and societies is likely to have more interest in the cult of the supreme being. Horton believes that religion and the social matrix are so intertwined that a change in the sociocultural setting will stimulate a change in the religious sphere.

Indigenous groups are constantly adapting their religious ideology in response to changing religious, social, political, and economic factors; people are active and creative in making these changes, even without the introduction or imposition of outside forces. Thus, Horton asserts that initial responses to Christianity and Islam were based on the relative emphasis of the group and/or individuals on microcosm and macrocosm, on cults of the lesser spirits and the cult of the supreme being. Groups that focus primarily on the microcosm are unresponsive; groups emerging into the macrocosm are especially responsive to Christianity or Islam, because these religions provide extensive rituals and beliefs relevant to the larger world. The degree of elaboration and responsiveness to outside elements is determined by the active adaptation of the people themselves.

The Religious Factor in Context

Horton's theory of conversion, first articulated in 1971, has stimulated extensive debate. The earliest critique came from Humphrey J. Fisher, who centered his criticism on the fact that Horton was chiefly concerned with Christian conversion and had only slight interest in conversion to Islam in Africa.[14] Fisher also believes that Horton downplays the role of "pure" Islam and Christianity in the lives of Africans. He rejects Horton's rather simple scheme of explanation of differential response. The major point of Fisher's critique is that Horton fails to recognize the distinctively religious dimension of Christianity and Islam.

Fisher offers a three-fold scheme of the development of Islam in Africa and articulates the difference of conversion in each phase. The three phases are quarantine, mixing, and reform. In the quarantine phase, which can last hundreds of years, Muslim traders, merchants, and religious teachers or ritualists move into an area but are more or less isolated from the wider society. The relatively small numbers who do convert are often slaves, because they are detached from their traditional society and are thus more available for new religious options. During the quarantine period, converts are numerically few because one must break with traditional society in order to become a Muslim, and the price of such a break is high.

Mixing begins when there is a breakdown of barriers to conversion. Fisher notes that conversion during the mixing phase is often more like the "adhesion" described by A. D. Nock than conversion; adhesion requires a less radical break with the past.[15] It is not uncommon in Africa for a person to be involved in multiple cults and to engage in various ritual activities. Becoming a Muslim is fairly easy in such contexts. Indeed, Islam allows relative ease of admission, unlike Christianity, which generally requires a long period of training. The admission ritual is simply to state the confession: "There is one God and Mohammad is God's prophet."

A reform phase often emerges in the form of *jihad* (or holy-war) movements, which demand exclusive loyalty to Islam and the doctrinal and behavioral purity of "high" Islam. During this phase, syncretist elements of traditional indigenous cultures are vigorously denounced and purged. Fisher believes that a major factor initiating the reform phase is literacy. As more Muslims become trained in the Koran and other Muslim texts, they discover discrepancies between Islam in a mixed environment and the pure Islam of the past. One might say that a second, intensified conversion takes place. The initial adhesion to Islam is replaced with a vigorous, pure Islamic conversion that demands movement from indifferent acceptance to deep commitment and purity. Fisher observes: "The reformed Islam which was imposed alike upon the newly converted, the reconverted and the recalcitrant was based upon the literary monuments of the Muslim heritage. It involved, sometimes, a sharp and even cruel insistence upon proper standards, and an equally sharp break with local traditions."[16]

Diffusion of Innovation

Richard W. Bulliet proposes the use of the "diffusion of innovation" theory for interpreting the nature of conversion.[17] This concept was developed initially in the biological sciences, and later employed in sociology to explain how new technology was adopted in various parts of the world. Through extensive use of biographical dictionaries extant in Muslim cultures, Bulliet carefully examines evidence of name changes, considered to be a significant indicator of conversion, and their relationship to the pace and sequence of conversion in Iran, Iraq, Egypt, Tunisia, Syria, and Spain.[18] He empirically establishes that conversion to Islam took place in a way that is consistent with the diffusion of innovation theory.

The theory supposes that a population's adoption of a new concept generally takes place in accordance with the standard distribution curve, which can be visualized in the familiar statistical bell curve or the S-curve for the summation of standard distribution. The bell or S-curve is divided into intervals known as standard deviations. Statistical percentages predict the probability of adoption. Diffusion of innovation theory proposes that the first to embrace a new option are "innovators," who comprise about 2.5 percent of the population. The next group are the "early adopters," who make up some 13.5 percent of the population. The third group are the "early majority," 34 percent of the total. The "late majority" are the fourth group, also 34 percent of the total. Fifth, and last, are the most reluctant or resistant 16 percent of the population, the "laggards."

Diffusion of innovation theory is based on an assumption that adoption of something new is based on access to information. As increasing numbers of people adopt the novelty, there is a bandwagon effect, characterized by more and more interest in and less and less resistance to the innovation. Bulliet stresses a potential significance of this approach to conversion: "What is useful about this division into categories is that it suggests that people who converted at different times had very different motives and experiences."[19]

Using the diffusion of innovation theory, Bulliet constructed a hypothetical timetable for the conversion process to Islam, a process that took place over four centuries. For his detailed study of conversion to Islam in Iran, he reports that the innovators were those 2.5 percent who converted to Islam before 695 C.E. These innovator converts were slaves, prisoners of war, and others of very low social status. As non-Arabs, they were required to become *mawali* (that is, fictive members of Arab tribes), but they were considered inferior to real Arabs and were discriminated against and stigmatized. Few converts adopted Muslim names in this period. Between 695 and 762, the early adopters comprised an additional 13.5 percent of all the eventual converts. Stigmatization gradually diminished but was still practiced by the community that the convert rejected in order to become a Muslim. The early adopters began using biblical names, considered by Bulliet to be safe vis-à-vis the Christian and Jewish communities. Bulliet adds that "the early adopters were largely people who were able to change residence upon conversion. Within this group could be found artisans, merchants, and religious and state functionaries; but what is most important is the general exclusion from the group of rural landowners."[20]

Between 762 and 820, the early majority began to emerge and comprised 34 percent of the total number of converts. Bulliet reports: "With the removal or lessening of bars to conversion, such as ostracism or persecution by non-Muslims, the primary factor in the determination of the conversion process during this period was probably the dissemination of information. Increasingly, Islam was regarded as a permanent and irreversible aspect of Iranian life, and the idea spread that adherence to Islam was an absolute good in a manner analogous to the absolute advantage of a superior technological process or device."[21]

Between 772 and 869, more than 60 percent of the conversions took place. The bandwagon effect is clearly evident during the early majority and late majority phases. The late majority (again, 34 percent of the total) were converted between 820 and 875. The laggards, the last 16 percent, were converted between 875 and 1009. As more and more people in Iran converted to Islam, there was a remarkable increase in the use of five distinctively Muslim names: Muhammad, Ahmad, Ali, al-Hasan, and al-Husain. With the bandwagon effect converts could publicly identify their new allegiance through their names and suffer no negative consequences.

Differential Motivation and Experiences

Several important issues emerge from Bulliet's work. First, he suggests that conversion processes are different at different times in history. Some scholars of conversion continue to conceptualize it as a static phenomenon that is universal and invariant, and some theologians argue for one particular mandatory model. Bulliet has shown that conversion is a dynamic process that varies according to place and time. The type of people converted, the nature of their experience, and I would add the consequences of their conversions, are different at different times and in different places. Second, he demonstrates that conversion is a cumulative process. In other words, the conversion of large numbers of people generates momentum and expands the process over time.

Missionary Adaptations

What change does the personal and dynamic encounter effect upon the advocate? Such interaction has consequences not only for the potential converts—those who convert and those who resist—but for the advocates as well. The missionary wants to be effective, and therefore assesses the situation and modifies strategies and tactics in order to be more successful in particular settings. Some missionaries change in ways that are more profound than mere methodology would warrant.[22] Steven Kaplan nominates six types of missionary change: tolerance, translation, assimilation, Christianization, acculturation, and incorporation.[23] Even though his study focuses on missionaries in Africa, these types may be considered relevant around the world.

Tolerance

Tolerance is often an expedient and/or a functional necessity for the advocate. Confronted with beliefs and practices that he or she finds more or less repugnant, the missionary must face the reality of these beliefs and practices and hope that tolerance of them will permit the persuasion process eventually to change such objectionable behaviors and attitudes.

Translation

To communicate the new religious message in a manner that is understandable, the missionary engages in translation. Kaplan means more than merely translation from one language to another. He points to the creativity of missionaries in finding comparisons and analogies with indigenous culture and customs that will familiarize the message, clothe the new story in recognizable garb.

Assimilation

Some missionaries, especially after they have developed more in-depth knowledge and experience of a particular setting, engage in assimilation. Kaplan notes that missionaries will sometimes utilize the traditions and rituals of an indigenous culture in the practice of Christianity (as, for example, in burial rituals). For some modern missionaries, the incorporation of local practices is a major step forward, though their predecessors, especially during the nineteenth century, were initially repelled by the customs they encountered. After learning the language and developing relationships with the local people, however, some found that the indigenous way of life actually had many positive aspects, and assimilation of indigenous forms into worship became more and more common.

Christianization

Christianization is another strategy used by missionaries. Particular indigenous rites and practices are "cleansed" of any "un-Christian" elements and transformed so that they become officially "Christian." Thus, the missionaries move from mere respect for the indigenous culture to a more affirmative stance. This was the pattern with European pagan customs, and is much the same when African practices are "sacralized" or legitimized into the Christian way of life. The form of a ritual—otherwise African—may be pagan in origin, but the content is securely Christian.

Acculturation

The strategy of acculturation owes most to reduction of cultural arrogance and intolerance. Preservation, or in some cases restoration, of traditional elements of tribal life is recognized to have inherent human value. The advocate's ethnocentrism and cultural blindness are transformed, or at least significantly mitigated, so that the missionary becomes an important agent in the conservation and promotion of indigenous cultures. Some missionaries may "go native," jettisoning their own Western culture and fully embracing the way of life of the people they are serving.[24]

Incorporation

To Kaplan, the ultimate change is for the missionary to be so impressed by indigenous concepts that he or she introduces these into normative Christianity. Incorporation of such worldviews, values, and rituals is sometimes so complete that the advocate develops a view of Christianity very different from the one originally brought into the missionary setting. Two representatives of this process are John V. Taylor and Vincent J. Donovan. Taylor, an Anglican priest, reports in his superb book *The Primal Vision* that his experience in Uganda transformed his view of Christianity.[25] Donovan's *Christianity Rediscovered* narrates his confrontation with Masai life and thought and their effects on his understanding of Christianity and the missionary enterprise.[26]

Potential Converts and Convert Adaptations

The constellation of events that may transpire between the two poles of rejection and acceptance is ferociously complex. Keshari N. Sahay provides us with a useful set of categories for describing and interpreting the contours of encounter over a long period of time. Sahay conducted extensive research on the conversion process of the Uraon tribal people in Chotanagpur, India.[27] Lutheran missionaries arrived in the area in the 1840s, but conversions were few until the arrival of Constant Lievens, a Roman Catholic. Lievens's success, according to Sahay, was attributable to his service as a legal advocate of the impoverished and oppressed people. Sahay contributes to our discussion five varieties of how the encounter took shape for the Uraons who became converts: cultural oscillation, scrutinization, combination, indigenization, and retroversion.

Oscillation

In the early stages of encounter, incipient converts fluctuated between traditional beliefs and their new commitment to Christianity. Their affiliation was nominal and, for most of them, their knowledge of Christianity was extremely limited. For some, the motivation for conversion was to receive material benefits, especially legal assistance against oppressive landlords. However much they wanted to be Christians, the new converts remained deeply attached to their Sarna traditions. In times of trouble they returned to the old ways of healing. Sahay reports that 83 percent of Roman Catholic converts and 93 percent of Lutheran converts still acknowledged belief in witchcraft and sorcery.

Scrutinization

As time went by, the Uraon converts, because of their new beliefs, eliminated more and more elements of their tradition that were considered incompatible with Christianity. As their knowledge grew, they became more aware of conflict between belief systems, and in order to establish their new identity as Christians, they often made public gestures that would distinguish them from nonbelievers. For example, the *chundi* (the topknot of hair) was cut off. Christian converts also rejected the use of tattoos, except for a small cross on the forehead. Some "secular" traditions were retained, but specifically "religious" elements of their old traditions were eliminated. Many people experimented with the new beliefs and tested the efficacy of traditional rituals.

Combination

Another strategy mixed various elements of Christianity with local Uraon traditions. An important element of tribal culture was dancing, but some European and American missionaries worried that dancing stimulated inappropriate sexual activity. After a period of conflict over the issue, both sides became willing to compromise, and the missionaries accepted dancing as an integral part of the culture.

Indigenization

Christian (or, more accurately, Western in some cases) traditions were incorporated into the local way of doing things. For instance, when a disapproved-of ritual or activity was eliminated from the traditional culture, people sought an equivalent practice among the missionaries and then made it part of their own lives. Hence, fusion and replacement took place.

Retroversion

After a generation of two of Christianization, the people sometimes re-evaluated elements of their culture that had been suppressed and decided that it was legitimate to re-adopt certain practices. For instance, vermilion, a crucial element in traditional weddings and festivals, had been eliminated by the Uraons. In later times, converts decided it was compatible with Christian principles to use the precious stone once again. Sahay concludes that when Christian identity was consolidated among the Uraons and they were more mature in their faith, they were more affirmative toward nonconflicting traditions that they had previously rejected.

Sahay's model is another useful way to see the process of how the advocate and the potential convert respond to one another, and to understand better the nature of that encounter over time.

Interaction

Chapter 8

For people who continue with a new religious option after the initial encounter, their interaction with their adopted religious group intensifies. Potential converts now learn more about the teachings, life-style, and expectations of the group, and are provided with opportunities, both formal and informal, to become more fully incorporated into it. The intensity and duration of this phase differs from one group to another. Some faiths insist on a very long period of education and socialization; others focus more on brief, intense periods during which potential converts are encouraged and/or required to make a decision.

In the interaction stage, the potential convert either chooses to continue the contact and become more involved, or the advocate works to sustain the interaction in order to extend the possibility of persuading the person to convert. Once again there is a spectrum of passivity and activity by the potential convert, as well as manipulation and persuasion by the advocate. Some groups, such as Orthodox Jews, do not encourage conversions, and a potential convert must be very assertive in seeking a rabbi willing to provide training in Judaism. Thus, hurdles are erected by the religious authority. Other groups like Southern Baptists, the Unification Church, or the Church of Jesus Christ of Latter-Day Saints are eager to bring in new members (although they are not indiscriminate), and they will seek ways to persuade and encourage the potential convert. The Roman Catholic Church has instituted a program called the Rite of Christian Initiation for Adults, a one-year progression of classes, retreats, liturgies, spiritual direction, and community life designed to introduce potential converts to the Roman Catholic Church and to teach them the theology, liturgy, organization, and way of life of the church.[1] Most Roman Catholics do not, however, actively go out into the community seeking people to participate in the RCIA. It is more a program for those who, on their

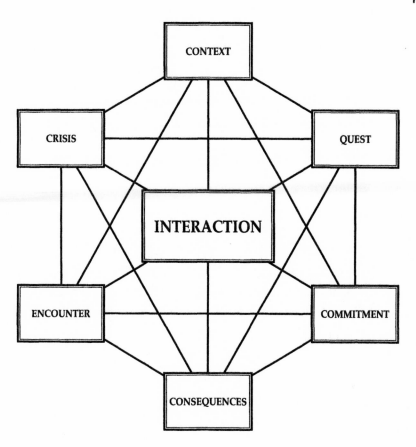

Figure 12 *Stage 5: Interaction.*

own initiative, come to the church seeking information and desiring conversion.[2]

Encapsulation

A fuller understanding of effectiveness in the interaction stage may derive from a discussion of the nature of encapsulation processes (studied extensively by sociologists Arthur Griel and David Rudy), which create a sphere or matrix in which crucial elements of conversion operate.[3] These processes employ four components: relationships, rituals, rhetoric, and roles.

Encapsulation seems particularly important because of the way in which different religious groups create and maintain "worlds" of their own. When I observe such a group I am sometimes reminded of a television report years ago about that small boy in Houston, Texas, whose immune system was completely ineffective. In order to protect the child, physicians constructed a large plastic bubble in which the boy could be shielded from all outside bacteria and viruses. Similarly, I have found that both liberal and conservative religious groups create encapsulated worlds of their own, not unlike the bubble in which that child lived. Within those bubbles their beliefs, actions, and experiences have special meaning and value. Outside those spheres, however, it is often difficult to communicate unique spiritual concepts, much less affirm their validity and value. In the conversion process, a potential adherent is invited and/or persuaded (some might say coerced) into these self-contained worlds in order to begin or strengthen the process of conversion—not unlike the African missionary stratagem of isolated compounds.[4]

Encapsulation strategies (the degree to which potential converts are isolated or restricted from communication with outsiders, alternative ideologies, books, newspapers, radio, and television) can be a crucial feature of the interaction stage. Although it sounds sinister, encapsulation is a procedure employed to some extent by everyone who wants to teach something new. Every classroom is a form of encapsulation in that it creates an environment in which there can be concentration on the topic at hand, control of noise and competing ideas, and minimal interruption. If to change people it is necessary to control the flow of information, the issue is not *whether* but *how* people use encapsulation—that is, the degree and kind of encapsulation used.

If the religious group is affirmative of the wider world, it will tend to have fairly flexible boundaries and exercise less control over communication and social interaction within and outside the group. Groups that reject or are suspicious of the world, rigidly excluding outsiders, tend to exert much more extensive pressure to control communication and social interaction. To some degree, the amount of control considered necessary by a group is determined by the perceived status of that group within the macrocontext. If the group is considered "deviant" vis-à-vis the wider world, it is likely that the group will feel compelled to encapsulate itself and repudiate the "evil" world.

The degree of encapsulation is also influenced by the theology of the group. When a group sees the world as the domain of evil, darkness, and Satan, as fundamentalist Christians often do, they will vigorously seek to isolate and separate themselves and potential converts from that evil world. Their mode of conversion will emphasize the convert's sinfulness and the extent to which the convert's past was vile and perverse, contaminated because of immersion in the world of evil.[5]

Another valuable way of understanding encapsulation is to appreciate the conversion motif being used by the group or community. Lofland and Skonovd's six conversion motifs introduced in chapter 1 are relevant here: intellectual, mystical, experimental, affectional, revivalist, and coercive. In the intellectual, the experimental, and sometimes the mystical types of conversion, the potential convert is most active in seeking out new possibilities and feels considerably less social pressure to conform. Encapsulation is likely to be correspondingly loose, as these types of conversion are chiefly advocated by groups that do not manipulate potential converts but rather open themselves to seekers and encourage free pursuit of spiritual goals. Affectional, revivalist, and coercive motifs of conversion are prone to very high levels of group pressure, and they often employ methods that either render people vulnerable or exploit existing vulnerabilities to win converts. This self-conscious manipulation of emotional gratifications and vulnerabilities clearly approaches brainwashing and coercive persuasion, tactics that are most effective under conditions of strict encapsulation. This description may make one feel very uncomfortable; nevertheless, it is indisputable that in order to foster religious involvement and commitment, even well-intentioned people can and often do deliberately manipulate others through careful deployment of emotional rewards and punishments.[6]

Three varieties of encapsulation—physical, social, and ideological—impose conditions that are not entirely distinct from one another but rather

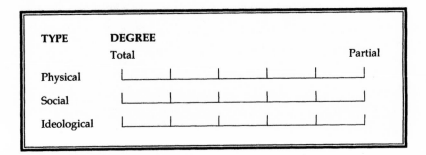

Figure 13 *Encapsulation processes.*

overlap and reinforce one another.[7] Again, it is a matter not of a simple either/or but of a both/and combination, which may be represented as a continuum of processes.

Physical encapsulation may be achieved by removing people to distant locations or remote areas where communications can be controlled, so that no sources of information are available to the potential convert except those that the advocate deems important, suitable, or reinforcing. Physical isolation can also be achieved by actual barriers other than distance, as in monasteries, convents, mission compounds, and religious communities and ghettos.

Social encapsulation means directing the potential convert into life-style patterns that limit significant contact with "outsiders." Certain churches expect members to spend all their discretionary time in various church sponsored or sanctioned activities, such as Bible study, worship, and prayer. Some groups, like the Hare Krishnas, Sikhs, and Orthodox Jews, foster social encapsulation by wearing unusual or specialized items of apparel, which serves as an obvious distinction and/or reminder, both to followers and outsiders, of the member's chosen "otherness" in status and role.

Ideological encapsulation involves cultivation of a worldview and belief system that "inoculates" the adherent against alternative or competitive systems of belief. Members and potential converts both are reminded of the purity and sacredness of their beliefs, the destructiveness of beliefs of the outside world, and often, the special responsibility that adherents bear for

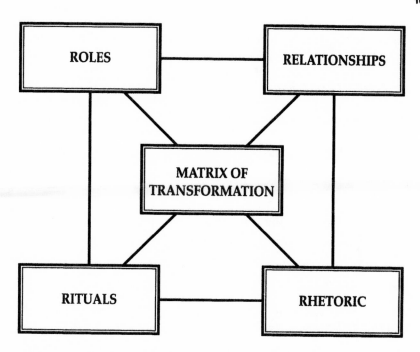

Figure 14 *Matrix of transformation.*

preserving the "truth." In many cases, people are trained explicitly to be critical of the assumptions, methods, and values of the "enemy" ideology. I remember being taught by an especially conservative professor during my undergraduate college days about "liberal" forms of biblical interpretation. He gave us details of particular perversions that were foisted upon the unwary, and instructed us in how to analyze and criticize the point of view of liberals who were undermining the authority of the Bible. This is ideological inoculation, a closing and rigidifying of the mind-set, no matter how well-intentioned.

When a sphere of influence has been created by encapsulation, the four dimensions of interaction are deployed:

1. *relationships* create and consolidate emotional bonds to the group and establish the day-by-day reality of the new perspective;

2. *rituals* provide integrative modes of identifying with and connecting to the new way of life.

3. *rhetoric* provides an interpretive system, offering guidance and meaning to the convert; and

4. *roles* consolidate a person's involvement by giving him or her a special mission to fulfill.

In other words, with whom does the convert now interact, what unique thing does the convert actually do, how does the convert think and speak differently, and what does the convert believe he or she has newly become? These four elements interact and reinforce one another in the conversion process, though groups may differ in the degree to which each component is stressed.[8]

Relationships: "Blessed Be the Ties That Bind"

Kinship and friendship networks are fundamental to most conversions, just as they are influential in resistance and rejection.[9] In my research I have observed the degree to which relationship patterns are controlled and the degree to which there is continuity and intensity in relationships before and after the conversion process. I would argue that relationships are important to most but not all conversions, and that relationship dynamics need to be more systematically examined.

Relationships may be crucial to the conversion process in a variety of ways. Some scholars have theorized that formation of close personal relationships during conversion enables converts to feel accepted at a deep level, and that such personal affirmation releases energy that gives vitality to the new orientation.[10] Others have theorized that an experience of group acceptance enables people to transcend conflict, enhances self-esteem, and offers a new perspective on life. In any case, most social scientists agree that relationships—both friendship and kinship—are primary avenues of proselytizing.

Many people become involved in religious organizations through a network of friends and/or family. Powerful faith-group relationships can serve a compensatory function; that is, those who have suffered deprivation in their families or other social backgrounds find the nurture gained in a supportive group to be extremely important to them. Relationships can also be both catalysts and matrices for growth and development. The stimulation, safety, and support found in an atmosphere of love are helpful to people who are confronting the issues of their lives and discovering and experimenting with new possibilities. Finally, relationships can provide confirmation and consolidation of one's religious orientation. When loving friends and family affirm the worldview, life-style, and goals of a shared religious organization, this reinforcement is crucial to the creation of a "real" world. Overall, relationships provide an environment of security that nurtures, supports, encourages, and sustains the new life of the convert. Not all converts establish relationships *before* conversion, but many do, and thus it is important to note this common pattern. In interviews I conducted with more than fifty converts, I found that relationships were very important to the conversion process, with only three or four exceptions. For many, a relationship with a friend or family member was crucial in leading the person to a new perspective or way of life.

Several important dynamics are at work in the role of relationships within the conversion process. For one thing, a friend is generally perceived to be trustworthy. (The literature on persuasion describes this trustworthiness of the advocate as "source reliability.") Religious beliefs often seem very strange and out of the ordinary to the uninitiated, but when someone known and trusted espouses those beliefs, one is more inclined to entertain their validity and even explore them for oneself.

Another theme that emerged in my interviews is that personal relationships are often important for validation of a new belief system. A potential adherent can see first-hand that someone known to him or her has really changed. It is not uncommon to hear people say that they had known Mr. X years ago and now find him "completely different." Such observations are important in establishing worthiness in the theology being advocated.

Charles Colson tells such a story in his autobiography, *Born Again*.[11] Colson knew Tom Phillips, the president of Raytheon Company, and remembered how different he had seemed after some sort of religious experience. Phillips had initially told Colson something of what had happened but Colson had not really been interested until later, after his indictment in the Watergate scandal. On 12 August 1973, Phillips told Colson the details of his conversion at a Billy Graham crusade. Phillips then began to describe what Colson needed to do to be saved. Phillips's love, support, warmth, and genuine compassion touched Colson deeply and became a turning point for him. Colson began to study the Bible, read Christian authors like C. S. Lewis, and talk with other Christians. Over the next few months the love and attention of Christian friends provided the environment in which Colson's conversion was nurtured.

I do not propose that personal relationships are the one and only "cause" of conversion; historically, there are many obvious exceptions. I do believe, however, that in today's world they more often than not provide the environment in which faith can be nurtured. Even when a conversion is intellectual in content, the presence of friendships or a system of support provides a critical milieu in which the person can explore intellectual and spiritual issues. C. S. Lewis's own conversion, richly analyzed by himself and others, is generally seen as the fruit of an intellectual quest; indeed, that is the way he describes it himself. But when one reads biographical works on Lewis or his own autobiography, *Surprised by Joy*, it is evident that his relationships with university and professional colleagues (the "Inklings") provided a supportive environment in which issues of faith could be explored. I do not minimize the volitional intellectual dimensions of Lewis's conversion, but I think one must acknowledge and credit the environment of mutual support that made the changes in Lewis's life plausible and meaningful. One wonders what might have happened if people like H. V. V. Dyson and J. R. R. Tolkien were not available at the critical juncture of Lewis's internal struggle.[12] It is certainly clear that Lewis played an important role in the conversions of other people, perhaps the best known being that of Sheldon Vanauken, whose autobiography, *A Severe Mercy,* details his conversion and the influence of his friendship with Lewis.[13]

Psychologist Chana Ullman has systematically studied the importance of relationships to the conversion process.[14] She interviewed and tested seventy people in her research project: forty converts to four different groups (Bahai, Judaism, Roman Catholicism, and Hare Krishna), and thirty people from Judaism and Catholicism who were not converts but active lifelong members. The results startled her. She had initiated the research as an investigation of conversion as an intellectual process in which people examine the assumptions of their beliefs and the nature and validity of a new belief system, and then make a commitment. She discovered that the converts—in contrast to the lifelong members—had in common long histories of relational and emotional problems in childhood, adolescence, and immediately prior to their conversion.

Ullman's core finding, however, was that the converts, to a statistically significant level, had absent, weak, or abusive fathers. This serious psychological deprivation and abuse appeared to motivate and inform the person's conversion. In many cases, the convert established a powerful relationship with a guru, rabbi, priest, or other person in the group to which they were converting, and these relationships were, according to Ullman, absolutely central to their conversion.

Sociologist Janet Jacobs's research on deconversion or apostasy found similar results.[15] Her subjects had been members of many different groups, and Jacobs questioned them not only about their departure but also about how they got involved in the first place. Like Ullman, she found that personal relationships with group leaders and/or members were decisive in both the conversion and deconversion processes. In fact, Jacobs interprets the conversion and deconversion processes as falling in and out of love: emotional need drew the convert into the group, and when gratification of those needs failed or the person felt severely mistreated by the group, he or she would with great reluctance leave. Severing the emotional bond was often difficult, if not nearly impossible.

The importance of relationships is also demonstrated in the process of conversion to Islam in some parts of Africa. Arens reports that one of the ways Islam has become important in sub-Saharan Africa is through a patronage system. A stranger is introduced to a village by a patron, and between them a father-son relationship develops in which reciprocal obligations are mutually accepted. The "father" sponsors his "son," and the "son" thereby becomes part of the extended kinship network. If the sponsor is a Muslim, the "client" too becomes a Muslim, as an integral part of becoming a full member of the community. The stranger thus receives access to the community, and the sponsor gains prestige and power by the elaboration of his social ties throughout the community. This pattern may well owe more to material expedience than to deep emotional fervor, and Western Christians may harshly criticize such arrangements as clearly not being "genuine" conversions. I would argue, however, that many conversions in the missionary field, and also on our own shores (if we were willing to examine the issues objectively), reflect similar dynamics.[16]

This stressing of the importance of relationship is not to question the validity and value of these conversions, but rather to observe the actual process of conversion that takes place for many people. During the fall of 1989 and spring of 1990, I conducted participant-observation research on a movement known as the Boston Church of Christ, which has a disciple relationship as a central element in both outreach and the maintenance of members.[17] The group works very hard at reaching out to new people, establishing friendships with them, and sharing the gospel with them, with the goal of fostering trust, candor, and submission. These churches are known as "discipling ministries," and they stress the importance of learning the Bible and following the life of Christ in a concrete, intimate relationship with someone who loves and cares for you. The discipleship relation is thus central to the conversion process.

A provocative point of view on this topic is presented by Jarle Simensen. His study of Norwegian missionaries among the Zulus in South Africa led him to believe that the process of conversion can be seen as a relational transaction between the missionary and the convert. Exchanges are undertaken by both parties. The missionaries gratify spiritual, educational, and health-care needs, and the converts in return give attention, attendance, and adherence to the new religious belief system.[18]

The charismatic leader is also important in the relationship dimension of conversion.[19] In many cases a charismatic leader is not directly involved with the convert, but his or her image and personality play an important role in conversion. The perceived power and energy of the charismatic leader— either actual or imagined—are powerful catalysts in the conversions of many people. For years I have been fascinated by the popularity of Billy Graham. Friend and foe alike recognize that Graham is charismatic: more people respond to the "invitation" at the end of a rally when Graham is there than when the other evangelists in his organization are present. Several years ago I attended a Graham crusade in San Jose, California. Thousands of people had flocked to hear him, even though the San Francisco Bay Area is one of the most secular regions of the United States. Many were there simply because they wanted to "experience" Billy Graham the individual. When a man embodies his message as potently as does Graham, there is a powerful attraction for many people.

I have talked with many converts who say that the inspiration received from watching their guru, leader, preacher, or teacher energized them to greater commitment in their own way of life. In some cases, it was the leader who was the proximate catalyst for the conversion. Several years ago a recent convert to Christianity reported that while randomly sampling television channels on a Sunday morning, she happened to catch Oral Roberts and stopped to listen. Her life was transformed. Even though she is now critical of Roberts's theology and organization, she acknowledges with some embarrassment that the stimulus for her faith conversion was watching Oral Roberts on television.

Ritual: Choreography of the Soul

Victor Turner's brilliant anthropological work, best represented in *The Ritual Process*,[20] alerted scholars to the need for serious study of the importance of ritual in religious life. In the past, many researchers have tended to dismiss or denigrate ritual as merely dull and largely vacuous repetition of religious words and actions. Without rejecting the validity of this view regarding *some* rituals, scholars have come to recognize that ritual can play a vital part in religious life. Indeed, some argue that ritual precedes all other aspects of religion: people first *perform* religiously, and then *rationalize* the process by way of theology. Whichever comes first, it is clear that ritual may have an important effect on the conversion process. It is my view that religious action—regularized, sustained, and intentional—is fundamental to the conversion experience. Ritual fosters the necessary orientation, the readiness of mind and soul to have a conversion experience, and it consolidates conversion after the initial experience.

Ritual is crucial in several ways. It offers a form of knowledge that is distinctive from, but as important as, cognitive knowledge; one might call it embodied, or holistic, knowledge. The first time I witnessed an ordination service in the Roman Catholic tradition, I was taken aback when I saw the young men lying prostrate on the floor, vowing their obedience to the bishop. As I look back on that experience, I can appreciate that what those men learned through their prostration was very different from what they might have learned by merely reciting their vows with a handshake. Similarly, kneeling to pray is a truly different experience from praying while sitting or standing. It is not that one experience is superior to another, but that the physical, mental, and experiential process, and one's internal response, is different in each circumstance.

Theodore W. Jennings asserts that ritual is a way of acquiring, transmitting, and displaying forms of knowledge. "Ritual action is a means by which its participants discover who they are in the world and 'how it is' with the world."[21] Ritual enables the potential and recent convert to begin to understand and embody the new way of life that conversion requires. For many Christian groups, the potential or new convert is considered to be "living in darkness" and thus is seen as needing a great deal of knowledge about the

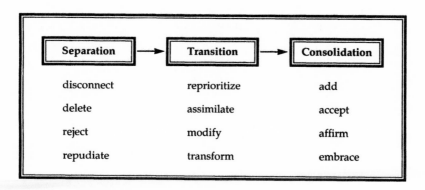

Figure 15 *Ritual processes.*

new life he or she is considering. Ritual not only helps teach important lessons about that new life but also functions as repetitive reinforcement.

Ritual helps people to learn to act differently. From the details of when to bow, kneel, and stand, to how to carry a Bible or address the minister, priest, or rabbi, to more profound truths and teachings, ritual is crucial in revealing the nature of worship, obedience, and celebration. Jennings asserts that "ritual serves as a paradigm for all significant action."[22] Attitudes toward life, other people, the world, and God are informed by the power of ritual in the life of the convert.

Ritual actions consolidate the community through singing, recitation, and gestures in unison, which instill a deeper sense of belonging. Ritual is also a way to tell the story of the new faith to outsiders. Communication of the group's faith is a way of informing and inviting others to participate. Ultimately, ritual is seen by the believer as a "dance with God," a pattern of actions that incline the person to see God as creator and sustainer of the universe and of the individual, a continuing partner in the business of life.

Ritual provides experiential validation of the religious belief system being advocated. I would argue that where there is no agreed-upon religious authority, ritual experience is central to the validation of the doctrines of a movement. Ritual, which may include various meditation techniques, can enable a person to have direct, personal experience of a spiritual phenomenon that is then interpreted by the group as a confirmation of the doctrine being advocated.

James Downton's research on conversion to the Divine Light Mission noted the importance of performing certain rituals so that a person could experience personally the nature of the doctrine being taught. "Seeing the light" was made possible by a technique in which the person pressed against the optic nerve in the top part of the eyeball. "Tasting the nectar" took place when a person rolled his or her tongue back in order to taste liquids flowing past the uvula.[23]

Many Christian groups require baptism by total immersion, a dramatic re-enactment of death and rebirth which confirms that, in the process of being "born again," the old self dies and a new self is created. Many converts report that during the symbolic cleansing of their baptism they felt that their burden of sin was literally lifted from their body.

Conversion strategies typically employ two basic types of ritual: deconstructive and reconstructive. Social scientists have explored the nature of what they often call "degradation ceremonies,"[24] rituals designed to break a person down so that the spirit is more malleable by the new group, and/or to break old patterns of behavior considered destructive or counterproductive to the person. Outsiders generally perceive deconstructive rituals as negative, but there is clearly a difference of opinion between insiders and outsiders on this issue. Social psychologists Elliot Aronson and Judson Mills found in their research that the severity of initiation into a group actually increased people's liking of and loyalty to the group. Drawing on cognitive-dissonance theory, they speculated that the greater the price one pays for entrance, the more an individual values membership.[25]

It could be hypothesized that the greater the change demanded by a group, the more rigorous and drastic would be the rituals of breaking with the past and of deconstructing qualities deemed inimical to the new commitment. Virginia H. Hine discusses the role of "bridge burning" in her theory of conversion and commitment.[26] The more one has to reject, the more drastic the new identity. Of course, not all conversions require dramatic and total life shifts. Groups differ in the degree of change required.

David L. Preston conducted intensive research on a Zen group. He reports that the various techniques and rituals used in Zen were important elements in learning the Zen way of life and philosophy. Particular techniques produced specific physiological results in people, and these symptoms were then interpreted according to Zen theory. The philosophy was thus grounded in the bodily experience of the person who was undergoing Zen conversion. Conversion in that context was not some dramatic, instantaneous experience but rather a gradual process in which a person learned how to act like a Zen practitioner, produce the appropriate experiences, learn the theory, and then interpret those experiences in the appropriate manner. Thus experience induced by ritual was used to vindicate the theory being taught.[27]

Stephen R. Wilson's research on a Yoga group confirms and extends Preston's conclusions. Wilson notes that ritual used in Yoga is designed not just to socialize the person into a new group but, more important, to transform a person's assumptive world. Deconstruction of the normal categories of everyday life is achieved through a process of meditation that modifies or eliminates habituated patterns of perception of oneself and the world. The meditation process seeks to disassemble fundamental elements of personality and to rearrange them into a new person and a new mode of perceiving reality.[28]

It is evident that deconstruction can be voluntarily engaged or externally imposed. Margaret Singer, Richard Ofshe, and Philip Cushman consider deconstructive processes to be fundamentally destructive and manipulative.[29] They see the use of deconstructive ritual as an attempt to elicit submission and obedience from malleable followers, and they condemn these practices as unadulterated methods of mind control and systematic coercion. Whatever one's judgment on the methods, it is clear that they are powerful tools in teaching a person techniques that are destructive of old patterns and an old way of life. The core issue is whether a convert adopts these methods as a conscious, deliberate choice, or is seduced into their use and thus manipulated to do things that were not a part of the original commitment.

On the other side of the coin, there are rituals of construction, affirmation, healing, and growth. Many groups use singing, dancing, unison reading, and other methods to build a sense of group solidarity. A person enacting this kind of ritual transcends the self and becomes a part of the larger community, empowered by a sense of connection with others. Other rituals may provide a sense of healing and forgiveness. Within Christian communities various rituals of forgiveness give people an experience of "unburdening" themselves of their sins. Following confession they experience the affirmation of forgiveness and group solidarity. Alienation from self and God is overcome through such ritual.

Prayer is also a central ritual for many Christians and Muslims, fostering a sense of intimacy with the deity through the experience of talking with God, using either structured prayer or free-form, spontaneous prayer. Connecting with the creator of the universe in a personal, intimate way is a powerful experience for most converts.[30] Communion (the Lord's Supper, or Eucharist), is another Christian ritual of affirmation. By ritually drinking the blood of Jesus and eating his flesh, the person may have a profound sense of connection with the Savior of the world. Remembering the suffering and resurrection of Christ reminds Christians that current suffering will ultimately be transformed into victory.

Rhetoric: The Language of Transformation

The specific language of conversion has recently become of central interest to scholars. The work of James Beckford, Brian Taylor, David Snow, and Richard Machalek is especially noteworthy.[31] Rhetoric includes the various linguistic interpretations of a person's actions, feelings, and goals. I use the category to point to the importance of the way in which people's language changes during the conversion process. For some people, the language of conversion is informed by a formal theology. Others use the language of the Bible, of metaphor, of hymns, and other linguistic tools both to induce their conversion and to interpret the conversion process.

We have thus far emphasized actual changes in people's behavior and in their relationships, but equally vital are a person's *conceptualization* and *interpretation* of those changes. Which comes first can never be answered to everyone's satisfaction. It is my view that all these processes are transpiring at the same time. For some converts their rhetoric or system of interpretation changes first, and is then followed by changes in actions, roles, and relationships. For others the starting point may be changes in actions, roles, or relationships, which later require changes in interpretation.

The language of a potential convert begins to change, sometimes quite dramatically, as the person interacts with a group. It is, of course, true that we are all changed linguistically as we interact with a new group, but the language process is highlighted in religious conversion because words are so important in religious groups. Religion itself, after all, is a system for explaining the world as it is and one's place in it. By way of simple illustration, in many Christian groups a person's primary designation is that of "sinner." Not many people appreciate this designation, yet in conservative Christian churches one learns very quickly that one is a sinner. The precise meaning of the word varies from group to group, but its use is mandatory. There is a logic in the rhetoric employed by groups. If a group emphasizes the redemption of the world by the sacrifice of Jesus Christ, then a member must own the label *sinner*, must somehow experience that reality in his or her own life. As the interaction process continues, the person learns to recognize various thoughts, feelings, and actions as "wrong." These wrong events in his or her life are manifestations of the sinful nature of the potential convert. Some groups stress the wretchedness of the individual more than others do. For some, sin is essential to the human condition in the sense that we are all alienated from God because we are imperfect, while God is perfect. For others, the notion of sin carries with it a sense of utter vileness, degradation, and pollution. Human beings are thus seen as fundamentally perverted, and only through the intervention of God's grace can redemption become manifest.

Whatever the details of the nature of sin, in the interaction phase potential converts learn to speak the language of the group so that they are in tune with the ethos and goals of the movement. Among certain groups a rather elaborate language is devoted to the conversion process itself. Definitions of selfhood, interpretations of the human predicament, and ideas of how the profound gulf between the self and God can be bridged are all expressed through the group's language.

Rhetoric includes not only the more discursive language of theology but the language of metaphor and symbol as well. Needless to say, the language of theology, as demonstrated above, is not mere ordinary discourse but is riddled with metaphor. By using the term *metaphor* I do not belittle the language of theology but rather point to its importance as a vehicle of transformation.

Ralph Metzner has done extensive work on the nature of metaphor in various world religions.[32] In his view, metaphor is not only a linguistic tool but also a vehicle for the transformation of consciousness. The language used by a group is not sheer verbiage but constitutes the very basis upon which consciousness is formed and transformed. The rather violent and dramatic language of death and rebirth in Christianity, as well as in other religions, is formative in giving Christians the sense that conversion is dramatic. The old must pass away and the new must come into being by divine intervention. Conversion then takes place, in part, through the process of learning a new language and learning to apply that language in situations that make it relevant to the convert and to the community to which the convert is speaking.

In addition to changes in a person's metaphor, Snow and Machalek point to changes in a person's system of attribution. Attribution is the process of assigning motives for actions, both one's own and others'. Ordinarily, people use various systems of interpreting life events. Snow and Machalek believe that a convert learns to focus on a single system of attribution as he or she traverses the interaction phase. If I had an automobile accident I might interpret it in several ways: I made a foolish mistake; the other driver was stupid and caused the accident; the traffic light was out of order and thus it was the city's fault and not that of either driver; there were evil spirits at work causing mischief in the lives of the two victims; or the event was planned by God as a way of forcing me and the other driver to acknowledge our finitude, align our lives with God, and stop living selfishly. Snow and Machalek believe that the "true" convert will change and utilize only one system of interpretation, the one required by the group or common to its worldview.

For many religions Snow and Machalek's ideas are accurate. Some groups, however, permit more than one interpretation of an event. For instance, while conservative groups might demand that a person interpret the car accident in one particular way, a liberal group might allow for a variety of interpretations or at least a multileveled interpretation. In either case, the convert often uses language in a new way to describe and interpret many different aspects of life. In general, the convert's interpretation is a transcendent perspective on ordinary experience and illustrates life as a dramatic struggle of good and evil and as being of ultimate significance. Life is not merely a chance collection of events but a meaningful process of bringing people into relationship with God.

Roles: Enactment of Vision and Vocation

Sociological approaches to conversion stress the importance of role change in the conversion process.[33] A role is defined as the behavior expected of the occupant of a given position or status, and it implies (but does not always require) internal beliefs and values congruent with that role. Originally derived from the thought of George H. Mead and based on the metaphor of the theater, role has become an important theoretical concept in both social psychology and sociology. A role has two features: "(1) *expectations* (beliefs, cognitions) held by certain persons in regard to what behaviors are appropriate for the occupant of a given position, and (2) *enactments* (i.e., conduct) of a person who is assigned to, or elects to enter, a given position."[34]

David G. Bromley and Anson Shupe, for example, propose that rather than looking at internal, psychological processes, the role approach sees conversion as a change in expectations, values, and norms within a social network. Roles are derived from institutions and beliefs, not from personality or innate character. Roles are reciprocal. People interact with one another and provide gratifications that are mutually beneficial.[35]

Robert Balch goes even further. Based on his participant-observation research of a UFO cult, Balch argues that many people become involved in a group and essentially "playact." In other words, people may talk and act like converts when they are engaging in interaction with members, but they are merely experimenting with the new option, trying out the role. Like Shupe and Bromley, Balch does not accept the traditional psychological interpretation of major personality changes being involved in conversion—at least not in the early stages. People adopt the role of the convert and perform accordingly, and internal changes may then follow.[36]

An important role for the convert is to be the "student" of a teacher, an older member who knows the ropes of the organization and is able to teach the convert about behaviors and beliefs that are expected in the group.[37] This teaching may be formal or informal, but the relationship is based on one person knowing more and being willing to share it with an interested person who is seeking assistance, who is willing to play the role of novice. In some traditions, the teacher-student relationship is formalized, as in the Boston Church of Christ with its clear-cut notion of discipleship roles: one person is the teacher and another is the student. One is more advanced in the faith, the other less advanced. Yet in real terms, everyone is in both roles simultaneously. Even the "lead evangelist" of the congregation has a discipleship role with someone above him.

Role also functions in the conversion process as a means for a person to see himself or herself in a new way. In the Christian tradition, for example, the convert is characterized as having been rebellious and alienated from God, seeking only the gratification of selfish desires. Conversion restores a person to the role of "child of God," who seeks to do the will of God and is a "soldier for Christ." Evangelical groups often expect that new converts begin immediately to share their faith with others. They are told that "every real Christian is a missionary," and that every disciple should seek to share the gospel with others. The Christian is "an ambassador for Christ" and must learn to present the gospel in any situation.

Role change is an internalization and integration of the changes in relationships, rhetoric, and ritual. Role combines and appropriates all the elements that make the new way of life, new set of beliefs, and new network of relationships crucial to conversion.

The interaction phase of the conversion process is intense and crucial to the potential convert, as a rebirthing process should be. A sphere of influence has been created through encapsulation techniques. In that sphere, new or existing networks of relationships are fostered, religious ritual is enacted, a new rhetoric is learned, and new roles are embodied. These dynamic processes culminate in the commitment phase.

Commitment

Chapter 9

The sixth stage of conversion, commitment, is the fulcrum of the change process. Following a period of intensive interaction, the potential convert faces the prospect, the choice, of commitment. Commitment includes several important facets. A specific turning point or decision is often required and/or experienced, and this commitment decision is often dramatized and commemorated—sealed with a public demonstration of the convert's choice. Commitment rituals like baptism and testimony are important, observable events that give witness to the convert's decision.

Many traditions employ various rituals of rejection, transition, and incorporation at the commitment stage. These rituals are powerful in that they not only provide a kind of ultimate shaping for a person's experience of the conversion process but also provide a means by which to consolidate a person's beliefs and involvement in a group. Commitment rituals both express a person's transformation and allow the person to participate in that transformation.

Not all groups have such requirements, and for some groups these demonstrations are optional. Still other groups demand compliance with extensive rules and regulations when the convert makes a formal or informal, explicit or implicit decision to become a member of a religious community.[1] Understanding the variety of these rituals and their precise settings, metaphors, and methods will enable the scholar of conversion to describe better the nature of the commitment stage, and to generate sophisticated theoretical analysis as well as cultivate a profound personal understanding. The five most common elements of the commitment stage are decision making, rituals, surrender, testimony manifested in language transformation and biographical reconstruction, and motivational reformulation.

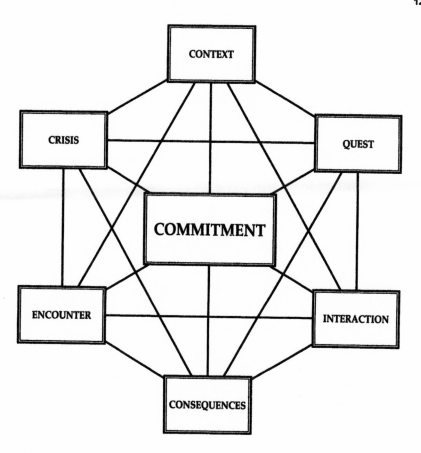

Figure 16 *Stage 6: Commitment.*

Decision Making

Decision making is an integral part of the commitment stage and is often the occasion for an intense and painful confrontation with the self.[2] Within the biblical tradition, a paradigmatic call to decision is found in Deuteronomy 30:15–20:

See, I have set before you today life and prosperity, death and adversity. If you obey the commandments of the Lord your God that I am commanding you today, by loving the Lord your God, walking in his ways, and observing his commandments, decrees, and ordinances, then you shall live and become numerous, and the Lord your God will bless you in the land that you are entering to possess. But if your heart turns away and you do not hear, but are led astray to bow down to other gods and serve them, I declare to you today that you shall perish; you shall not live long in the land that you are crossing the Jordan to enter and possess. I call heaven and earth to witness against you today that I have set before you life and death, blessings and curses. Choose life so that you and your descendants may live, loving the Lord your God, obeying him, and holding fast to him; for that means life to you and length of days, so that you may live in the land that the Lord swore to give to your ancestors, to Abraham, to Isaac, and to Jacob.[3]

The biblical tradition is filled with examples of dramatic decisions that affect a person's destiny. It is no accident that making a decision for Christ is a major theme in evangelical theology. Yet at the same time that a potential convert may be attracted to Jesus Christ and the new religious community, he or she may still be enmeshed in old ways of life. Vacillation between two worlds can be very painful.[4] The decision to cross the line into a new life, on the other hand, can be an occasion for tremendous joy, for generating a new feeling of freedom that can itself be a powerful experience confirming the theology being embraced.[5]

Decision making involves the evaluation of alternatives. The potential convert, his or her extended network of relationships and patterns of behavior, and his or her internal weighing of pros and cons, desires and fears, all help shape the outcome. C. David Gartrell and Zane K. Shannon propose that decision making in the conversion process is a result of several factors.[6] The potential convert's perceptions of the expected rewards of conversion are crucial. Evaluation of these possible rewards derives from the person's own life experience and values as well as those of friends and relatives. In addition, the potential convert weighs the social rewards (consisting of approval, respect, love, relief of fear and tension) and the cognitive benefits (ultimate meaning and solutions to practical problems). Decision making is thus not entirely an internal process but an experience of social interaction with friends and family.

As we noted when discussing the encounter stage, initial participation in a religious group is often facilitated by the existence or establishment of emotional bonds between a potential convert and the advocate and/or the group. It appears that a person's decision whether to make a long-term commitment to a group may largely be determined by the degree of connection the person feels with the new group, as opposed to the degree of emotional connection he or she feels outside the group. The study by Marc Galanter and his colleagues of the Unification Church is provocative. They found that after participating in a recruitment workshop, potential converts acquired a virtually uniform level of Unification Church beliefs. In other words, everyone who completed the workshop was persuaded to affirm the belief system. However, the major factor ultimately influencing an individual's commitment to the group was not level of belief but whether the person had stronger relationships with people in the group than he or she had with people outside the movement.[7]

Rituals

As Theodore R. Sarbin and Nathan Adler and Robert C. Ziller have recognized, rituals that may be a part of the commitment stage are powerful methods by which new learning takes place. Baptism in Christianity, for example, is an explicit, experiential process by which one declares the old life to be dead and the new life to be born.[8] In some religious traditions, requirements to modify one's clothing, diet, or other patterns of common daily behavior can serve this same function of reinforcing the rejection of old patterns and behaviors and the incorporation of new behaviors into one's life.

At the heart of conversion ritual is the difficult combination of saying no and saying yes. Conversion implies that a person is "turning away from" the

past and "turning to" a new future. Ritual witnessed by others can be powerful in advertising the new condition of the person or persons who are converting. One of the most dramatic conversions in the twentieth century took place
on 14 October 1956.[9] An estimated five hundred thousand people gathered
near Nagpur in the western Indian state of Maharashtra. Led by B. R. Ambedkar, hundreds of thousands of Mahars renounced their Hindu faith and embraced Buddhism. Dressed in white robes, the people followed Ambedkar in
reciting the Buddhist oaths administered by Chandramani Mahasthavir, the
oldest and most revered Buddhist monk in India. The massive gathering of
people, the white robes, and the recitation of oaths were simple but powerfully effective rituals in transforming the Mahars from being Untouchables to
being Buddhists. A generation later debates still rage about the converts'
motives and the ultimate effects of their conversion, but the fact remains that
14 October 1956 was a turning point in the history of Buddhism in India. The
mass conversion was revolutionary, marking the revitalization of Buddhism
in the land of its origin.[10] Whatever one's evaluation of Ambedkar and the
Buddhist conversion movement, the public conversion ritual enacted a break
with the past and initiated a new beginning for thousands of people.[11]

From an institution's point of view, commitment ritual is designed to
create and sustain loyalty to the group.[12] From the individual's point of view,
commitment ritual provides public testimony of the culmination or consummation of a process that may have been going on for a period of time. Commitment rituals are, in the words of Virginia Hine, "bridge-burning events,"[13]
effective because they serve three functions. First, the convert enacts the ritual
ceremony and thus embodies the transformation process. Dramatizing
change, acting out the role, is more effective than merely talking about
change. A public proclamation of the rejection of an old way of life (however
subtle or implicit) and an embracing of the new consolidates the conversion
process. Hine asserts that the bridge-burning rituals of conversion provide
the individual with powerful subjective experiences that confirm the ideology
of the group and transform the convert's self-image. New members of the
movement are ritually reaffirmed in their convictions, transported into their

new roles and status. Seeing the initiation ritual enacted reminds other members of their own commitment to a new way of life; they re-experience their own transformation. Finally, outsiders are sometimes offended or bewildered by the "absurdity" or irrationality of the rituals; such reactions help to define a sense of boundaries between the convert and the outside world.

Hare Krishna followers, for example, shave their heads and don orange robes, thus announcing their rejection of ordinary ways of living within the United States. Conversion to Judaism requires total immersion in water before witnesses, and men must be ritually circumcised. Jewish theology affirms that these ceremonies, along with other procedures, mean that the person's previous life is abolished, and that the convert becomes a new being.[14] Christian baptism is filled with imagery of death and rebirth. Saint Paul could write, "Don't you know that all of us who were baptized into Christ Jesus were baptized into his death? We were therefore buried with him through baptism into death in order that, just as Christ was raised from the dead through the glory of the Father, we too may live a new life" (Romans 6:3–4). Baptism, then, specifically memorializes and re-enacts that turning point. Even though debates continue about the theological implications of baptism and the necessity of baptism for salvation, most Christian churches see baptism, whatever its precise form, as the dividing line between the community of faith and the world.

Elaborate initiation rituals developed during the first four centuries of Christian history. Henry Ansgar Kelly has documented the significance of these ceremonies in *The Devil at Baptism*, in which he shows that demonology shaped much of the environment of early Christianity.[15] As a result, rituals of conversion demanded extensive education in the doctrines and practices of the early church, including dramatic rituals renouncing Satan and rites of purification. The children of light had to be completely cut off, set apart from the offspring of darkness. In more recent times, missionaries have used bridge-burning rituals as a method of cutting the convert off from previous religious involvements. Alan Tippett studied rituals of rejection in the missionary field. Based on his experience in the South Pacific, Tippett believed that those tribal groups that burned their previous objects of worship were less likely to return to paganism than those who did not ritualize their radical break with the past.[16]

It should come as no surprise that such rituals are still practiced today. Many conservative Christian groups see the conversion process as a radical break with a life in service to the Devil, however unwitting, and the forging of a new allegiance to Christ. Few Protestant groups use the elaborate rituals of the early church, but their ideology requires no less a repudiation of the world of evil and no less an affirmation of their allegiance to faith and commitment to Christ.[17]

A fascinating insight into the ceremonies involved in the commitment process can be found in Alan Morinis's work.[18] Morinis examined ordeals of initiation in which groups required the mutilation of the body (such as circumcision, scarification, beatings, amputation of fingers, removal of teeth and so forth) in a deliberate attempt to induce pain. He theorizes that inducement of pain serves two functions: to heighten self-awareness and to demonstrate powerfully that to become a part of the group the individual has to sacrifice something of the self. Although no Christian group that I know of requires mutilation of the physical body as part of the conversion process, psychic pain and trauma are often intensely present in Christian conversion. Stories of religious converts are steeped in agonized description of struggles with sin and alienation from God. The emphasis in conservative Christianity on one's inherent sinfulness and depravity before turning to God may be one way to create the same painful effect induced by mutilation rituals.

There is, I believe, a long history of this pain-inducing process in Christian religious experience generally, a "tradition" consciously perpetuated by Protestantism in the United States. David Kobrin, for instance, provides a description of the stages of conversion expected (demanded?) in seventeenth-century colonial America.[19] His rich case study of the First Church in Milford, Connecticut, in the early 1600s is illuminating. The four stages of conversion he details began with a vivid conviction of sin. A person needed to be keenly aware of the exact nature of his or her sinfulness. Self-analysis based on the Bible, sermons, and theology provided revelation and exposition of the precise extent of one's personal sinfulness. Next, a potential convert needed a sense of compunction, owning that profound wounded-ness had resulted from one's sin. Awareness of sin was not enough—a person had to feel absolute and total revulsion for his or her horrible predica-ment. Compunction was presumed to foster a profound desire to be separated from the source of pollution, sin.

The third phase was a sense of humiliation, of recognition that there was nothing good in the sinners that would enable them to reform or save them-selves, that they were destitute of inner resources for improvement. Absolute dejection made it possible to enter phase four, faith, which permitted recep-tion of Christ's saving grace. Grace was an utter mystery but was received with joyful gratitude because it was established in the belief system as the only solution to the sinner's plight. In this process there could be no omission of any steps, nor any lack of attention or severity in the experience of any stage. Any psychic torture experience was testimony to the rightness of the doctrine and was regarded as lending efficacy to the experience. Jerald Brauer asserts that the Puritan conversion experience was "a terrible and awful or-deal."[20]

The Boston Church of Christ (sometimes called the discipling or multiply-ing ministry movement) is one contemporary movement that seeks to foster a conversion process similar to that of the Puritans in its emotional intensity. "Bringing to brokenness" is a theme that emerges in the one-on-one relation-ship between the Christian and the potential convert. The advocate shows the potential recruit various passages in the Bible listing sins that are sources of alienation from God. Galatians 5:19–21 and 2 Timothy 3:1–5 are commonly used. As potential converts reflect on these lists of sins, they are asked if any are present in their own lives. As in the case of the Puritans, keen, painful awareness and admission of one's sinful predicament is believed necessary to generate the desire to break with the bonds of sin, that is, with the past. I would also assert that an underlying purpose of this focus on personal sinfulness is to shatter one's previous identity, in order to reconstruct a new identity based on the church's interpretation of the Bible.[21]

My point in emphasizing this aspect of Christian conversion is that the induction of psychological and spiritual pain is inherent in many forms of Christian conversion. Its effect on the convert is expected to be shattering, literally life-transforming. Death of the previous persona is required, and rebirth through the power of God is offered as the only alternative to utter depravity and destruction.[22]

Surrender

Surrender is the inner process of commitment and is one of the most difficult aspects of conversion to understand. It is also very likely the aspect hardest for a convert to achieve in any lasting, pervasive sense. The experience of surrender is, for many converts, *the* turning point away from the old life and the beginning of a new life, produced not by one's own controlling volition but by the power of God's grace. Paradigmatic for total submission to God in the Christian tradition is Paul's statement that "I have been crucified with Christ, and I no longer live, but Christ lives in me. The life I live in the body, I live by faith in the Son of God, who loved me and gave himself for me" (Galatians 2:20). Outsiders may be perplexed, but insiders see such surrender as absolutely essential to a new life. Many religious traditions require that a convert submit to the authority of a guru, teacher, institution, or other form of authority that will guide the convert's actions, associations, and beliefs. In some traditions detailed prescriptions and proscriptions must be rigorously followed. The discipline required is astounding to many people, but the religious rationale is that these particular steps are required in order to attain a spiritual consciousness superior to ordinary consciousness.

Surrender is an inner yielding of control, an acceptance of the authority of the leader, group, or tradition, which enables the convert to devote himself or herself completely to the group. Getting to the point of surrender can be extremely difficult, and several elements must be considered to understand this process. These are not discrete and neat chronological steps but rather psychological and spiritual influences that intermingle and overlap in the actual phenomenology of the surrender process. I see five elements of surrender. (1) The potential convert may first feel a desire for surrender, which can originate in a wish to be compliant with the requirements of the group, or from a profound understanding that surrender is necessary on the path of spiritual transformation. (2) Surrender entails conflict between a need for self-control and a desire for surrender and transformation. Desire and fear are opposed in this conflict: the convert is attracted to the new life option yet wishes to avoid the insecurity that accompanies yielding of control. (3) Conflict is generally resolved through what might be called "giving up" or "giving in," which may require the figurative "leap of faith." (4) The resolution of conflict brings an experience of liberation, relief, and breakthrough. (5) Surrender tends to be fragile and precarious, requiring a continual sifting through the other four elements. Surrender needs to be constantly re-affirmed and re-experienced, human beings being what they are.

Desire

The desire for surrender can emerge pragmatically from a recognition that it is required by the religious group. That is one extreme; at the opposite end of the spectrum is a recognition, an insight, that the path to spiritual growth is paved with surrender. Neither kind of desire necessarily arises spontaneously; it is more typical for a person to learn the importance of surrender through interaction with people who teach and embody it in their own lives. Spiritual literature is replete with admonitions and illustrations of the necessity of desire for surrender. Emilie Griffin, in her splendid book *Turning: Reflections on the Experience of Conversion,* explores the nature of this desire.[23] It can emerge through nostalgia for a lost past. Alienation can be a catalyst for a profound desire to give up oneself to union with God or reconciliation with family and friends. Success in one's chosen life goals may bring an awareness that there must be something beyond such achievement. For others, desire may come from undifferentiated stirrings of restlessness and vague yearnings for "something more."

Conflict

Conflict pervades the surrender process. A common metaphor underlying the conversion process is that of war, of battle between the forces of light and the forces of darkness. God and Satan contend for the soul of each individual. This warfare may be intensely felt in the heart of a potential convert. Surrender requires the person to confront directly what he or she will be giving up for the benefits of the new option. This process is never easy. Surrender, in fact, seems paradoxical, and it cannot occur simply as a matter of will. Fundamental ego preservation drives one to equate surrender with loss, not victory. A person will remind himself or herself of the benefits of surrender and of the dire consequences if that option is rejected; nevertheless, internal and external forces stand in the way of total surrender. Conflict may center around existing relationships, activities, and basic beliefs, on the one hand, and the option of a transcendent reality, on the other hand. Anguish is keenly felt when a person firmly believes in the new reality but is still wedded in various ways to old patterns and perceived needs, which can be quite persistent.

The nature of conflict varies with different people and traditions. Evangelical Christians require an admission of sinfulness, a confession of the divinity of Jesus Christ, a yearning for God to forgive, and an invitation for Jesus to enter the person's life and heart. Intellectual acknowledgment of sinfulness is relatively easy; deep emotional awareness of one's sinfulness comes only with struggle. Thoughts of one's good deeds and basic decency are challenged by a confrontation with one's enumerated sins of a lifetime. Exploring the nature and consequences of personal sins is often resisted, but it is one way that a person struggles to understand his or her predicament. In groups that do not polarize good and evil in such sharp terms, there is an approach to conflict that is more gentle. Letting go of obstacles and en-cumbrances that stand in the way of surrender is more common than ago-nized conflict. Affirmation of ambivalence may be allowed. Whether through repudiation of an evil element of life or through the letting go of some burden, the promise of victory through surrender is the reward held out to converts for right resolution of this conflict.

"Giving In": Relief and Liberation

The initial reaction to surrender is often an enormous burst of both en-ergy and relief. Energy that was consigned to maintain the conflict is now channeled into the new life, and the convert may feel incredible vitality and empowerment, with the possible effect that he or she can resolve major problems easily. The person feels a sense of power, and the belief that God is alive and within him or her becomes an experienced reality. This sense of empowerment and presence is a powerful vindication of the existence of God and/or the transcendent, and it provides hope for transformation, healing, and renewal. The convert may feel a sense of ease in doing what the religion dictates even though just a few weeks or days earlier there was great inner and outer resistance.

Harry M. Tiebout, in his studies of Alcoholics Anonymous, provides some interesting insights into this process.[24] He contends that people will often struggle with an issue or a problem for a long period of time, and that their anguish and fear depletes them. Powerlessness is a frightening condi-tion to admit. When participating in A.A., one finally confesses the reality that one is an alcoholic and is completely helpless to change that reality by oneself. Paradoxically, upon a genuine acknowledgment of that helplessness, one is empowered to begin the process of dealing with alcoholism.

A similar process is, I believe, sometimes at work in Christian conver-sion. When a person confronts his or her predicament as a lost sinner, sur-render to that knowledge and to Jesus Christ as a deliverer is the very point at which energy becomes available for a new life. Tiebout's psychoanalytic interpretation, centering on the concept of energy, reaches a similar conclusion. He recognizes that much energy is deployed to maintain an inner struggle. With surrender, energy is freed to be used in other aspects of the person's life.[25] Marc Galanter proposes a similar process, the "relief effect," which takes place when a person identifies with a group.[26]

Sustaining Surrender

On a more profound level, surrender is more than either a verbal agreement or a single public action; it is an inner process of submission to God (and, for some, to the authority of the Church) that continues over a lifetime. It is an inner resolve to shift loyalties, and the process is never complete. Old urges return, sometimes with greater power than before. Few people experience surrender as a final achievement, without reservations or backsliding. Surrender is a process in which the person disconnects himself or herself from old ways and patterns and gradually is able to consolidate the new life into a firmer, growing commitment.

The battle within the convert usually continues. When people cannot maintain a sense of euphoria and empowerment, an inevitable loss of energy may initiate a new crisis. They may worry that their conversion was not valid, and they may be plagued with old temptations and doubts. For example, I met many converts to evangelical Christianity when I taught at Trinity College in Deerfield, Illinois, between 1975 and 1978. As I observed these young converts I developed the notion of "postconversion depression," an inevitable tapering off from the emotional peak of decisive commitment. This issue is a serious problem for any tradition that advocates total, complete, and sudden conversion.

The human reality seems to be that the power of the conversion experience will eventually dissipate for most people, and thus maintenance procedures become important to protect a person either from severe depression or from abandoning the new religious commitment altogether. Some religious traditions recognize the problem and prepare people to surrender and commit afresh in response to each new struggle, to have more patience with themselves and more willingness to face the reality that lives shaped over many years will require a long process of reshaping according to new ideas, relationships, and life-styles. Other traditions, such as most of the conservative, evangelical Protestant movements in the United States, appear less well equipped to deal with this postconversion phenomenon, resulting in many converts dropping out a few months after their conversion experience, or sinking into a slough of dissatisfaction in which their conversion seems to avail little.

Testimony: Language Transformation and Biographical Reconstruction

As we recall, testimony is the narrative witness of a person's conversion, and it entails two interacting processes: language transformation and biographical reconstruction. We have seen that conversion is in part the adoption of a new rhetoric or language system. Since language is a powerful tool for the transformation of one's consciousness and perception of the world, it is not surprising that testimony is the adaptation of this modified rhetoric to explain one's conversion experience, to tell one's own story.[27]

Personal testimony is a common method for publicly displaying commitment.[28] Indeed, certain groups require testimony in order to discern the person's appropriateness for inclusion in the group. Other groups encourage but do not require it, while some groups make no formal use of testimony. Those that require testimony vary according to the specificity and rigidity of what is considered an "acceptable" or an "unacceptable" conversion story.

Testimony is a rich resource for understanding the nature of conversion. Learning to give one's testimony of conversion is often an integral part of the conversion process itself.[29] The convert's testimony serves as an opportunity to demonstrate his or her language transformation and biographical reconstruction. Testimony can also be a potent reminder of the community's basic values and goals. The community can celebrate a new convert's experience as well as have a sense that the group's theology and methods are vindicated by the testimony of a "good" convert. Audience and speaker form a powerful matrix of support and reinforcement.

The metaphor we discussed in the encounter stage, that of adopting the story of a new group as one's own, is carried forward into the commitment stage, where it is more fully appropriated, so that a convert undergoes an experience of biographical reconstruction. Although all of ordinary human life can be seen as a subtle process of reorganizing one's biography, in religious conversion there is often an implicit or explicit requirement to reinterpret one's life, to gain a new vision of its meaning, with new metaphors, new images, new stories.

This idea has very pertinent application to the psychology of conversion, but it is primarily sociologists who have investigated notions of biographical reconstruction.[30] James Beckford and Brian Taylor have found that religious groups may require that people learn to tell their conversion story to the satisfaction of the group. The convert learns what is expected by listening to other testimonies and gradually begins to see his or her life within the common perspective. The individual appropriates a new frame of reference, which helps him or her learn to be a new person.

For example, Beckford observed that Jehovah's Witnesses have a distinctive way of telling their conversion stories.[31] Rather than the typical evangelical script of a deep sense of sin, crisis, and surrender to Christ, he found that they would tell of their conversion as entailing progressive enlightenment and discovery of cognitive truth, as achievement and work within an organization. Their conversion was a gradual process of learning about the Witnesses and about the Bible as they interpreted it. To be a good convert one had to be a "truth seeker." As knowledge increased, the potential convert engaged in a self-directed, deliberate program of self-reform. This was no sudden conversion "from the sky." Furthermore, conversion was intimately involved with working within the organization to further the goals of the institutional church, especially through dissemination of church literature or "publishing" the truth of God's will, literally "witnessing."

Beckford also noted that over the many years he has systematically studied the Jehovah's Witnesses, both their institution and the type of conversion stories told have changed. Thus testimony becomes more than a story of individual change; it also reflects the ongoing process of institutional change.

The individual who is learning a new language is both overtly and covertly molded by the group. Some groups require specific language and even tone; others merely affirm that which they admire or like and ignore or gently admonish the person who is not going along with the group. This subtle process of interplay between speaker and audience is complex and powerful, because the convert usually is quite sincere about what he or she is saying and may adopt subtle or even significant modification out of genuine desire to speak the "truth." Research has shown also that when a person talks before a group there is more likelihood that the speaker's beliefs will undergo some adjustment than when a person merely reads silently, unbound by any public statement. It is therefore understandable that religious leaders require new converts to communicate orally and publicly their new commitment or way of life.[32]

Groups that do not require public testimony are generally less demanding, and hence the changes expected and manifested may be fewer and less dramatic than in groups that require a powerful conversion experience and a report on that experience. This, however, is not necessarily the case.

Motivational Reformulation

One of the most fascinating topics in the study of conversion and commitment is the nature of people's motivation for conversion.[33] This is a concern for scholars of conversion as well as for those who are advocates. Motivation reaches a peak of importance at the commitment stage, because advocates often question the motivation of the potential convert. Also, it is my view that motivation itself is transformed in the process of language transformation and biographical reconstruction. Is the convert manifesting genuine motivation for conversion or seeking instead to gain something extrinsic to the religious life? Even if the person is motivated by "spiritual" goals, an advocate may sometimes question the convert's true motives.

Motives, after all, are not simple and single. They may be multiple, complex, and often quite malleable. For instance, when a person first comes into contact with a religious movement, his or her motives for conversion may be to achieve prestige, a sense of belonging, or other extrinsic rewards. After a period of interaction, however, the person may change his or her rhetoric of motives, as deep spiritual or religious yearnings and aspirations are triggered. People change over time, and so do their motives. Indeed, change is the essence of conversion. There is certainly no one motive for conversion. Motives that start out as multiple, interactive, and cumulative are likely to be further transformed in the process of personal and spiritual growth and development or through the acquisition of a new vocabulary that is more in line with the requirements and expectations of the group.

I propose the following hypotheses about motivation:

1. Motives for conversion vary from person to person;

2. motives for conversion are multiple, interactive, and cumulative;

3. different groups have (and communicate) different norms for what they consider to be right and wrong motives;

4. groups vary in the latitude of motives allowed, encouraged, or fostered;

5. initial motivation for joining a group or converting are refined as the person interacts with the group—for membership to be sustained and conversion to be maintained, it is necessary for there to be a convergence of the convert's initial and present motives for converting;

6. each person converts when it is to his or her *perceived* advantage: satisfaction, benefit, fulfillment, improvement, and/or compulsion;

7. for conversion to continue, motives must be sustained; and

8. motives are selected, emphasized, reprioritized, and deleted according to the implicit or explicit rules of testimony and the rhetorical system of the group into which one is converting.

Consequences

Chapter 10

The consequences of conversion are complex and multifaceted, in both their study and explication. We can delineate five approaches to the exploration of consequences: the role of personal bias in assessment, general observations, and in-depth looks at sociocultural and historical consequences, psychological consequences, and theological consequences of conversion. Assessment of the consequences of conversion necessarily embodies both descriptive and normative elements, and there is free movement between the two in my discussion.

Personal Bias in Assessment of Consequences

Two potential sources of bias need to be accounted for in assessing conversion. The particular religious community under consideration will naturally have its own set of evaluative criteria. These must be articulated as clearly and completely as possible to assess an individual's conversion in terms of the internal criteria developed by the group. This approach is important for many reasons, chief among which is to highlight the fact that the process of converting is, after all, a religious conversion within a religious community and tradition.

Beyond that, however, is the necessity to recognize that scholars are not immune from bias, which they must make as explicit as possible.[1] It is important to recognize that evaluations, whether from theological orientations or from the human sciences, are normative. That is to say, assessments of any kind proceed out of a particular perspective in which values and philosophies are present, either explicitly or implicitly. No perspective is purely "scientific." In the field of conversion studies, assessments are *always* made from a values orientation. One example is the tendency within psychology to be vigilant for pathology; hence, most psychological evaluations of conversion

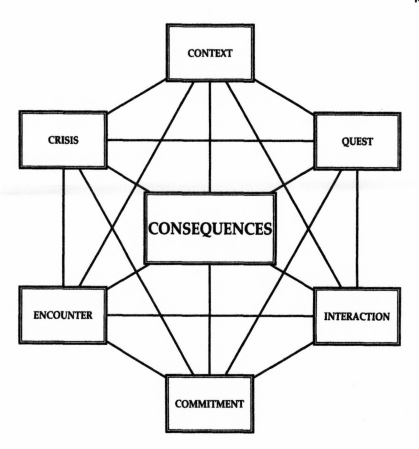

Figure 17 *Stage 7: Consequences.*

assess the outcome as an inadequate coping with resolution of guilt, or hostility, and so forth. The psychological literature on conversion (with the exception of Christian psychologists and a few within the humanistic or transpersonal perspective) generally portray conversion in a negative light. I do not totally reject such evaluations; I think that some conversions are, from a psychological point of view, immature and regressive. For research to have maximum value for peers and other readers, however, the person making the assessment must acknowledge that his or her values may have an impact on the interpretation of the data, and that one's own disciplinary ethos tends to shape interpretation. A study of conversion should reveal whether the investigator is religious or open to an alternative reality advocated by the group, even though the scholar is agnostic, humanistic, or atheist.

Can a devout Roman Catholic "objectively" evaluate the merits of a convert to the Church of Jesus Christ of Latter-Day Saints? Can a Mormon assess the validity and value of a conversion to Islam? Can a nonbeliever affirm the validity and value of a conversion to a perspective that radically questions his or her own fundamental assumptions about the nature of reality. These considerations can be addressed only if the reporting scholar uses the following questions, or something very similar, to reveal the investigator's point of view:

Am I religious or not?

Am I religious in a way that is the same as or similar to that of the person I am assessing?

If I am not religious, what is my personal response to the nature of the religious conversion I am studying?

Am I repulsed or attracted?

What is my fundamental agenda in studying such phenomena?

In addition, the scholar should articulate as explicitly as possible the criteria by which his or her own discipline operates. What constitutes mental health in psychology? To what degree is the conversion judged to promote mental health from the assessor's point of view? Scholars should also recognize that while an assessment on the basis of an external value system may not be adequate to the task, their being explicit and candid about their own values and biases can help make the assessment as fair as possible and allow the reader to bear these biases in mind.

Nature of Consequences

The consequences of conversion are determined in part by the nature, intensity, and duration of the conversion and the response to conversion in a person's or a group's context. One of the most dramatic conversions in the history of Christianity was that of Saul of Tarsus, erstwhile persecutor of Jews who came to believe that Jesus was the Messiah. Saul became Paul in an experience that set in motion a profound and fundamental shift from persecution to advocacy.[2] The experience was brief, but the intensity was very great, and the nature of the phenomenon was, if we follow the report of Luke, a direct experience of the risen Christ. Many scholars consider Paul's conversion to be the paradigm of the sudden conversion in Christianity.[3]

For most people, conversion is not so dramatic or intense. I once talked with a man who reported that he had been reared as a Southern Baptist yet had never been comfortable with that tradition. When he became an adult he found that most of his friends were Jewish. For several years he attended various synagogues but was not quite sure how to reconcile his understanding of Jesus with Judaism. One day at temple, the answer came. The rabbi delivered a sermon in which he asked, Where would Jesus be most comfortable if he came to San Francisco tonight? Would Jesus feel at home at Saint Mary's Cathedral (Roman Catholic), Grace Cathedral (Episcopal), or other churches in the city? Finally the rabbi asserted that Jesus would surely feel most at home in that very synagogue. This statement confirmed to the discontented Baptist that he too was most at home in the synagogue. Even though this event was not a thunderous revelation or a dramatic turning point for him, it generated an insight that enabled him to begin the formal process of becoming a Jew.

How many aspects of life are affected by conversion? How extensive are the changes conversion brings? To what extent are converts alienated from or reconciled to the wider world? Conversion to a mainline Protestant church may require few major changes in one's life. Conversion to Orthodox Judaism, however, requires one to change eating patterns, acquire a new set of associates, possibly modify job commitments, and follow a new and complex set of rituals. Conversion to Orthodox Judaism also requires the convert to sever many if not all previous ties, even within his or her own family.

When evaluating degree of change, one must look beyond the immediate results. Many contemporary scholars believe that authentic conversion is an ongoing process of transformation. Initial change, while important, is but the first step in a long process, a pilgrimage. More profound changes may come in the months, and even years, after the initial conversion takes place.

Donald J. Gelpi, a Jesuit theologian, has developed a sophisticated approach to the normative interpretation of conversion.[4] Building upon the work of Bernard Lonergan and the American philosophical tradition, Gelpi writes: "I use the word 'conversion' . . . to mean the decision to assume responsibility for a distinguishable area of experienced growth and development. Converts turn from irresponsible to responsible living. . . . By 'conversion' I mean the double decision to repudiate irresponsible behavior and to take responsibility for the subsequent development of some aspect of my own experience. 'Responsibility' means accountability. Responsible people measure the motives and consequences of their actions against norms and ideals they recognize as personally binding. They also recognize that they must answer to others for their motives and for the consequences of their decisions."[5]

Gelpi proposes five dimensions of conversion: affective, intellectual, ethical, religious, and social. Affective conversion means taking responsibility for one's emotional life, with its passions, feelings, and intentions. Examining the nature of one's emotions challenges one to grow into emotional maturity by confronting and eliminating such things as racism and sexism. Moving from selfishness to the love of others demands a fundamental shift in emotional valence.

Intellectual conversion requires the person to confront all forms of false ideology and consciousness that distort understanding and interpretation. Logic and rigor are required of the intellectual convert.

Ethical or moral conversion challenges the person to move from mere gratification of immediate personal needs to living by consistent principles of justice. Moving from a personal hedonistic calculus to other-directed living by and for justice is mandatory in this type of conversion.

Religious conversion challenges the person to live for the "one true God" and not mere idols. Religions that foster self-indulgence and oppression of others are corrupt. True religion challenges an individual to transcend personal gratification and the creation of permissive gods in our own image. According to Gelpi, religious conversion is a response to historical self-revelation and self-communication by God. Christian conversion is a subtype of religious conversion.

A fifth type of conversion is sociopolitical. After years of exploring the topic of conversion, Gelpi has recently advocated sociopolitical conversion as mandatory. Genuine conversion requires that the person move and grow beyond mere personal conversion. Engaging the social institutions and systems of the wider world requires yet another level of conversion, and entails acknowledging accountability and taking responsibility, to the fullest degree possible, for the quality of life produced by these institutions. While the substance of the other forms of conversion are important, the core evaluation of social conversion is justice for all. For Christian converts, then, challenging institutions to live according to the ethics of Jesus Christ would be a consistent, logical goal.

Gelpi recognizes that there is a difference between initial and ongoing conversion. Initial conversion is the first phase of moving from irresponsible to responsible behavior in some area of experience. Ongoing conversion is the interaction between various dimensions of conversion and the continuous process of change throughout life. Integral conversion is a commitment to living out these fundamental changes in all areas of life—emotional, affective, ethical, intellectual, and social. Authentic conversion is a movement from mere personal conversion to a living out of conversion in the social world.

Gelpi's normative approach to conversion is very valuable and is congruent with the important work of Walter Conn and Jim Wallis.[6] A careful assessment of conversion in terms of religious, intellectual, emotional, ethical, and sociopolitical dimensions gives us a starting point in the development of a sophisticated normative interpretation of conversion. This approach transcends parochial denominational perspectives that have dominated past scholarship, and it offers a way of bringing the human sciences and religious studies together.

Sociocultural and Historical Consequences of Conversion

Conversions not only have personal consequences for the individual, but (especially as a cumulative phenomenon) may also include sociocultural consequences for the convert's group. Anthropologist Paul Turner examined the effects of conversion to Protestantism on the Tzeltal Indians of Oxchuc in Chiapas, Mexico.[7] More than one-half of the town's four thousand inhabitants converted. As a result, Turner noticed changes in the levels of poverty, disease, and illiteracy. Roman Catholicism in the area was relatively weak, because no priest was living there. In addition, the Indians had been exploited by Spanish colonialism, so conversion to Protestantism was an appealing option. Besides being land poor, the Indians were heavy users of alcohol. Intoxicants were available only through the landowners, who charged extremely high prices. Hence, debt was often heavy.

Converts, however, were required to abstain from all alcohol. With a decrease in the use of alcohol, people began to save some money and to improve their lot in life. In addition, the high cost of participating in the indigenous fiestas, which were rejected by converts, had previously prevented people from breaking out of the cycle of poverty. And converts who had been taught to repudiate the system of witchcraft were relieved of heavy payments for protection from evil forces.

Through the introduction of modern health-care methods and the rejection of traditional methods of healing, people began to live healthier lives, employing basic principles of hygiene, sanitation, and improved diet. Missionaries taught lay people basic medical skills that enabled local people to take an active role in their own health care, which soon led to improved health and longevity.

Most of the people in the Oxchuc region knew only the rudiments of

Spanish, so missionaries translated the Bible into the local Indian vernacular, introducing the Indians to the world of the Scriptures in their own language. Previously, most of the people had been illiterate. Now, through learning to read their own language, they also became interested in Spanish—the dominant language of the wider world of Mexico. In addition to the effects of conversion in alleviating poverty, disease, and illiteracy, Turner reports, the converts became more involved in their community. The passivity and hopelessness of the past were replaced by an active and hopeful engagement with their predicament.

Turner's assessment of the consequences of conversion in one-half of the population of a small town is positive. It is very possible, however, that his own involvement in the area as a member of the Wycliffe Bible Translators colored his evaluation.[8] Jayashree B. Gokhale assesses the consequences of conversion in a different way.[9] Her work focuses on the conversion of millions of Hindus to Buddhism, stimulated by the leadership of B. R. Ambedkar. We recall that on 14 October 1956 more than five hundred thousand Maharashtrian Untouchables, led by Dr. Ambedkar, repudiated Hinduism and embraced Buddhism. Gokhale believes that the consequences of the conversion were mixed. Originally, Ambedkar sought to transform the Untouchables' conception of themselves as a people on the lowest rung of the socio-economic hierarchy. The Mahars were essentially village servants who were considered unclean because of their work, such as removing dead animals from the streets.

Becoming Buddhist changed the people's self-understanding, especially as it related to their previous fatalistic attitude to their plight, and stimulated families to sacrifice for their children's education. Nevertheless, conversion did not enable the people to escape the caste system. Caste Hindus, as well as other groups of Untouchables, still considered the Mahars to be a part of the prevailing social system and, indeed, reviled them for their pretensions to be Buddhists, attacking them for their rejection of their social and economic "duties." The practical political, economic, and social consequences were thus not as far-reaching as envisioned by Ambedkar. While the conversion dramatically changed Mahar self-understanding and stimulated the search for education, the social consequences fostered resentment, violence, and consolidation of the Hindu caste system against the Mahars, now simply renamed as a Buddhist caste.

We must bear in mind that the effects of conversion are not always direct, radical, or total. Because of the commonly expressed ideology of conversion, people expect immediate, dramatic results. I would argue that the cumulative effects of conversion over time are as significant historically as the more obvious and immediate consequences. Even though the social results of Mahar conversion to Buddhism are rather limited, who knows what the eventual cumulative effects will be? In 1951 the Indian state of Maharashtra had a Buddhist population of 2,487. The 1961 census, five years after Ambedkar's mass conversion, reported 2,789,501 Buddhists.[10] For some scholars, such as Trevor Ling, the Ambedkar movement is a part of a larger Buddhist revival.[11] It is possible that the Buddhist revival, among other forces, is eroding the hegemony of Hinduism, not only over the minds of Indians but also over the political structure.

Cumulative effects of conversion, though sometimes difficult to track, are particularly profound when there is massive historical change, as in the case of the Christianization of the Roman Empire, the conversion of the Philippines, and the Islamization of the Middle East and Java. Many people, because of their own biases, reject the use of the term *conversion* to talk about these major waves of historical change. I would argue that the term is appropriate because the changes, while not always obvious, are significant nonetheless.

Conversion of the Roman Empire took more than four centuries. Even though the Christian movement was relatively small (some would argue less than 10 percent of the known population of the empire) at the time of Constantine's conversion in the fourth century, the shift was profound. Ramsay MacMullen's *Christianizing the Roman Empire* discusses the nature of that process.[12] For the first time, an emperor became a convert to Christianity. What was once just a small Jewish sect was now the official state religion of the

Roman Empire. The resources of the empire were henceforth available both to support Christian enterprises and to suppress pagans. The persecuted became the persecutors.

Nevertheless, MacMullen raises some provocative questions in his essay "What Difference Did Christianity Make?"[13] He focuses his attention on the immediate consequences of the "conversion of the Roman Empire" during the years 312–412 C.E. MacMullen's goal was "to discover how broad patterns of *secular* life changed as a result of the population being now believers." Based on his view that Christianity fostered a morality that extended to all areas of life, he sought to discern the effects of the reputed conversion of massive numbers of people in the empire. He chose five specific areas as potential barometers: sexual norms, slavery, gladiatorial shows, judicial penalties, and corruption. After detailed analysis of the sources, he found that there were virtually no consequences of conversion in the areas of attitudes toward slavery, gladiatorial shows, and government corruption, especially bribery. Attitudes about these aspects of life continued to reflect the prevailing standards of most of the pagan world.

The most significant effects are seen in sexual norms and judicial penalties. In the realm of sexuality, there was clearly a broadening of condemnation of any behavior that would foster "licentiousness," but, as elsewhere, there was often a double standard applied to the elite versus the ordinary people. What is rather more startling is MacMullen's description of the remarkable increase in judicial savagery. First, civil law was expanded to govern many more aspects of life, especially private morality and religious beliefs. Second, punishments were more brutal. Capital punishment and torture became much more widespread between 312 and 412.

What is one to make of MacMullen's evaluation of the consequences of conversion? My first reaction was dismay. How is it possible that so little changed, and that what did change was not always for the better in the first one hundred years after Christianity became the *official* religion of the Roman Empire?[14]

Assessment of the consequences of conversion requires the very long view and perhaps a willingness to see things that we would prefer not to see. Conversion of the Roman Empire was a very complex process that had different effects in different regions of the empire, and the nature of the consequences was determined by many factors. Moreover, conversion of institutions, societies, and cultures is far more difficult to evaluate than the effects on individuals and smaller groups.

We should also note that many historians and theologians have overestimated the effects of Christianity during its first four hundred years. Many effects were geographically specific and thus isolated from broader currents of life in the empire. Furthermore, the consequences of conversion may have been severely limited because the nature of Christianity itself was modified when it became official. Is it possible that the fundamental nature of Christianity was modified as the religion grew beyond the bounds of sectarian Judaism and entered the Hellenized world of the Roman Empire?

Such issues are profoundly disturbing, as we cannot explore them without considering what "genuine" Christianity and "genuine" conversion are. Whatever our stance, it is disconcerting, from a faith standpoint, that the conversion of the Roman Empire did not profoundly transform the ancient world.

Alistair Kee, in *Constantine versus Christ*, asserts that Constantine was not converted to Christianity but instead converted Christianity, co-opting it to the Roman Empire.[15] The case of Constantine raises major questions about how one determines criteria by which to assess the validity and value of a conversion. Kee believes that Constantine "corrupted" Christianity in terms of the way of life, ethical standards, and beliefs of Christians portrayed in the literature of the New Testament.

A similar problem arises in the assessment of the conversion projects of various Western nations during the colonial period. Did the Spanish convert the people of the Philippines to genuine Christianity or to a form of thought and value control used by the Spanish to dominate much of the world at the time? To answer that question requires a specific theological point of view. What I do know is that the missionary enterprise had significant consequences in the area that came to be known as the Philippines. Vicente L. Rafael's *Contracting Colonialism* explores the issues with sophistication and depth.[16] Whatever one's theological stance, the impact of the Spanish mission on the development of the Philippine nation has been profound. As the only Christian nation in Asia, the Philippines has a distinctive identity in the Pacific and has, for better or worse, also sustained a unique relationship with Spain and later with the United States. The impact of Roman Catholic language, theology, institutions, and ethos has shaped the destiny of the Philippine people. After 1898, the United States dominated the Philippines. With U.S. hegemony, Protestants attempted with little success to convert people away from the Roman Catholic Church. Kenton J. Clymer summarizes that frustrated enterprise in his *Protestant Missionaries in the Philippines, 1898–1916.*[17]

Religious Landscapes

Another major consequence of the conversion process is the shaping of what might be called the "geography" of religion. An example would be Daniel Doepper's study of the impact of Islam and Roman Catholicism upon the Philippines.[18] Islam arrived in the Philippines two hundred years before Christianity. To this day, Mindanao and the Sulu are firmly rooted in Muslim tradition, generating a unique religious and political impact on the Philippine nation. Spanish missionaries were most successful in converting people of the lowlands, by gathering them into larger communities and making religious education and nurture accessible to more and more people. Inhabitants of the highlands were less affected.

During the revolution of 1898, a schism from the Catholic Church occurred in the formation of the Philippine Independent Church, which was most successful in those areas where people felt that religious leaders had exploited the people by undercutting the development of strong indigenous leadership. When the United States came to dominate the Philippines (after the Spanish-American War), those areas remote from Roman Catholic control and those areas that were poorly served by the Roman Catholic Church were most open to Protestant missionaries from the United States. Even though they form a small minority, Protestants, Moslems, and various independent churches belie the common notion that the Philippines is a Roman Catholic nation. Many of these patterns continue to shape the nature of religious and political life in the Philippines today.

Unintended Sociocultural Consequences

One of the most interesting aspects of studying the sociocultural and historical consequences of conversion is to examine results that missionaries did not expect and over which, in most cases, they despaired. For instance, scholars have argued that missionary education in many parts of the world, especially in Africa, was designed to convert students, to introduce these students to modern education, and in some cases, to "civilize savages." In actual practice, the teaching of European languages, cultures, and philosophy often created an elite who eventually used their Western education and ideology to challenge the foundations of colonialism.

Nationalism

Brendan Carmody, among many others, has noted that missionary education was designed to convert and train the local populace.[19] However, European languages and ideas also taught people about democracy or Marxism, and thus created groups of politicized intellectuals who could then marshal these political ideas and their new knowledge of the colonial system to seek independence through revolution or diplomacy.

Another consequence of conversion was the creation of transtribal alliances that eventually served as crucial catalysts in the development of nationalist sentiments and goals. Norman Etherington notes in his study of missionary work in South Africa that most of the early converts were rejects from tribal groups in the area.[20] They were, in the judgment of the indigenous people and the missionaries, the dregs of that society. Paradoxically, through development of mission stations and the protection provided by the colonial missionaries, these people acquired education and a variety of skills that eventually gave them elite status in the society.

Preservation of the Vernacular

The translation of the Bible into indigenous languages has often had the paradoxical effect of preserving indigenous cultures. Lamin Sanneh has written extensively on the topic, most recently in his outstanding work, *Translating the Message.*[21] While Sanneh does not deny that missionaries often denigrate indigenous peoples and cultures, he does assert that the missionary impulse to translate the gospel into the vernacular of even the most isolated and small language group communicates in a profound way that the language and culture of those people are worthy of bearing such a revered message. Moreover, the painstaking effort to record the language and to write dictionaries and grammars has preserved languages that otherwise might have disappeared through the onslaught of modernization, secularization, and colonialization. Being able to read the Bible in their own language also enables indigenous peoples to see for themselves what God had to say in the Scriptures. In many cases this experience leads them first to doubt missionaries who are not consistent with the Bible, and may result in the development of independent churches. It is likely also to promote the general idea that authority may be criticized or challenged.

Secularization

One of the most interesting and paradoxical consequences of religious conversion is that it may stimulate the secularization process.[22] Elmer S. Miller, in a study of several tribal groups in Argentina, found that Protestant missionaries intending to convert local people to their version of Christianity unintentionally occasioned an intensive secularization of the peoples' worldview.[23] The indigenous worldview was rich with interpretations of "supernatural" causes for all sorts of events and life experiences. Indeed, the whole of life was pervaded by a sense that the world teemed with spirits, both benign and malevolent. Missionaries sought to eliminate these "superstitions" as much as possible. By introducing systematic, formal education, they dismissed the belief that knowledge could be infused or revealed through a spirit companion, dreams, or visions. They taught that disease was caused by germs, not by spirits, witches, or sorcery. Diagnosis and remedy were scientific, not magical. Economics, now shaped by the missionary store and modern methods of agriculture, was the result of hard work and proper calculation. Fecundity was controlled by scientific methods, not the power of the local shaman. Religion, through the missionary chapel, was limited to a person's relationship with God and the community of the faithful. Miller concluded that by encouraging a form of religion that diminished and restricted the role of the supernatural, the missionary unintentionally became a force for secularization.

Psychological Consequences of Conversion

Keeping in mind one's own biases and assumptions, a psychological evaluation of conversion must ask whether there has been progress, regression, or fixation. One study that explores these questions was conducted by Robert B. Simmonds.[24] He asked whether conversion to a Jesus movement was a genuine conversion or merely the replacement of an addiction to drugs with an addiction to Jesus. Given the emphasis on "dependence on Jesus" and obedience to group leaders and group norms, Simmonds felt that the subjects of his study exhibited no real change in personality, but merely a substitution of one arguably healthier addiction for another.

David F. Gordon's study of a fundamentalist group is also instructive.[25] Generally speaking, psychologists are very suspicious of notions of surrender, self-abandonment, and subordination to a group, because such notions often are presumed to indicate a weak ego and immaturity. Gordon found, however, that the people in his study had, in fact, made significant positive changes in their lives, because they had surrendered ways of functioning that were unproductive and had learned new, more adaptive patterns for living. Thus the "dying to self" advocated by the group was psychologically effective in enabling people, paradoxically, to gain ego control and strength. Psychological studies of this kind demonstrate how complicated the process of assessment may prove to be.

Joel Allison found in his research (conducted in the 1960s) on the conversion of male seminary students that their conversions were "progressive."[26] By "progressive" he meant that they were able to advance developmentally away from enmeshment with their mothers. Because of dead, absent, or weak fathers, these young men had become too dependent on their mothers. In their cases, identification with God provided them with the psychological means by which to gain a new form of independence. Needless to say, such findings raise provocative questions about gender issues. It should be noted, however, that Chana Ullman found similar patterns in her research (conducted in the 1980s) that included women.[27]

Another approach to the psychological assessment of conversion is the perspective of "faith development" presented by James W. Fowler and Romney M. Moseley.[28] This perspective contends that the conversion process for a particular person can be examined in terms of criteria appropriate to the age and developmental stage of the person involved. Conversion and developmental processes can relate to one another in many different ways. For example, movement from one developmental stage to another can be the occasion for a conversion. Likewise, conversion can foster movement to a new stage of development. Many conversions, however, do not require growth to a new stage but are merely reflections of the developmental stage of the person before the conversion. In other words, a person's developmental level serves as a filter through which the conversion is processed, setting parameters for what can be accomplished through that conversion and influencing what is attractive to the potential convert. Using developmental stages as a lens through which to observe conversion, one can make evaluations as to whether the convert has progressed, regressed, or remained the same developmentally as a result of conversion.

"Brainwashing" and New Religious Movements

Most sociologically oriented research asserts that there is little pathology to be found in converts to New Religious Movements.[29] Many psychiatrists, psychologists, and social workers, however, report that great harm has been inflicted and cite a variety of supporting symptoms.

What is the reason for this remarkable discrepancy?[30] A primary reason for the optimism of sociological perspectives might be that most of the empirical social-science research has been done only with *current members* of New Religious Movements. It could be argued that objective, accurate results among this population are impossible because the people have been "brainwashed." Another possibility is that the convert, because she or he is functioning in a tightly knit group, is able to cover or contain pathology. These considerations would seem to apply equally, however, to study of mainline religious groups.

The pessimism of the psychological perspective may derive from the fact that most research done by therapists is with those who have left various groups. Therapists work with people who, for one reason or another, have rejected a group or drifted away from it, or in some cases have been forcibly ejected from it. Is there not a difference in the findings on marriage if one is studying those currently married and those who have recently been divorced? How is one to determine the consequences of conversion to a New Religious Movement when there is such a fundamental difference among researchers in orientation and in the people studied?

Stories of Conversion

Another approach to the consequences of conversion is that conversions, especially within the Christian tradition, typically generate stories of that process which may then stimulate conversion in others. These stories as they are retold orally and composed as autobiographies become the paradigms by which people interpret their own lives.[31] One particularly influential conversion in the history of Christianity is that of Augustine. His autobiography, *The*

Confessions, has stood for fifteen centuries as a powerful shaper of religious consciousness in the history of Christianity.[32] Several converts have told me they were converted in the process of reading *The Confessions*. A professor of English literature, raised as a Jew, told me that while he was in graduate school he read Augustine, and through that experience began the process of becoming a Christian.

Autobiography, perhaps better than any other genre, engages people on a very personal level. Conversion autobiographies stimulate imitation and provide reinforcement. Conversion stories touch the lives of people in ways that theological reflection rarely does. The tradition of conversion stories is derived, at least in part, from the Book of Acts in the New Testament. The conversions of Paul, Cornelius, the Philippian jailer, and Lydia point to the personal impact of religious change. Every story of conversion calls for a conversion, confirms the validity of conversion, and shapes a person's experience of conversion.

Theological Consequences

Evaluation of conversion from within a religious tradition is a crucial element in assessing the consequences of conversion. Aharon Lichtenstein asserts that two levels of assessment are common.[33] The first, and most direct, is the ritual or behavioral dimension. Has the candidate for conversion fulfilled the ritual requirements for conversion? In the case of Judaism, for example, evidence of male circumcision, presence of a rabbinical court, agreement to obey the Torah, and immersion are relatively simple and straightforward. The second dimension is more elusive: Is there a profound quest for God? Is the person sincere? What is actually going on inside the person? Are the person's motives "pure" or is the person being compliant for extrinsic rewards? This inner process, according to Lichtenstein, is much more difficult to judge.

The convert to Judaism engages the community and God through ritual procedure and personal experience. Ritual should be seen not as mere rigid requirements for compliance to the community but rather as a primal connection to the community of Jewish faith—past, present, and future. By following the procedures of the community, the person is forging connections with a new people. The inner process is, according to Lichtenstein, like a new birth. The convert is born into Judaism as a servant of God and a citizen of the Knesset Yisrael, the community of Israel.

Missionaries often come under harsh criticism for their over-optimistic evaluation of conversion. In some cases, critics will charge that a missionary reported inflated numbers of converts to supporting agencies. In other cases the charge is that a missionary was merely naive and attributed sincerity to converts whose motives were in fact suspect. While one would be foolish to reject the notion that missionaries never distort their evaluations, more often than not missionaries are extremely careful in their assessment of the validity of a conversion. Missionary journals and reports are filled with the struggles of missionaries on this topic. How could they determine whether a conversion was genuine? What were the criteria? Did the converts really understand what had taken place? Were the fruits of the conversion consistent with the convert's oral confessions of faith?[34]

Theological Consequences Reported by Converts

Over the past twelve years I have had the opportunity to talk with about two hundred converts to many different orientations. I would like to summarize, from a phenomenological point of view, the nature of the consequences reported by converts. I seek to focus on religious experience, not creedal statements.

As these converts talk about their experiences, a common theme they express is a sense of relationship with God. They report that whereas previously they were either unaware of or alienated from God, the gulf between them and God is now bridged. God is no longer an abstract concept but a living reality. Although the details given by converts may differ, there is a sense of intimacy and connection that was not there before. Some use traditional terms like "Father" to describe their God, others choose "Mother," "friend," "companion," "guide," or other terms that denote a closeness of relationship. Love is also a common theme. Some converts report that after their conversion they felt a source of love embracing them, a love so powerful that they were empowered to love others more fully.

Another common theme among converts is that through conversion they have a sense of relief from guilt.[35] Some converts, especially those in conservative Christian churches, had previously experienced a pervasive sense of sin. For others, the sense of guilt was primarily a keen realization that their actions had harmed other people and hence somehow violated their relationship to God. Conversion was an experience that enabled them to experience a "lifting of the burden of sin" and feel a sense of liberation from the pain of their actions. Few converts believed that the consequences of their sins were magically removed (as in the case of harm caused to others), yet they did feel profoundly that God had removed their culpability. Not all converts focus on guilt, but a substantial number do.

Another common theme is that converts gain a sense of mission and a reason for living. For some, there is a clear focus: I am called by God to be a missionary or a worker for social justice or some other specific task. It is no surprise that for many converts there is a specific call to ministry. The classic case of Saul of Tarsus is a good illustration of this element of conversion. He became Paul not for the sake of his own soul merely; he was "turned around" to share the good news with the gentile world. Many people experience a profound new awareness that their life is not theirs to be spent in selfish indulgence; they have gained a purpose, whether it be sharing the good news of salvation or simply being a loving person who serves others for the sake of God.

Other converts celebrate involvement with and membership in a new community. The "family" of God is now their home. This family is often felt to be distinctive even though it is universal and inclusive of many different kinds of people. This sense of belonging both supports the person's sense of identity and gives the person a network of people to serve and of which to be a part.

For yet others, conversion is an avenue to understanding the nature of reality. One convert told me that the turning point in his conversion journey came after a long presentation in his church. During a break he went outside and walked around, thinking. Suddenly he realized that for the first time in his life he perceived a deep meaning to the whole human drama. The new theology gave him a structure for the beginning, middle, and end of human history. It was no mere abstract schema, for he now saw where he fitted into the picture. This new sense of meaning and order to his life was crucial in sustaining his commitment.

For others, conversion is a profound revolution, not only in the way they view the self but also in the way they view the whole cosmos. The person may feel that the core of his or her being has been changed. Converts often affirm the centrality, power, and foundational quality of their experience. I do not mean to assert that all converts have this experience, but many do. They feel that their lives are beginning all over again and that they now think, act, and intend differently. God is now the center, and the self is transformed. For certain converts there is a sense that a formerly fragmented self or soul is now united. Internal warfare has come to an end, and they have a sense of peace.

Other converts report less dazzling consequences. Some assert that their conversion was just the beginning of a long journey. God's grace turned them from one path to another. They saw no bright lights, had no sudden revelations; indeed, no inner sense of power propelled them into acts of sainthood. Rather, a gentle sense of God's presence gave them the courage to take the next step in the journey.

How Long Does It Last?

A common question that arises in conversion studies has to do with how long conversion lasts.[36] This question assumes, unfortunately, that conversion is a static, once-and-for-all event rather than a dynamic interaction that takes place in an interlocking set of reciprocal systems. Conversions may be valid given their immediate particular context and situation, but when that

situation changes, the person may also change and other forces take prece-
dence over the new commitment. Such a malleable view of the human person
and such a liberal view of theological commitment is not popular. But is a
conversion real only if it changes a person permanently? There are, of course,
situations in which there is change that is clearly mere compliance with situa-
tional variables. In these cases there is no inner or sincere change, but only an
impetus toward self-protection or even direct exploitation or expediency. In
fact, I would argue that people who convert and remain the same are not
really on a spiritual path of transformation. They have enshrined the conversion as a sacred moment and relive that event over and over again, but it has
little power to transform their lives. Change is persistent and important and
continuous, and most religious traditions expect and foster change by providing ideology and techniques for the ongoing development and maturation of
their members. Unfortunately there are also pernicious measures used by
some religions to keep people under control and docile.

Repetition of Conversion

In the Christian tradition, some people are very critical of those who
"come forward" at every revival meeting. The outsider may say that a person
is not genuinely converted or otherwise would not need to repeat the conversion over and over. It is my view that within conservative Christian circles the
return to the "sawdust trail" or the "mourner's bench" is a manifestation of
deep spiritual urges that are not being met in any other manner. In other
words, people come forward because there is no other method by which they
find the sense of renewal and support they need for their spiritual development. I think that there is a paucity of mechanisms by which deeper spiritual
issues can be confronted and engaged. In some conservative Christian circles
the conversion theme is not only dominant but the single ritualized mechanism available to the person seeking spiritual revitalization.

It is also possible that the centrality of conversion for conservatives is
imperative because the distinction between the world and the Christian is so

great that they must constantly remember the gulf, and provide avenues by which to make sure they are on the correct side of it. By constantly reminding the congregation of that gulf, members are kept vividly aware that they are both in the world and in the church, and that they must constantly expunge the world from their very being.

Conclusion

As we have seen, conversion is a complex, multifaceted process involving personal, cultural, social, and religious dimensions. While conversion can be triggered by particular events and, in some cases, result in very sudden experiences of change, for the most part it takes place over a period of time. People change for a multitude of reasons, and that change is sometimes permanent and sometimes temporary. Certain contemporary theologians believe that genuine conversion transpires over an entire lifetime.

The stage model serving as the organizing framework for this book is a heuristic construction designed to integrate the perspectives of anthropology, psychology, sociology, and religious studies. Even though a temporal sequence transpires in conversion processes, the order of the stages is *not* universal and invariant. The stage model serves to organize the cluster of themes, patterns, and processes operative in religious change. Let us try to summarize its parts.

The Stages

Context: The Ecology of the Conversion Process

Context, the most comprehensive of all the stages, is the dynamic force field in which conversion takes place. Context encompasses the modes of access and transmission, provides the models and methods of conversion, and also contains sources of resistance.

Human beings are intimately connected with the world in which they live. Organized religions, among other institutions, are the vehicles through which the methods and models for conversion are conveyed. While people may feel alienated from society and the church, we are all influenced by the dynamic force field of the context. Forces of resistance and attraction fill the intellectual, spiritual, and cultural climate of society. Religious organizations, as well as other cultural media (whether books, magazines, television, or movies) convey messages to people every day that changing one's life is either desirable or undesirable. Reading a book, talking with a friend, attending a lecture, or participating in a synagogue, church, mosque, or meditation center puts us all within the contextual sphere that is the ecology of conversion. Although people are aware of these influences, they usually avoid change. Resistance is pervasive.

We have a tendency to split the person and the environment. We forget that the political, religious, economic, social, and cultural worlds are shaped by people. Conversely, people are shaped by the socialization processes of the wider world. The networks of relationships and the cumulative effects of education, training, and institutional structures all influence the potential convert. It is against this background of influences that people begin their trajectory to conversion through such things as conversations with others or mystical visions that serve as catalysts for further searching, leading eventually to commitment to a religious orientation.

Crisis: Catalyst for Change

Crisis provides an opportunity for a new option. Crises force individuals and groups to confront their limitations and can stimulate a quest to resolve conflict, fill a void, adjust to new circumstances, or find avenues of transformation. Experiences in life often cause crises. Disorientation in life sometimes triggers the search for new options. The crises can have many sources, and they vary in intensity, duration, and scope. The crisis may be the major force for change, or it may be simply the catalytic incident that crystallizes the person's situation.

Quest: Active Search

Human beings actively seek solutions to their problems and strive to find meaning, purpose, and transcendence. Questing for something more or something better than one's present situation seems to be endemic in human beings.

While sometimes a convert is passive in conversion because of extreme personal vulnerability or a coercive environment, most converts are actively engaged in seeking fulfillment. Quest is, to some degree, influenced by a person's emotional, intellectual, or religious availability. The potential convert, like all other people, is motivated by the desire to experience pleasure and avoid pain, maintain a conceptual system, enhance self-esteem, establish gratifying relationships, and attain a sense of power and transcendence.

Encounter: Advocate and Potential Convert in Contact

The encounter stage brings people who are in crisis and searching for new options together with those who are seeking to provide the questors with a new orientation. Congruence of interests are not always found, however. Advocates and potential converts relate dialectically to one another. Depending on the differences between each partner's relative power and particular circumstances, the encounter can proceed to interaction.

Encounters are complex exchanges that generally do not lead to conversion. Resistance based on powerful personal or group proclivities result in either outright rejection of the new option or mere apathy toward it. Advocates are often persistent and creative. Seeking new ways to elicit the interest of potential converts, they seek to understand them better and communicate better with them. Potential converts as active agents are also skillful in seeking out what it is that they want and rejecting what they do not desire.

Interaction: The Matrix of Change

Once sufficient mutual interest is established or created, interaction involves more intense levels of learning. Relationships are often the most potent avenues of connection to the new option. In some cases, establishing a new relationship forms the foundation upon which a new way of life is built. Rituals enable the potential convert to experience religion beyond the merely intellectual level. Rhetoric provides the convert with a system of interpretation relevant not only to the religious sphere of life but also, in some cases, to

STAGE 1 CONTEXT	STAGE 2 CRISIS	STAGE 3 QUEST	STAGE 4 ENCOUNTER

Macrocontext
• Systems of access and control
 	
Microcontext
• Degree of integration and conflict
 	
Contours of context
• Culture
• Social
• Personal
• Religious
    Valence of dimension
 	
Contextual influences
• Resistance and rejection
• Enclaves
• Paths of conversion
• Congruence
• Types of conversion
    Tradition transition
    Institutional transition
    Affiliation
    Intensification
    Apostasy
• Motifs of conversion
    Intellectual
    Mystical
    Experimental
    Affectional
    Revivalism
    Coercive
 	
Normative: proscriptions and prescriptions
	Nature of crisis
	• Intensity
	• Duration
	• Scope
	• Source: internal/ external
	
	Catalysts for conversion
	• Mystical experiences
	• Near-death experience
	• Illness and healing
	• Is that all there is?
	• Desire for transcendence
	• Altered states of consciousness
	• Protean selfhood
	• Pathology
	• Apostasy
	• Externally stimulated crises
		Response style
		• Active
		• Passive
		
		Structural availability
		• Emotional
		• Intellectual
		• Religious
		
		Motivational structures
		• Experience pleasure and avoid pain
		• Conceptual system
		• Enhance self-esteem
		• Establish and maintain relationships
		• Power
		• Transcendence
			Advocate
			• Secular attributes
			• Theory of conversion
			• Inducements to conversion
			
			Advocate's strategy
			• Strategic style
			    Diffuse
			    Concentrated
			• Modes of contact
			    Public/private
			    Personal/ impersonal
			
			Benefits of conversion
			• System of meaning
			• Emotional gratification
			• Techniques for living
			• Leadership
			• Power
			
			Advocate and Convert
			• Initial response
			• Resistance
			• Diffusion of innovation
			• Differential motivation and experiences
			
			Missionary adaptations
			
			Convert adaptations

Figure 18 *The converting process summarized.*

the totality of a person's life. Playing a role that conforms to reciprocal expectations in a social setting enables the potential or new convert to experience and enact a new way of life, frequently with a sense of mission; a new sense of self often emerges through the internalization of a new role as a convert.

Commitment: Consummation and Consolidation of Transformation

Commitment is the consummation of the conversion process. The decision to commit is often expected. A psycho-spiritual experience of surrender

STAGE 5 INTERACTION	STAGE 6 COMMITMENT	STAGE 7 CONSEQUENCES
Encapsulation Sphere of Change • Physical • Social • Ideological	Decision making Rituals • Separation • Transition • Incorporation	Personal bias in assessment
Relationships • Kinship • Friendship • Leadership • Disciple/teacher	Surrender • Desire • Conflict • "Giving In": relief and liberation • Sustaining surrender	Nature of consequences • Affective • Intellectual • Ethical • Religious • Social/political
Rituals–choreography of the soul • Deconstruction • Reconstruction	Testimony: biographical reconstruction integrating personal and community story	Sociocultural and historical consequences of conversion
Rhetoric–systems of interpretation • Attribution • Modes of understanding	Motivational reformulation • Multiple • Malleable • Interactive • Cumulative	Religious landscapes
Roles–reciprocal expectations and conduct • Self and God • Self and others		Unintended sociocultural consequences • Nationalism • Preservation of the vernacular • Secularization
		Psychological consequences • Progression • Regression • Stasis
		Stories of conversion
		Theological consequences

empowers the convert with a sense of connection with God and the community. Some groups require that a person engage in specific rituals that enable him or her to separate from the past, move to a new "world," and consolidate that new identity through rituals of incorporation. In the liminal or transitional period, the convert learns more intensively how to think, act, and feel like a new person. Central to the converting process is the convert's reconstruction of his or her biographical memory and deployment of a new system of attribution in various spheres of life. The convert becomes a full member of the new community through rituals of incorporation.

Consequences: Effects of Converting Processes

Throughout the process of change, there are consequences of conversion. The convert is more or less aware of the nature of the experiences he or she is going through. From the first experience of crisis and quest or, in other cases, from the first encounter with a new option, the convert is exploring, experimenting, and in some sense "negotiating" the new possibility. After a period, certain consequences are more obvious than others. For some people the consequence is a radically transformed life. Their patterns of beliefs and actions are significantly different from what they were before. Others gain a sense of mission and purpose, and yet others acquire a very quiet sense of security and peace. The conversion process can also have a destructive effect. One may find that the new orientation is not what one expected. In some cases, the convert realizes that he or she has been manipulated for the sake of the group's own goals. In any case, conversion is precarious; it must be defended, nurtured, supported, affirmed. It needs community, confirmation, and concurrence. As converts develop spiritually, their understanding becomes more sophisticated and they review, reinterpret, and revalue their experience.

Major Themes and Issues

One of the major findings of this book is that perennial debates which involve either/or assertions are inadequate. Debates about whether conversion is sudden or gradual, partial or total, internal or external, and the like, can be resolved by acknowledging a spectrum of possibilities. Conversion is malleable. It is a complex process that transpires over time, shaped by the expectations of those advocating a certain type of conversion and the experience of the person who experiences the process. While we may often discern general patterns, it is impossible to assert that every single convert goes through precisely the same experience. Groups differ, individuals differ, and modes of interacting between the person and the group differ.

Phenomenologically there are some elements of conversion processes that are sudden and some that are gradual. The issue is complicated by the fact that many people have a fixed idea of what is relevant to the conversion process, and therefore tend systematically to eliminate data that would not fit with that image of conversion.

One of the most complex issues in conversion studies is the comparison between an individual's experience and the expectations of the cultural-social-religious milieu. Some believe that conversion is a universal experience with clear-cut boundaries and guidelines for discerning the genuine from the fraudulent. Eugene V. Gallagher's *Expectation and Experience: Explaining Religious Conversion* is a fine study of precisely this issue.[1] Building upon the work of Wayne Proudfoot, Gallagher observes that it is probably impossible to discover what the "pure" conversion experience is—assuming that such a thing exists—given the pervasive influence of expectations as to what conversion is.[2] I would argue that the separation of pure experience from expectations is a false split. Such a split assumes that some pristine aspect of human consciousness or the divine-human encounter is transcultural. Rather, human experience is by definition shaped by the milieu; there is a constant dialectic between human experience and the person's environment.

One of the most important ways in which experiences and expectations are formulated is through the religious traditions upholding ideologies, theologies, and liturgies that formulate norms for religious change.[3] I shall illustrate this through Christianity, but I believe it applies to all religions. The central effect of theology on conversion is the creation of norms for what is expected in the conversion process and the shaping of expectations and experiences of converts. There are several types of theology. In general, theology is the disciplined effort to articulate beliefs and ways of life in fresh and challenging ways so that the religious message can be accepted and understood by people of various cultures. Formal theology is the kind of theology that is normally practiced in academic settings by those trained in theology and philosophy. Academic theologians are engaged in a very sophisticated process of conceptualizing the faith of the Christian community in the intellectual tradition of philosophy and contemporary thought. Even though their writings are rarely read by people in the pews, the authors of highbrow theological books and articles are the professors who shape the clergy who then go on to serve the Church as teachers, preachers, and pastors.

A second level of theology is the kind of speech and writing used by preachers, teachers, and pastors in the local congregation. I would argue that their form of theology is the most directly influential in shaping the conversion experience of the "ordinary" convert.

A third level of theological influence is less clearly defined, but influential nevertheless: hymns, liturgy, and the Bible. These are as important as the sermons of pastors. For years people have sung songs, recited prayers, and read the Bible. The images, ideas, feelings, stories, and emotions are important in creating an ethos for the conversion process. Even if a particular leader does not emphasize certain aspects of conversion, there are many things in liturgy and the Bible that influence the consciousness of the people. I would argue that traditions convey models of conversion and exert more direct influence than the formal theology of the intellectuals.

The notion of conversion encompasses several different types of interrelated phenomena. Conversion may be seen as a process such as the "Christianization" or "Islamization" of a region. Some people speak of the "conversion of the Roman Empire" or the "conversion of the Philippines." Conversion may be viewed as movement between religious traditions (tradition transition), and as movement between religious options within a particular tradition (institutional transition). Conversion sometimes involves the joining of a group, with the convert having little or no connection to any prior religious involvements (affiliation). It may also be conceived of as an intensification process within a religious tradition (intensification). While some argue that these are totally different phenomena, I believe that there is an underlying unity to these processes that overrides the distinctions.

I believe that all these uses of the word *conversion* are appropriate, and that the various meanings are intimately intertwined. The conversion of a geographical region lays the foundation or provides the setting for a religious option to be available to people. In other words, the conversion of a geographical area encourages change through its religious, cultural, personal, and social infrastructures.

Movement from one tradition to another becomes possible either when there is an encounter between two previously unknown cultural-political systems (as in the case of European missionaries in the colonial period) or in settings in which the infrastructure for contact has already been established. Islam and Christianity, for example, are available in many parts of Africa, and the indigenous people are often expected to make a choice as to which religion to give their allegiance.

In other words, the process of change involved in conversion is built upon an infrastructure that includes support systems and suppression, access and repression, encouragement and discouragement. Intensification is the process of personal renewal and the deepening of conviction within one's religious community. Hence, it is assumed that the person is already, to some minimal degree, involved in the community of faith, but that his or her spiritual experience becomes more profound.

I think that all these notions are related and interconnected. Radical, total transformation of the individual—which includes the person's emotions, intellect, morals, religion, and social commitments—is made possible through the vast complex network of relationships, rituals, roles, and rhetoric that already exists in the person and group. In other words, for the type of conversion to take place, the infrastructure and superstructure must be in place. The institutions, teachers, leaders, and doctrines of the organization are in a sense taken for granted. The conversion they urge is an intensification of the principles and practices that are already available.

Movement between groups may or may not elicit a profound spiritual experience in the convert. However, it is clear that these changes from one group to another may be, and often are, significant in the ongoing spiritual or religious transformation that the person is experiencing.

To be a convert in a missionary situation—especially when the person has had little or no previous connection with religion—is a change that requires major readjustments in a person's life. For certain people that change is merely expedient; for others it entails a profound new understanding of and relationship to God. While some may expect the new convert to be as deeply transformed as the person who has been nurtured in a tradition since birth, this is asking a great deal. Some people in missionary settings are profoundly transformed, some are not.

Future Research

There are very few studies of women's conversion experiences to offset the assumed generic (but almost always male) research to date. Important issues need to be addressed: Do women experience conversion differently from men? If so, what are those differences? To what extent are women's experiences distorted, denigrated, or denied by any patriarchal requirements of the conversion stereotype? Such questions have scarcely even been raised in the literature to date, much less adequately addressed.

Susan Juster is among the few who have considered this issue in a sustained manner. Her splendid essay "'In a Different Voice': Male and Female Narratives of Religious Conversion in Post-Revolutionary America"[4] explores the nature of conversion experiences among Evangelicals between 1790 and 1830. Although Juster finds "an androgynous model of regeneration that ultimately echoes the Biblical affirmation that in Christ there is neither . . . male nor female,"[5] one can hardly consider this result determinative and conclusive without a variety of corroborating research.

Similarly, there is the intriguing question of why gay and lesbian people should benefit from conversion to faiths that, on the institutional level at least, discourage and even damn them. Yet there is an active and growing movement toward Christianity and Judaism among gay and lesbian people. This movement in some respects challenges the very foundational assumptions of the established religious organizations and could, in the future, prove either revolutionary as it demands response or irrelevant as it withers away or is co-opted. Perhaps something between the two may occur. In any case, it is a fallow field as far as active research is concerned.

Another topic in conversion studies that needs to be addressed is the nature of conversion in the formation and transmission of religious traditions. With the exception of studies by Norman Gottwald, Jacob Milgrom, Donald Gray, and W. Montgomery Watt, few have sought to connect the conversion process with the experience of founders. Such studies to date have focused on Judaism, Christianity, and Islam, and the nature of conversion in the early stages of a religious movement.[6] The nature of the experience of the founders of a religious tradition is important in discerning the basic orientation to change and how (or if) that experience becomes normative. It would also be important to trace the changes in the normative nature of conversion in the evolution of particular religious traditions.

There should also be a study of the systematic history of conversion in the development of religions. The elements of such a history are currently available.[7] A history of conversion—implied in much of what I have written in this book—would underscore the variety of notions, but it would also locate the underlying unities. Sorting out the normative and descriptive aspects of such a history would be complicated, but it is, I believe, crucial at this stage in conversion scholarship.

Finally, the fields of psychology, sociology, and anthropology must develop a new model so that we can appreciate more keenly the actual experience of people in the modern world. I concur with Edward E. Sampson's view that psychology needs to formulate a new theory of the person operating in a global context.[8] The old paradigms are inadequate to a full understanding of religious change in modern life.

Conversion is paradoxical. It is elusive. It is inclusive. It destroys and it saves. Conversion is sudden and it is gradual. It is created totally by the action of God, and it is created totally by the action of humans. Conversion is personal and communal, private and public. It is both passive and active. It is a retreat from the world. It is a resolution of conflict and an empowerment to go into the world and to confront, if not create, conflict. Conversion is an event and a process. It is an ending and a beginning. It is final and open-ended. Conversion leaves us devastated—and transformed.

Notes

Preface

1 For an overview of my experiences in Jerusalem, see my "Reflections on Conflict in Israel and the West Bank," *Pacific Theological Review* 21 (1987): 48–56.

2 For an astonishingly candid self-revelation by a scholar of conversion, see Bennetta Jules-Rosette's "Conversion Experience: The Apostles of John Maranke," *Journal of Religion in Africa* 7 (1976): 132–64.

3 See Sallie McFague, "Conversion: Life on the Edge of the Raft," *Interpretation* 32 (1978): 255–68; Jim Wallis, *The Call to Conversion: Recovering the Gospel for These Times* (San Francisco: Harper and Row, 1981).

4 Anton T. Boisen, *Out of the Depths: An Autobiographical Study of Mental Disorder and Religious Experience* (New York: Harper and Brothers, 1960). See also Charles V. Gerkin, *The Living Human Document* (Nashville: Abingdon Press, 1984).

Introduction

1 For descriptions and assessments of the contemporary religious scene, see Frank Whaling, ed., *The World's Religious Traditions: Current Perspectives in Religious Studies* (New York: Crossroad, 1984); Frank Whaling, ed., *Religion in Today's World: The Religious Situation of the World from 1945 to the Present Day* (Edinburgh: T. and T. Clark, 1987); Richard T. Antoun and Mary Elain Hegland, eds., *Religious Resurgence: Contemporary Cases in Islam, Christianity, and Judaism* (Syracuse, N.Y.: Syracuse University Press, 1987); and Richard L. Rubenstein, ed., *Spirit Matters: The Worldwide Impact of Religion on Contemporary Politics* (New York: Paragon House, 1987).

2 I use the terms *religion* and *religious* in what Peter L. Berger calls a substantive, not a functional, manner. Even though a good argument can be made that functional definitions of religion are somewhat useful, I prefer to define religion in relation to the human concern, both individual and collective, with the spiritual, transcendent, or supernatural realm of existence. In other words, I use *religion* to refer to Hinduism, Buddhism, Judaism, Christianity, Islam, and so forth. For a helpful discussion of this

topic, see Berger's "Some Second Thoughts on Substantive versus Functional Definitions of Religion," *Journal for the Scientific Study of Religion* 13 (1974): 125–34.

3 Emefie Ikenga-Metuh, "The Shattered Microcosm: A Critical Survey of Explanations of Conversion in Africa," *Neue Zeitschrift für Missionswissenschaft* 41 (1985): 241–54. See also H. Byron Earhart, "Toward a Theory of the Formation of the Japanese New Religions: A Case Study of Gedatsu-Kai," *History of Religions* 20 (1980): 175–97. Both studies emphasize the importance of multiple factors in the creation of theories.

Chapter 1

1 James R. Scroggs and William G. T. Douglas, "Issues in the Psychology of Religious Conversion," *Journal of Religion and Health* 6 (1967): 204–16.

2 For a fine survey of various approaches to the definition of conversion in the history of Christianity, see Marilyn J. Harran, *Luther on Conversion: The Early Years* (Ithaca, N.Y.: Cornell University Press, 1983), 15–53.

3 A. D. Nock, *Conversion* (New York: Oxford University Press, 1933), 1–16.

4 For examples of definitions that are too rigid and narrow, see Richard V. Travisano, "Alternation and Conversion as Qualitatively Different Transformations," in *Social Psychology through Symbolic Interaction*, ed. Gregory P. Stone and Harvey A. Farberman (Waltham, Mass.: Ginn-Blaisdell, 1970), 594–606. See also David A. Snow and Richard Machalek, "The Convert as a Social Type," in *Sociological Theory 1983*, ed. Randall Collins (San Francisco: Jossey-Bass, 1983), 259–89; and Snow and Machalek, "The Sociology of Conversion," *Annual Review of Sociology* 10 (1984): 167–90.

5 See Aharon Lichtenstein, "On Conversion," *Tradition* 23 (1988): 1–18, trans. Michael Berger.

6 My orientation to these issues has been influenced by Roland Robertson's *Meaning and Change: Explorations in the Cultural Sociology of Modern Societies* (New York: New York University Press, 1978). See especially his chapter "Conversion and Cultural Change," 186–222.

7 William James, *The Varieties of Religious Experience: A Study in Human Nature* (New York: Modern Library, 1902 and 1929).

8 Few people, especially secular intellectuals, wish to be consciously aware of constant subjection to the authority of a superior being, even a god. I see my own reservations about an honest appraisal of the religious domain emerge when I am with a

convert who reports a powerful experience of God and I sense that that experience, if true, might have a powerful determining influence on me. Something in me would rather continue flight from God, and live in the relatively tame and safe world of the intellectual who has the illusion of control.

9 William R. Garrett, "Troublesome Transcendence: The Supernatural in the Scientific Study of Religion," *Sociological Analysis* 35 (1974): 167–80.

10 Richard W. Bulliet, *Conversion to Islam in the Medieval Period* (Cambridge, Mass.: Harvard University Press, 1979).

11 Ramsay MacMullen, *Christianizing the Roman Empire: A.D. 100–400* (New Haven: Yale University Press, 1984).

12 Jerald C. Brauer, "Conversion: From Puritanism to Revivalism," *Journal of Religion* 58 (1978): 227–48. While Brauer's assessment of varying consequences is accurate, I am unable to accept his claim that the motivations, morphology, and methods of conversion would be identical.

13 I have not been able to trace the precise origins of this typology of conversion, which I began using in the early 1980s. V. Bailey Gillespie in *The Dynamics of Religious Conversion* (Birmingham, Ala.: Religious Education Press, 1991), 14–15, mentions the typology but does not supply references.

14 John Lofland and Norman Skonovd, "Conversion Motifs," *Journal for the Scientific Study of Religion* 20 (1981): 373–85.

15 John Lofland and Rodney Stark, "Becoming a World-Saver: A Theory of Conversion to a Deviant Perspective," *American Sociological Review* 30 (1965): 862–75.

16 For an excellent description of revival meetings, see Ted Ownby, *Subduing Satan: Religion, Recreation, and Manhood in the Rural South, 1865–1920* (Chapel Hill: University of North Carolina Press, 1990), especially 144–64. See also Norman Pettit, *The Heart Prepared: Grace and Conversion in Puritan Spiritual Life*, 2d. ed. (Middletown, Conn.: Wesleyan University Press, 1989).

17 See Lofland and Stark, "Becoming a World-Saver." Alan R. Tippett, "Conversion as a Dynamic Process in Christian Mission," *Missiology* 2 (1977): 203–21. See also Robert F. Berkhofer, Jr., "Protestants, Pagans, and Sequences among the North American Indians, 1760–1860," *Ethnohistory* 10 (1963): 201–32.

18 Clifford Geertz, *The Interpretation of Cultures* (New York: Basic Books, 1973); see especially 3–30.

Chapter 2

1 For two excellent resources on the importance of the cultural context, written from an evangelical Protestant perspective, see Hans Kasdorf, *Christian Conversion in Context* (Scottsdale, Pa.: Herald Press, 1980), and Charles H. Kraft, *Christianity in Culture* (Maryknoll, N.Y.: Orbis Books, 1979). For a Roman Catholic point of view, see Louis J. Luzbetak, *The Church and Cultures* (Maryknoll, N.Y.: Orbis Books, 1988).

2 John A. Gration, "Conversion in Cultural Context," *International Bulletin of Missionary Research* 7 (1983): 157–63.

3 Anthony F. C. Wallace, "Revitalization Movements," *American Anthropologist* 58 (1956): 264–81; "Mazeway Resynthesis: A Biocultural Theory of Religious Inspiration," *Transactions of the New York Academy of Sciences*, 2d. series, 18 (1956): 626–38; and "Mazeway Disintegration: The Individual's Perception of Socio-Cultural Disorganization," *Human Organization* 16 (1957): 23–27.

4 For a more recent assessment of revitalization movements and the psychological and neurological bases of the phenomenon, see Barbara W. Lex, "Neurological Bases of Revitalization Movements," *Zygon* 13 (1978): 276–312.

5 Eldridge Cleaver, *Soul on Fire* (Waco, Tex.: Word Books, 1978). For a fascinating contrast, see his earlier book, *Soul on Ice* (New York: McGraw-Hill, 1968).

6 It should be noted that Cleaver's role in the Black Panther Party is controversial. His views on women and homosexuality, among other things, have been sharply criticized. I am grateful to Elizabeth L. Morgan for pointing out these issues.

7 Cleaver, *Soul on Fire*, 211–12.

8 William G. McLoughlin, *Revivals, Awakenings, and Reform* (Chicago: University of Chicago Press, 1978). The process can also be viewed from a Jungian point of view; see John Weir Perry, *Roots of Renewal in Myth and Madness* (San Francisco: Jossey-Bass, 1976).

9 Geertz, *Interpretation of Cultures*, 255–310.

10 For an extremely sophisticated and comprehensive examination of the processes involved in European expansion and exploration, see Eric R. Wolf, *Europe and the People without History* (Berkeley: University of California Press, 1982). For a brilliant examination of the contemporary scene, see Theodore H. Von Laue, *The World Revolution of Westernization: The Twentieth Century in Global Perspective* (New York: Oxford University Press, 1987).

11 See Morton H. Fried, "Reflections on Christianity in China," *American Ethnologist* 14 (1987): 94–106. For a brief history of Christianity in China, see G. Thompson Brown, *Christianity in the People's Republic of China* (Atlanta: John Knox Press, 1986). For a fascinating study of the Chinese response to early missionaries, see Jacques Gernet, *China and the Christian Impact: A Conflict of Cultures,* trans. Janet Lloyd (New York: Cambridge University Press, 1985). For assessments of Christianity in Japan, see Richard H. Drummond, *A History of Christianity in Japan* (Grand Rapids, Mich.: Eerdmans, 1971), and Tetsunao Yamamori, *Church Growth in Japan* (South Pasadena, Calif.: William Carey Library, 1974).

12 Abdullahi Ahmed An-Na'im, "The Islamic Law of Apostasy and Its Modern Applicability," *Religion* 16 (1986): 197–224.

13 The debate over secularization is extremely complex. For an overview, see Larry Shiner, "Six Meanings of 'Secularization,'" *Journal for the Scientific Study of Religion* 6 (1968): 207–20.

14 See Andrew M. Greeley, *Unsecular Man: The Persistence of Religion* (New York: Schocken Books, 1971) and *Religious Change in America* (Cambridge, Mass.: Harvard University Press, 1989).

15 See Bryan Wilson, *Religion and Secular Society* (Harmondsworth, U.K.: Penguin Books, 1966), and *Contemporary Transformations of Religion* (London: Oxford University Press, 1976).

16 See David Martin, *A General Theory of Secularization* (New York: Harper and Row, 1978).

17 See Peter L. Berger and Thomas Luckmann, *The Social Construction of Reality* (Garden City, N.Y.: Doubleday, 1967); also Berger's *Sacred Canopy* (Garden City, N.Y.: Doubleday, 1969), and *Facing Up to Modernity* (New York: Basic Books, 1977).

18 Peter L. Berger, *The Heretical Imperative* (Garden City, N.Y.: Doubleday, 1979). For a more general assessment of religion and modernity, see Berger's *Sacred Canopy.*

19 Robert Jay Lifton, "Protean Man," *Partisan Review* 35 (1968): 13–27.

20 Philip Cushman, "The Self Besieged: Recruitment-Indoctrination Processes in Restrictive Groups," *Journal for the Theory of Social Behavior* 16 (1986): 1–32.

21 Stephen M. Sales's study in the early 1970s is the only one I know of that examines empirically the relationship between the larger environment and motivations for conversion. He studied economic fluctuations in Seattle, Washington, and the rates of

church attendance in various types of churches. He found that conversion rates to authoritarian churches increased when there were economic problems in Seattle. See Sales's "Economic Threat as a Determinant of Conversion Rates in Authoritarian and Nonauthoritarian Churches," *Journal of Personality and Social Psychology* 23 (1972): 420–28.

22 For a brief, general survey of Buddhism, see E. Zurcher, *Buddhism: Its Origin and Spread in Words, Maps, and Pictures* (London: Routledge and Kegan Paul, 1962).

23 For an illuminating interpretation of conversion processes and the spread of Christianity in the first century, see Wayne A. Meeks, *The First Urban Christians: The Social World of the Apostle Paul* (New Haven: Yale University Press, 1983). An excellent analysis of conversion between A.D. 100 and 400 can be found in MacMullen's *Christianizing the Roman Empire*. For an overview of the worldwide spread of Christianity, see Stephen Neill, *A History of Christian Missions* (Harmondsworth, U.K.: Penguin Books, 1964, 2d ed., 1986, revised by Owen Chadwick).

24 The classic book on the spread of Islam is T. W. Arnold's *Preaching of Islam: A History of the Propagation of the Muslim Faith* (Westminster, U.K.: Archibald Constable, 1896). For a general survey, see F. R. J. Verhoeven, *Islam: Its Origins and Spread in Words, Maps and Pictures* (New York: St. Martin's Press, 1962). For a very readable examination of Islam, see Malise Ruthven, *Islam in the World* (New York: Oxford University Press, 1984).

25 James T. Duke and Barry L. Johnson, "The Stages of Religious Transformation: A Study of 200 Nations." *Review of Religious Research* 30 (1989): 209–24, and "Religious Transformation and Social Conditions: A Macrosociological Analysis," in *Religious Politics in Global and Comparative Perspective*, ed. William H. Swatos, Jr. (New York: Greenwood Press, 1989), 75–109.

26 David B. Barrett, ed., *World Christian Encyclopedia* (Nairobi: Oxford University Press, 1982).

27 Nock, *Conversion*, 9–10.

28 Charles H. Kraft, "Cultural Concomitant of Higi Conversion: Early Period," *Missiology* 4 (1976): 431–42.

29 Robert W. Balch and David Taylor, "Seekers and Saucers: The Role of the Cultic Milieu in Joining a UFO Cult," *American Behavioral Scientist* 20 (1977): 839–60. See also Robert W. Balch, "Looking Behind the Scenes in a Religious Cult: Implications for the Study of Conversion," *Sociological Analysis* 41 (1980): 137–43.

30 Tippett, "Conversion as a Dynamic Process in Christian Mission," 203–21.

31 Kraft, "Cultural Concomitant of Higi Conversion," 431–42.

32 Thousands of books and articles could be listed here to illustrate the point; two will suffice: Vicente L. Rafael, *Contracting Colonialism: Translation and Christian Conversion in Tagalog Society under Early Spanish Rule* (Ithaca, N.Y.: Cornell University Press, 1988), and Vincent J. Donovan, *Christianity Rediscovered: An Epistle from the Masai* (Maryknoll, N.Y.: Orbis Books, 1978). For a more complete bibliography see Lewis R. Rambo, "Current Research on Religious Conversion," *Religious Studies Review* 13 (1982): 146–59.

33 For excellent surveys of the issues, see Frank Newport, "The Religious Switcher in the United States," *American Journal of Sociology* 44 (1979): 528–52, and Wade Clark Roof and William McKinney, *American Mainline Religion* (New Brunswick, N.J.: Rutgers University Press, 1987).

34 Charles Selengut, "American Jewish Converts to New Religious Movements," *The Jewish Journal of Sociology* 30 (1988): 95–110.

35 The original idea for this type of conversion emerged in my reading about the Billy Graham crusades. While I agree with some of the assessments, I do believe that, at least for some people, there are profound experiences, which I shall label "intensification." See Ronald C. Wimberley et al., "Conversion in a Billy Graham Crusade: Spontaneous Event or Ritual Performance?" *Sociological Quarterly* 16 (1975): 162–70, and Weldon T. Johnson, "The Religious Crusade: Revival or Ritual?" *American Journal of Sociology* 76 (1971): 873–90. I would also argue that many of the conversions reported by William James in his classic book, *The Varieties of Religious Experience*, were actually the stories of people who were born and reared in a Christian context, so their conversion is more of an intensification process, not the conversion of totally nonreligious people. Current explorations of conversion often advocate this type of conversion. See Walter Conn, *Christian Conversion: A Developmental Interpretation of Autonomy and Surrender* (New York: Paulist Press, 1986), and Jim Wallis, *The Call to Conversion* (San Francisco: Harper and Row, 1981). The current return of secular Jews to Orthodox Judaism may also be seen as intensification. See Janet Aviad, *Return to Judaism: Religious Renewal in Israel* (Chicago: University of Chicago Press, 1983).

36 There have been few studies of apostasy, but more resources are becoming available. See David G. Bromley, ed., *Falling from the Faith: Causes and Consequences of Religious Apostasy* (Beverly Hills: Sage Publications, 1988), and Stuart A. Wright, *Leaving*

Cults: The Dynamics of Defection (Washington, D.C.: Society for the Scientific Study of Religion, 1987).

37 Models of conversion can be approached from many perspectives. Anne Hunsaker Hawkins uses the notion of archetype in her excellent book *Archetypes of Conversion: The Autobiographies of Augustine, Bunyan, and Merton* (Lewisburg, Pa.: Bucknell University Press, 1985). In the history of conversion in the United States, no models of conversion have been explored more than that of the Puritans. One of the classics in the field is Norman Pettit, *The Heart Prepared* (New Haven: Yale University Press, 1966). More recently, Patricia Caldwell, *The Puritan Conversion Narrative* (New York: Cambridge University Press, 1983), and John Owen King, *The Iron of Melancholy* (Middletown, Conn.: Wesleyan University Press, 1983) have stimulated new discussions. From my point of view, none is more rewarding than Charles Lloyd Cohen, *God's Caress: The Psychology of Puritan Religious Experience* (New York: Oxford University Press, 1986).

38 Olive M. Stone, "Cultural Uses of Religious Visions: A Case Study," *Ethnology* 1 (1962): 330.

39 Bill J. Leonard, "Getting Saved in America: Conversion Event in a Pluralistic Culture," *Review and Expositor* 82 (1985): 111–27.

Chapter 3

1 Luther P. Gerlach and Virginia H. Hine, *People, Power, Change: Movements of Social Transformation* (Indianapolis: Bobbs-Merrill, 1970). See also their "Five Factors Crucial to the Growth and Spread of a Modern Religious Movement," *Journal for the Scientific Study of Religion* 7 (1968): 23–40.

2 For a valuable survey of the debate, see James T. Richardson, "The Active vs. Passive Convert: Paradigm Conflict in Conversion/Recruitment Research," *Journal for the Scientific Study of Religion* 24 (1985): 163–79. The debate is especially harsh in terms of recruitment to new religious movements or cults. See Richardson's "Psychology of Induction: A Review and Interpretation," in *Cults and New Religious Movements*, ed. Marc Galanter (Washington, D.C.: American Psychiatric Association, 1989), 211–33.

3 For an excellent discussion of the issue, see William B. Bankston, H. Hugh Floyd, Jr., and Craig J. Forsyth, "Toward a General Model of the Process of Radical Conversion: An Interactionist Perspective on the Transformation of Self-Identity," *Qualitative Sociology* 4 (1981): 279–97.

4 Augustine, *The Confessions of St. Augustine*, trans. John K. Ryan (Garden City, N.Y.: Doubleday, 1960). See especially pages 202 and 203, the last few pages of book 8.

5 Lofland and Stark, "Becoming a World-Saver," 862–75.

6 *Ibid.*, 864.

7 See Bankston, Floyd, and Forsyth, "Toward a General Model," 279–97, and David A. Snow and Cynthia L. Phillips, "The Lofland-Stark Conversion Model: A Critical Reassessment," *Social Problems* 27 (1980): 430–47.

8 Max Heirich, "Change of Heart: A Test of Some Widely Held Theories about Religious Conversion," *American Journal of Sociology* 83 (1977): 653–80.

9 There is a vast literature on Paul's conversion. My purpose in this chapter is simply to illustrate the importance of religious experience as a crisis that is a catalyst for conversion. Consensus does not exist on the value of Luke's account in Acts and the autobiographical comments of Paul in his own epistles. For a fine survey of these issues, see Beverly Roberts Gaventa, *From Darkness to Light* (Philadelphia: Fortress Press, 1986). For the best recent study, see Alan F. Segal, *Paul the Convert* (New Haven: Yale University Press, 1990).

10 Two surveys and assessments of the issues may be found in Kenneth Ring, *Heading toward Omega* (New York: William Morrow, 1984), and Carol Zaleski, *Otherworld Journeys: Accounts of Near-Death Experience in Medieval and Modern Times* (New York: Oxford University Press, 1987).

11 It is interesting to note the ways in which conversion and healing are parallel and/or interactive processes. For more information, see Jerome D. Frank, *Persuasion and Healing*, rev. ed. (New York: Schocken Books, 1974); James Dow, "Universal Aspects of Symbolic Healing: A Theoretical Synthesis," *American Anthropologist* 88 (1986): 56–69; and Brock K. Kilbourne and James T. Richardson, "A Social Psychological Analysis of Healing," *Journal of Integrative and Eclectic Psychotherapy* 7 (1988): 20–34.

12 James V. Downton, Jr., *Sacred Journeys: The Conversion of Young Americans to Divine Light Mission* (New York: Columbia University Press, 1979), and "An Evolutionary Theory of Spiritual Conversion and Commitment: The Case of Divine Light Mission," *Journal for the Scientific Study of Religion* 19 (1980): 381–96.

13 Chana Ullman, "Cognitive and Emotional Antecedents of Religious Conversion," *Journal of Personality and Social Psychology* 43 (1982): 183–92.

14 Joel Allison, "Religious Conversion: Regression and Progression in an Adolescent Experience," *Journal for the Scientific Study of Religion* 8 (1969): 23–38; "Adaptive Regression and Intense Religious Experience," *Journal of Nervous and Mental Disease* 145 (1968): 452–63; and "Recent Empirical Studies in Religious Conversion Experiences," *Pastoral Psychology* 17 (September 1966): 21–34.

15 See Robert F. Weiss, "Defection from Social Movements and Subsequent Recruitment to New Movements," *Sociometry* 26 (1963): 1–20, and Janet Liebman Jacobs, *Divine Disenchantment: Deconverting from New Religions* (Bloomington: Indiana University Press, 1989).

16 The best book I have encountered on the process of leaving important roles is Helen Rose Fuchs Ebaugh's *Becoming an Ex: The Process of Role Exit* (Chicago: University of Chicago Press, 1988).

Chapter 4

1 Richardson, "The Active vs. Passive Convert." See also Roger A. Straus, "Religious Conversion as a Personal and Collective Accomplishment," *Sociological Analysis* 40 (1979): 158–65. The major and perhaps most popular argument for the passive view of the convert is in Flo Conway and Jim Siegelman, *Snapping: America's Epidemic of Sudden Personality Change* (Philadelphia: J. B. Lippincott, 1978). For a fascinating assessment of the complex arguments concerning the issues surrounding the "brainwashing" model of conversion, see Thomas Robbins, "Constructing Cultist 'Mind Control,'" *Sociological Analysis* 45 (1984): 241–56. For a very strong argument in favor of the active agency of the convert in the missionary setting, see Jack Goody, "Religion, Social Change, and the Sociology of Conversion," in *Changing Social Structure in Ghana: Essays in the Comparative Sociology of a New State and an Old Tradition*, ed. Jack Goody (London: International African Institute, 1975), 91–106. For a case study of the convert's active agency, see John C. Rounds, "Curing What Ails Them: Individual Circumstances and Religious Choice Among Zulu-Speakers in Durban, South Africa," *Africa* 52 (1982): 77–89. For a sophisticated theoretical discussion of the issue, see Lorne Dawson, "Self-Affirmation, Freedom, and Rationality: Theoretically Elaborating 'Active' Conversions," *Journal for the Scientific Study of Religion* 29 (1990): 141–63.

2 For an excellent article exploring this whole issue, see Richardson, "The Active vs. Passive Convert." Richardson does a fine job surveying the problems in this debate, but I disagree with him that there must be an either/or decision about whether a

convert is active or passive. Both modalities are clearly present in the research literature.

3 Roger A. Straus, "Changing Oneself: Seekers and the Creative Transformation of Life Experience," in *Doing Social Life,* ed. John Lofland (New York: John Wiley and Sons, 1976), 252–73. See also Straus, "Religious Conversion as a Personal and Collective Accomplishment."

4 There is an extensive bibliography on Ambedkar. For excellent summaries, see A. Bopegamage, "Status Seekers in India: A Sociological Study of the Neo-Buddhist Movement." *Archives européennes de sociologie* 20 (1979): 19–39; B. G. Gokhale, "Dr. Bhimrao Ramji Ambedkar: Rebel Against Hindu Tradition," *Journal of Asian and African Studies* 11 (1976): 13–23; J. B. Gokhale, "The Sociopolitical Effects of Ideological Change: The Buddhist Conversion of Maharashtrian Untouchables." *Journal of Asian Studies* 45 (1986): 269–92; and J. B. Gokhale, "Castaways of Caste," *Natural History* 95 (October 1986): 31–39.

5 See K. G. Daniel, "The Conversion of the 'Hill Arrians' of Kerala State in India from 1848 to 1878: The Implications for Twentieth-Century Evangelism in India" (D. Min. diss., San Francisco Theological Seminary, 1989). See the original descriptions by Henry Baker, Jr.: *The Hill Arrians* (London: British Book Society, 1862), and *The Hill Arrians of Travancore and the Progress of Christianity among Them* (London: British Book Society, 1862).

6 Perhaps the best biography of Augustine is Peter Brown, *Augustine of Hippo: A Biography* (Berkeley: University of California Press, 1967).

7 Interview with Margaret Singer by Lewis Rambo, Berkeley, 18 November 1989. Also presented at conversion seminar, Graduate Theological Union, 13 February 1990. See also Richard Ofshe and Margaret T. Singer, "Attacks on Peripheral versus Central Elements of Self and the Impact of Thought-Reforming Techniques," *Cultic Studies Journal* 3 (1986): 3–24.

8 See Frank K. Flinn, "Criminalizing Conversion: The Legislative Assault on New Religions et al.," in *Crime, Values, and Religion,* eds. James M. Day and William S. Laufer (Norwood, N.J.: Ables, 1987), 153–91, and Stephen G. Post, "Psychiatry, Religious Conversion, and Medical Ethics," *Kennedy Institute of Ethics Journal* 1 (1991): 207–23.

9 See David A. Snow, Louis A. Zurcher, Jr., and Sheldon Ekland-Olson, "Social Networks and Social Movements: A Microstructural Approach to Differential Recruitment," *American Sociological Review* 45 (1980): 787–801.

10 See Ernest Eberhard, "How to Share the Gospel: A Step-by-Step Approach for You and Your Neighbors," *Ensign* 4 (June 1974): 6–12. The overall Mormon missionary strategy, in the United States at least, is to appeal to the family unit as a whole. In fact, most Mormon television and radio promotions focus on issues of improving family life. Mormon missionaries often approach people with the question, Would you like to improve your family life? For an excellent study of conversion to the Church of Jesus Christ of Latter-Day Saints, see Linda Ann Charney, "Religious Conversion: A Longitudinal Study" (Ph.D. diss., University of Utah, Salt Lake City, 1986).

11 Marc Galanter, "Psychological Induction into the Large Group: Findings from a Modern Religious Sect," *American Journal of Psychiatry* 137 (1980): 1574–79.

12 Downton, *Sacred Journeys*, 101–15.

13 Balch and Taylor, "Seekers and Saucers," 839–60.

14 David F. Gordon, "The Jesus People: An Identity Synthesis," *Urban Life and Culture* 3 (1974): 159–78.

15 Steven M. Tipton, *Getting Saved from the Sixties: Moral Meaning in Conversion and Cultural Change* (Berkeley: University of California Press, 1982).

16 See Flavil Ray Yeakley, Jr., "Persuasion in Religious Conversion," unpub. diss., University of Illinois at Urbana-Champaign, 1975, or a version designed for use by churches, *Why Churches Grow*, 3d ed. (Broken Arrow, Okla.: Christian Communications, 1979).

17 Seymour Epstein, "The Implications of Cognitive-Experiential Self-Theory for Research in Social Psychology and Personality," *Journal for the Theory of Social Behavior* 15 (October 1985): 283–310. See also Seymour Epstein and Edward J. O'Brien, "The Person-Situation Debate in Historical and Current Perspective," *Psychological Bulletin* 98 (1985): 513–37.

18 James A. Beckford, "The Restoration of 'Power' to the Sociology of Religion," *Sociological Analysis* 44 (1983): 11–33.

19 Walter Conn, *Christian Conversion*. For excellent brief introductions to Conn's thought, see his "Adult Conversions," *Pastoral Psychology* 34 (Summer 1986): 225–36, and "Pastoral Counseling for Self-Transcendence: The Integration of Psychology and Theology," *Pastoral Psychology* 36 (Fall 1987): 29–48.

20 Carol Gilligan, *In a Different Voice: Psychological Theory and Women's Development* (Cambridge, Mass.: Harvard University Press, 1982).

21 One way to examine the issue of motivation is to take into account the extensive discussion of intrinsic and extrinsic religiousness. For a fine general survey of this approach, see Michael J. Donahue, "Intrinsic and Extrinsic Religiousness: Review and Meta-Analysis," *Journal of Personality and Social Psychology* 48 (1985): 400–19.

Chapter 5

1 The most extensive statistical data on missions can be found in the astonishing work of David B. Barrett. See his *World Christian Encyclopedia: A Comparative Study of Churches and Religions in the Modern World, A.D. 1900–2000* (Nairobi: Oxford University Press, 1982). See also his "Five Statistical Eras of Global Mission," *Missiology* 12 (1984): 21–37, and "Five Statistical Eras of Global Mission: A Thesis and Discussion," *International Bulletin of Missionary Research* 8 (October 1984): 160–69. Since 1985, Barrett has provided up-to-date statistics on world missions. See "Annual Statistical Table on Global Mission: 1985," *International Bulletin of Missionary Research* 9 (January 1985): 30–31; for 1986, 22–23; for 1987, 24–25; for 1988, 16–17; for 1989, 20–21; for 1990, 26–27; for 1991, 24–25; and for 1992, 26–27. For specific information on the impact of speaking in tongues on world evangelization, see his "Twentieth-Century Pentecostal/Charismatic Renewal in the Holy Spirit, with Its Goal of World Evangelization," *International Bulletin of Missionary Research* 12 (July 1988): 119–29. Barrett has also catalogued the various plans for world evangelization. See David B. Barrett and James W. Reapsome, *Seven Hundred Plans to World-Class Cities and World Evangelization* (Birmingham, Ala.: New Hope, 1986). For other information, see Barrett's "Getting Ready for Mission in the 1990's: What Should We Be Doing to Prepare?" *Missiology* 15 (1987): 3–14; "Forecasting the Future in World Mission: Some Future Faces of Missions," *Missiology* 15 (1987): 433–50; *Cosmos, Chaos, and Gospel: A Chronology of World Evangelization from Creation to New Creation* (Birmingham, Ala.: New Hope, 1987); *Evangelize! A Historical Survey of the Concept* (Birmingham, Ala.: New Hope, 1987); *Evangelize the World: The Rise of a Global Evangelization Movement* (Birmingham, Ala.: New Hope, 1988). See also David B. Barrett and Todd M. Johnson, *Our Globe and How to Reach It: Seeing the World Evangelized by A.D. 2000 and Beyond* (Birmingham, Ala.: New Hope, 1990).

2 See the remarkable historical study by James Axtell, *The Invasion Within: The Contest of Cultures in Colonial North America* (New York: Oxford University Press, 1985). Many missionaries report such changes, but two excellent examples are John V. Taylor, *The Primal Vision: Christian Presence amid African Religion* (London: SCM Press, 1963), and Donovan, *Christianity Rediscovered.*

3 See Frank Whaling, "A Comparative Religious Study of Missionary Transplantation in Buddhism, Christianity, and Islam," *International Review of Mission* 70 (1981): 314–33.

4 After completing this book, I discovered a fascinating study of missionaries by Julian Pettifer and Richard Bradley, *Missionaries* (London: BBC Books, 1990). Another new book that should be illuminating is Kenelm Burridge's *In the Way: A Study of Christian Missionary Endeavours* (Vancouver: University of British Columbia Press, 1991).

5 See Thomas O. Beidelman, "Social Theory and the Study of Christian Missions in Africa," *Africa* 44 (1974): 235–49; "Contradictions between the Sacred and Secular Life: The Church Missionary Society in Ukaguru, Tanzania, East Africa, 1876–1914," *Comparative Studies in Society and History* 23 (1981): 73–95; and *Colonial Evangelism* (Bloomington: Indiana University Press, 1982).

6 Richard M. Eaton, "Approaches to the Study of Conversion to Islam in India," in *Approaches to Islam in Religious Studies*; ed. Richard C. Martin (Tucson: University of Arizona Press, 1985), 106–23.

7 Beidelman, "Social Theory and the Study of Christian Missions in Africa," 240.

8 Ruth Rouse, "The Missionary Motive," *International Review of Missions* 25 (1936): 250–58.

9 For a fine case study of missionary motivation, see C. Tineke Carmen, "Conversion and the Missionary Vocation: American Board of Missionaries in South Africa," *Mission Studies: Journal of the IAMS* 4 (1987): 27–38.

10 R. Pierce Beaver, "American Missionary Motivation before the Revolution," *Church History* 31 (1962): 216–26.

11 For an example of a critique of such motives, see Francis Jennings, "Goals and Functions of Puritan Missions to the Indians," *Ethnohistory* 18 (1971): 197–212. It should be noted that scholars disagree sharply on these problems; see James Axtell, *After Columbus: Essays in the Ethnohistory of Colonial North America* (New York: Oxford University Press, 1988).

12 See William R. Hutchison, "A Moral Equivalent for Imperialism: Americans and the Promotion of 'Christian Civilization,' 1880–1910," *Indian Journal of American Studies* 13 (1983): 55–67, and *Errand to the World: American Protestant Thought and Foreign Missions* (Chicago: University of Chicago Press, 1987). Hutchison's work is brilliant in demonstrating the complex and conflicting motives behind the missionary enterprise. For a specific case study, see Kenton J. Clymer, *Protestant Missionaries in the Philippines,*

1898–1916: An Inquiry into the American Colonial Mentality (Urbana: University of Illinois Press, 1986).

13 For a contemporary Roman Catholic perspective, see Brian Cronin, "Missionary Motivation," *Milltown Studies* 23 (1989): 89–107.

Chapter 6

1 Ruth Mazo Karras, "Pagan Survivals and Syncretism in the Conversion of Saxony," *Catholic Historical Review* 72 (1986): 554. See also MacMullen, *Christianizing the Roman Empire*, 86–101.

2 Karras, "Pagan Survivals," 572.

3 For an excellent discussion of syncretism, see Carsten Colpe, "Syncretism," in *Encyclopedia of Religion*, ed. Mircea Eliade (New York: Macmillan, 1987), 218–27.

4 David B. Barrett's work is the best resource cataloging and assessing the scope of Christian world missions. Barrett not only collects data but also has very strong positions on what he considers to be the proper methods for world missions. See my note 1, chap. 5, for an extensive listing of Barrett's work.

5 See David R. Heise, "Prefatory Findings in the Sociology of Missions," *Journal for the Scientific Study of Religion* 6 (1967): 49–58.

6 See Irwin Scheiner, *Christian Converts and Social Protest in Meiji Japan* (Berkeley: University of California Press, 1970), and F. G. Notehelfer, *American Samurai: Captain L. L. Janes and Japan* (Princeton: Princeton University Press, 1985).

7 Joel S. Migdal has some fascinating insights into how and why people modernize, and I think his work is relevant to conversion as well. See his "Why Change? Toward a New Theory of Change among Individuals in the Process of Modernization," *World Politics* 26 (1974): 189–206. This article informs much of my thinking on the issue of marginality.

8 Snow, Zurcher, and Ekland-Olson, "Social Networks and Social Movements," 787–801.

9 This important point was first made explicit for me in the work of E. Burke Rochford, Jr. See his "Recruitment Strategies, Ideology, and Organization in the Hare Krishna Movement," *Social Problems* 4 (1982): 399–410, and *Hare Krishna in America* (New Brunswick, N.J.: Rutgers University Press, 1985).

10 See the fascinating work of Merrill Singer in "The Use of Folklore in Religious Conversion: The Chassidic Case," *Review of Religious Research* 22 (1980): 170–85, and "Chassidic Recruitment and the Local Context," *Urban Anthropology* 7 (1978): 373–83.

11 Many of my comments are based on information derived from R. Lanier Britsch, "Mormon Missions: An Introduction to the Latter-Day Saints Missionary System," *Occasional Bulletin of Missionary Research* 3 (January 1977): 22–27. The statistics are taken from "Statistical Report 1988," *The Ensign* 18 (1988): 20.

12 Epstein, "The Implications of Cognitive-Experiential Self-Theory," 283–310.

13 Susan F. Harding, "Convicted by the Holy Spirit: The Rhetoric of Fundamental Baptist Conversion," *American Ethnology* 14 (1987): 167–81.

14 Peter G. Stromberg, "The Impression Point: Synthesis of Symbol and Self," *Ethos: Journal of the Society for Psychological Anthropology* 13 (Spring 1985): 56–74. Stromberg's work is illuminating because he combines anthropology and psychology in a very creative way. See his "Consensus and Variation in the Interpretation of Religious Symbolism: A Swedish Example," *American Ethnologist* 8 (1981): 544–59; *Symbols of Community: The Cultural System of a Swedish Church* (Tucson: University of Arizona Press, 1986); and "Ideological Language in the Transformation of Identity," *American Anthropologist* 92 (1990): 42–56.

15 See the excellent work of Ullman in "Cognitive and Emotional Antecedents of Religious Conversion." See also "Psychological Well-Being among Converts in Traditional and Nontraditional Religious Groups." *Psychiatry* 51 (1988): 312–22; and *The Transformed Self: The Psychology of Religious Conversion* (New York: Plenum Press, 1989).

16 Rodney Stark and William Sims Bainbridge, "Networks of Faith: Interpersonal Bonds and Recruitment to Cults and Sects," *American Journal of Sociology* 85 (May 1980): 1376–95.

17 Benjamin Weininger, "The Interpersonal Factor in the Religious Experience," *Psychoanalysis* 3 (Summer 1955): 27–44.

18 This crucial point was originally made by Jacob Needleman, *The New Religions* (Garden City, N.Y.: Doubleday, 1970), 16–18.

19 For a more extensive discussion of this topic, see Lewis R. Rambo, "Charisma and Conversion," *Pastoral Psychology* 31 (1982): 96–108. My work on this issue is influenced most profoundly by Charles Camic, "Charisma: Its Varieties, Preconditions, and Con-

sequences," *Sociological Inquiry* 50 (1980): 5–23, and Joachim Wach, "Master and Disciple," *Journal of Religion* 42 (1962): 1–21. Also very useful is Kathryn L. Burke and Merlin B. Brinkerhoff, "Capturing Charisma: Notes on an Elusive Concept," *Journal for the Scientific Study of Religion* 20 (1981): 274–84.

20 See Beckford, "The Restoration of 'Power' to the Sociology of Religion" and Meredith B. McGuire, "Discovering Religious Power," *Sociological Analysis* 44 (1983): 1–10.

21 Harold W. Turner, "The Hidden Power of the Whites," *Archives de sciences sociales de religions* 46 (1978): 41–55.

Chapter 7

1 As I was completing final editorial changes for this book, I found Erik Cohen's "Christianity and Buddhism in Thailand: The 'Battle of the Axes' and the 'Contest of Power,'" *Social Compass* 38 (1991): 115–40. This excellent article explores issues similar to the ones I am examining.

2 I was made vividly aware of the rejection option by Steven Kaplan in a presentation he made to my seminar on conversion: "Rejection of Conversion," unpub. paper, Hebrew University of Jerusalem, 1985.

3 See Stark and Bainbridge, "Networks of Faith," 1376–95, and Eberhard, "How to Share the Gospel," 6–12.

4 Galanter, "Psychological Induction into the Large Group," 1574–79.

5 For a sensitive description of these issues, see Nancy Tatom Ammerman, *Bible Believers: Fundamentalists in the Modern World* (New Brunswick, N.J.: Rutgers University Press, 1987).

6 See Elizabeth Isichei, "Seven Varieties of Ambiguity: Some Patterns of Igbo Response to Christian Missions," *Journal of Religion in Africa* 1970 (3): 209–27.

7 *Ibid.*, 211.

8 *Ibid.*, 212.

9 *Ibid.*, 218.

10 *Ibid.*, 227.

11 See Norman A. Etherington, "An American Errand into the South African Wilderness," *Church History* 39 (1970): 62–71.

12 Robert L. Montgomery, "The Spread of Religions and Macrosocial Relations," *Sociological Analysis* 52 (1991): 37–53.

13 See the following essays by Robin Horton: "African Conversion," *Africa* 41 (1971): 85–108; "On the Rationality of Conversion, Part I," *Africa* 45 (1975): 219–35; and "On the Rationality of Conversion, Part II," *Africa* 45 (1975): 373–99.

14 Humphrey J. Fisher, "Conversion Reconsidered: Some Historical Aspects of Religious Conversion in Black Africa," *Africa* 43 (1973): 27–40, and "The Juggernaut's Apologia: Conversion to Islam in Black Africa," *Africa* 55 (1985): 153–73.

15 Nock, *Conversion*, 7.

16 Fisher, "Conversion Reconsidered," 37.

17 Bulliet, *Conversion to Islam*, 26–32. The most authoritative book on the diffusion of innovations is Everett M. Rogers, *Diffusion of Innovations*, 3d ed., (New York: The Free Press, 1983).

18 In addition to Bulliet's discussion, see Roger S. Bagnall, "Religious Conversion and Onamastic Change in Early Byzantine Egypt," *Bulletin of the American Society of Papyrologists* 19 (1982): 105–24, and G. H. R. Horsley, "Name Changes as an Indication of Religious Conversion in Antiquity," *Numen* 34 (1987): 1–17.

19 Bulliet, *Conversion to Islam*, 32.

20 *Ibid.*, 53.

21 *Ibid.*, 57.

22 See the very interesting article by Erik Cohen, "The Missionary as Stranger: A Phenomenological Analysis of Christian Missionaries' Encounter with the Folk Religions of Thailand," *Review of Religious Research* 31 (1990): 337–50. Cohen examines the way in which missionaries are often influenced in very significant ways by their involvement with another culture. Cohen's work, along with Kaplan's, provides important clues for exploring the way in which advocates are changed.

23 Steven Kaplan, "The Africanization of Missionary Christianity: History and Typology," *Journal of Religion in Africa* 16 (1986): 166–86.

24 For a fascinating discussion of "going native," see Cohen, "The Missionary as Stranger," 337–50.

25 Taylor, *The Primal Vision*.

26 Donovan, *Christianity Rediscovered.*

27 Keshari N. Sahay, "The Impact of Christianity on the Uraon of the Chainpur Belt in Chotanagpur: An Analysis of Its Cultural Processes," *American Anthropologist* 70 (1968): 923–42. For more complete details, see Sahay's *Christianity and Culture Change in India* (New Delhi: Inter-India Publications, 1986).

Chapter 8

1 For an excellent survey of the Rite of Christian Initiation of Adults, see Thomas H. Morris, *The RCIA: Transforming the Church* (New York: Paulist Press, 1989).

2 For further discussion of Roman Catholic approaches to evangelization and conversion, see Robert Duggan, ed., *Conversion and the Catechumenate* (New York: Paulist Press, 1984), and Kenneth Boyack, ed., *Catholic Evangelization Today* (New York: Paulist Press, 1987).

3 Arthur L. Greil and David R. Rudy, "Social Cocoons: Encapsulation and Identity Transformation Organizations," *Sociological Inquiry* 54 (Summer 1984): 260–78.

4 For a splendid sociological approach to the issue of encapsulation, see Berger's *Social Construction of Reality* and *Sacred Canopy.* For a social psychological perspective, see Roger A. Straus, "Religious Conversion as a Personal and Collective Accomplishment," *Sociological Analysis* 40 (1979): 158–165, and "The Social Psychology of Religious Experience: A Naturalistic Approach," *Sociological Analysis* 41 (1981): 57–67.

5 See Ammerman, *Bible Believers,* 72–102 and 147–166.

6 Lofland and Skonovd, "Conversion Motifs," 862–75.

7 This material is based on the work of Greil and Rudy, "Social Cocoons," 260–78.

8 My formulation of the interaction of relationships, rituals, rhetoric, and roles is an attempt to synthesize the very important work of Robert C. Ziller and of Theodore Sarbin and Nathan Adler. See Robert C. Ziller, "A Helical Theory of Personal Change," *Journal for the Theory of Social Behavior* 1 (1971): 33–73, and Theodore R. Sarbin and Nathan Adler, "Self-Reconstitution Processes: A Preliminary Report," *Psychoanalytic Review* 57 (1970): 599–616.

9 Virtually every social scientific study of conversion stresses the importance of relationships. One of the first to note the role of relationships was Weininger, "The Interpersonal Factor in the Religious Experience," 27–44. The most important article for the

empirical study of conversion is Lofland and Stark, "Becoming a World-Saver"; its emphasis on the "affective bonds" formed in conversion has stimulated extensive research. Also see a revised perspective on the topic in John Lofland, " 'Becoming a World-Saver' Revisited," *American Behavioral Scientist* 20 (1977): 805–18. Extensive empirical research includes Stark and Bainbridge, "Networks of Faith," and David A. Snow, Louis A. Zurcher, Jr., and Sheldon Ekland-Olson, "Further Thoughts on Social Networks and Movement Recruitment," *Sociology* 17 (1983): 112–20. More recently, Marc Galanter too has emphasized relationships, in *Cults: Faith, Healing, and Coercion* (New York: Oxford University Press, 1989). For a recent theoretical development relevant to this topic, see Lee A. Kirkpatrick and Phillip R. Shaver, "Attachment Theory and Religious Childhood Attachments, Religious Beliefs, and Conversion," *Journal for the Scientific Study of Religion* 29 (1990): 315–34, and Lee A. Kirkpatrick, "An Attachment Theory Approach to the Psychology of Religion," *International Journal for the Psychology of Religion* 2 (1992): 3–28.

10 See Weininger, "The Interpersonal Factor in the Religious Experience," 27–44.

11 Charles W. Colson, *Born Again* (New York: Bantam Books, 1976), 97–137.

12 See C. S. Lewis, *Surprised by Joy* (New York: Harcourt, Brace and World, 1955).

13 Sheldon Vanauken, *A Severe Mercy* (San Francisco: Harper and Row, 1977).

14 Ullman, *The Transformed Self*, 29–106.

15 Jacobs, *Divine Disenchantment*, 73–88.

16 W. Arens, "Islam and Christianity in Sub-Saharan Africa: Ethnographic Reality or Ideology," *Cahiers d'études africaines* 15 (1975): 443–56.

17 See Lewis R. Rambo, "Congregational Care and Discipline in the San Francisco Church of Christ: A Case Study," paper presented at the Christian Theological Seminary, Indianapolis, 3 March 1990.

18 Jarle Simensen, "Religious Change as Transaction: The Norwegian Mission to Zululand, South Africa, 1850–1906," *Journal of Religion in Africa* 16 (1986): 82–100.

19 I explore this issue more thoroughly in "Charisma and Conversion," 96–108.

20 See Victor W. Turner, *The Ritual Process: Structure and Anti-Structure* (Chicago: Aldine, 1969). See also the classic study of ritual by Arnold Van Gennep, *The Rites of Passage*, trans. Monika B. Vizedom and Gabrielle L. Caffee (Chicago: University of Chicago Press, 1960 [1908]).

21 Theodore W. Jennings, "On Ritual Knowledge," *Journal of Religion* 62 (1982): 113.

22 *Ibid.*, 118.

23 Downton, *Sacred Journeys*, 145–49, and "An Evolutionary Theory of Spiritual Conversion and Commitment," 381–86.

24 See H. Garfunkel, "Conditions of Successful Degradation Ceremonies," *American Journal of Sociology* 6 (1956): 420–24.

25 Elliot Aronson and Judson Mills, "The Effect of Severity of Initiation on Liking for a Group," *Journal of Abnormal and Social Psychology* 59 (1959): 177–81.

26 Virginia H. Hine, "Bridge Burners: Commitment and Participation in a Religious Movement," *Sociological Analysis* 31 (1970): 61–66.

27 David L. Preston, "Becoming a Zen Practitioner," *Sociological Analysis* 42 (1981): 47–55, and "Meditative Ritual Practice and Spiritual Conversion-Commitment: Theoretical Implications Based on the Case of Zen," *Sociological Analysis* 43 (1982): 257–70.

28 Stephen R. Wilson, "Becoming a Yogi: Resocialization and Deconditioning as Conversion Processes," *Sociological Analysis* 45 (1984): 301–14, and "In Pursuit of Energy: Spiritual Growth in a Yoga Ashram," *Journal of Humanistic Psychology* 22 (1982): 43–55.

29 Ofshe and Singer, "Attacks on Peripheral versus Central Elements of Self," 3–24, and Cushman, "The Self Besieged," 1–32.

30 Even though many converts speak of prayer, no one is more eloquent than Emilie Griffin in *Turning: Reflections on the Experience of Conversion* (Garden City, N.Y.: Doubleday, 1980). For a more extensive discussion of the topic, see her *Clinging: The Experience of Prayer* (San Francisco: Harper and Row, 1984).

31 See James A. Beckford, "Accounting for Conversion," *British Journal of Sociology* 29 (1978): 249–62; Brian Taylor, "Conversion and Cognition: An Area for Empirical Study in the Microsociology of Religious Knowledge," *Social Compass* 23 (1976): 5–22, and "Recollection and Membership: Convert's Talk and the Ratiocination of Commonality," *Sociology* 12 (1978): 316–24; and Snow and Machalek, "The Sociology of Conversion," 167–90. Clifford L. Staples and Armand L. Mauss conducted research to test Snow and Machalek's theory concerning rhetorical indicators of conversion. Staples and Mauss found that biographical reconstruction was the key change for converts. See "Conversion or Commitment? A Reassessment of the Snow and Machalek Approach to the Study of Conversion," *Journal for the Scientific Study of Religion* 26 (1987): 133–47.

32 Ralph Metzner, *Opening to Inner Light: The Transformation of Human Nature and Consciousness* (Los Angeles: Jeremy P. Tarcher, 1986), and "Ten Classical Metaphors of Self-Transformation," *Journal of Transpersonal Psychology* 12 (1980): 47–62.

33 For an excellent discussion of role theory and conversion, see David G. Bromley and Anson Shupe, "Affiliation and Disaffiliation: A Role-Theory Interpretation of Joining and Leaving New Religious Movements," *Thought* 61 (1986): 197–211. See Hans L. Zetterberg, "Religious Conversion and Social Roles," *Sociology and Social Research* 36 (1952): 159–66, for one of the first mentions of role-playing in the conversion process.

34 Theodore R. Sarbin, "Role: Psychological Aspects," in *Encyclopedia of the Social Sciences*, ed. David L. Sills (New York: Macmillan and Free Press, 1968), 546–52.

35 Bromley and Shupe, "Affiliation and Disaffiliation," 197–211.

36 Balch, "Looking Behind the Scenes in a Religious Cult," 137–43.

37 For a fascinating discussion of this topic, see Wach, "Master and Disciple," 1–21, and Lee Yearley, "Teachers and Saviors," *Journal of Religion* 65 (1985): 225–43.

Chapter 9

1 For excellent discussions of this issue, see Eileen Barker, "The Conversion of Conversion: A Sociological Anti-Reductionist Perspective," in *Reductionism in Academic Disciplines*, ed. Arthur Peacocke (London: Society for Research in Higher Education, 1985), 58–75; C. David Gartrell and Zane K. Shannon, "Contacts, Cognitions, and Conversion: A Rational Choice Approach," *Review of Religious Research* 27 (1985): 32–48; and William C. Tremmel, "The Converting Choice," *Journal for the Scientific Study of Religion* 10 (1971): 17–25.

2 For an interesting study of the effectiveness of conscious and overt decisions, see Christine Liu, "Becoming a Christian Consciously versus Nonconsciously," *Journal of Psychology and Theology* 19 (1991): 364–75.

3 Holy Bible, New Revised Standard Version (Grand Rapids, Mich.: Zondervan, 1988), 227.

4 No one portrays the struggle better than Paul W. Pruyser in *Between Belief and Unbelief* (New York: Harper and Row, 1974).

5 See the excellent discussion of decision making and choice in Barker, "The Conver-

sion of Conversion." Also see Gartrell and Shannon, "Contacts, Cognitions, and Conversion."

6 Gartrell and Shannon, "Contacts, Cognitions, and Conversion," 32–48.

7 Marc Galanter, Richard Rabkin, Judith Rabkin, and Alexander Deutsch, "The 'Moonies': A Psychological Study of Conversion and Membership in a Contemporary Religious Sect," *American Journal of Psychiatry* 136 (February 1979): 165–70.

8 See the excellent article by Lucy Bregman, "Baptism as Death and Birth: A Psychological Interpretation of Its Imagery," *Journal of Ritual Studies* 1 (Summer 1987): 27–42.

9 The story of Ambedkar's conversion movement may be found in many places. See my note 4, chap. 4, and Eleanor Zelliot, "Background on the Mahar Buddhist Conversion," in *Studies on Asia, 1966,* ed. Robert K. Sakai (Lincoln, Neb.: University of Nebraska Press, 1966), 49–63; "Buddhism and Politics in Maharashtra," in *South Asian Politics and Religion,* ed. Donald Eugene Smith (Princeton: Princeton University Press, 1966), 191–212; and "The Revival of Buddhism in India," *Asia* 10 (1968): 33–45.

10 See Trevor Ling, *Buddhist Revival in India: Aspects of the Sociology of Buddhism* (New York: St. Martin's Press, 1980), 67–92.

11 The long-term effects are discussed extensively in some of the references listed in my note 9. I discuss these issues in the next chapter.

12 Rosabeth Moss Kanter, "Commitment and Social Organization: A Study of Commitment Mechanisms in Utopian Communities," *American Sociological Review* 33 (1968): 499–517.

13 Hine, "Bridge Burners," 61–66.

14 See Aharon Lichtenstein, "On Conversion," *Tradition* 23 (1988): 1–18, trans. Michael Berger.

15 Henry Ansgar Kelly, *The Devil at Baptism: Ritual, Theology, and Drama* (Ithaca, N.Y.: Cornell University Press, 1985). See also Thomas M. Finn's "Ritual Process and the Survival of Early Christianity: A Study of Apostolic Tradition of Hippolytus," *Journal of Ritual Studies* 3 (1989): 69–85, and "It Happened One Saturday Night: Ritual and Conversion in Augustine's North Africa," *Journal of the American Academy of Religion* 58 (1990): 589–616.

16 Tippett, "Conversion as a Dynamic Process," 203–21.

17 See Nancy Tatum Ammerman, *Bible Believers,* for a very well done study of funda-

mentalist Christians, and Bruce B. Lawrence, *Defenders of God* (San Francisco: Harper and Row, 1989) for an examination of Christian, Jewish, and Islamic fundamentalism.

18 Alan Morinis, "The Ritual Experience: Pain and the Transformation of Consciousness in Ordeals of Initiation," *Ethos* 13 (1985): 150–74.

19 David Kobrin, "The Expansion of the Visible Church in New England, 1629–1650," *Church History* 36 (1967): 189–209.

20 Brauer, "Conversion: From Puritanism to Revivalism," 227–48.

21 For very interesting perspectives on this issue see Cushman, "The Self Besieged," and Ofshe and Singer, "Attacks on Peripheral versus Central Elements of Self."

22 For a study of a similar process of psychological pain induction, see George D. Bond's important article about meditation on death in Buddhism, "Theravada Buddhism's Meditations on Death and the Symbolism of Initiatory Death," *History of Religions* 19 (1980): 237–58.

23 Griffin, *Turning*, 31–50.

24 The theme of surrender is most clearly articulated by Harry M. Tiebout; see *Conversion as a Psychological Phenomenon* (New York: National Council on Alcoholism, 1944); "Therapeutic Mechanisms of Alcoholics Anonymous," *American Journal of Psychiatry* 100 (1944): 468–73; "Psychological Factors Operating in Alcoholics Anonymous," in *Current Therapies of Personality Disorders*, ed. Bernard Glueck (New York: Grune and Stratton, 1946), 154–65; "The Act of Surrender in the Therapeutic Process, with Special Reference to Alcoholism," *Quarterly Journal of Studies on Alcohol* 10 (1949): 48–58; *Surrender versus Compliance in Therapy* (Center City, Minn.: Hazelden, 1953); "Alcoholics Anonymous—An Experiment of Nature," *Quarterly Journal of Studies on Alcohol* 22 (1961): 52–68; and "What Does 'Surrender' Mean?" *Grapevine* (April 1963): 19–23.

25 Tiebout, "The Act of Surrender in the Therapeutic Process," 48–58.

26 Marc Galanter, "The 'Relief Effect': A Sociobiological Model for Neurotic Distress and Large-Group Therapy," *American Journal of Psychiatry* 135 (May 1978): 588–91.

27 Another way of explaining the process of biographical reconstruction is attribution theory. See Bernard Spilka, Phillip Shaver, and Lee A. Kirkpatrick, "A General Attribution Theory for the Psychology of Religion," *Journal for the Scientific Study of Religion* 24 (1985): 1–20, and Wayne Proudfoot and Phillip Shaver, "Attribution Theory and the Psychology of Religion," *Journal for the Scientific Study of Religion* 14 (1975): 317–30.

28 A number of people have been crucial in my own thinking on this topic. Brian Taylor was one of the first to point out the importance of the actual process of "telling the story" of one's conversion. See his "Conversion and Cognition: An Area for Empirical Study" and "Recollection and Membership." James A. Beckford's work has been influential in my approach; see "Accounting for Conversion." See also Meredith B. McGuire, "Testimony as a Commitment Mechanism in Catholic Pentecostal Prayer Groups," *Journal for the Scientific Study of Religion* 16 (1977): 165–68; J. Stephen Kroll-Smith, "The Testimony as Performance: The Relationship of an Expressive Event to the Belief System of a Holiness Sect," *Journal for the Scientific Study of Religion* 19 (1980): 16–25; Shimazono Susumu, "Conversion Stories and Their Popularization in Japan's New Religions," *Japanese Journal of Religious Studies* 13 (1986): 157–75; Elaine J. Lawless, "'The Night I Got the Holy Ghost': Holy Ghost Narratives and the Pentecostal Conversion Process," *Western Folklore* 47 (1988): 1–19; and Elaine J. Lawless, *God's Peculiar People* (Lexington: University Press of Kentucky, 1988).

29 One of the first to point out the nature of conversion stories was Olive M. Stone, in "Cultural Uses of Religious Visions," 329–48.

30 See also Snow and Machalek, "The Sociology of Conversion," 167–90, and Mordechai Rotenberg, "The 'Midrash' and Biographic Rehabilitation," *Journal for the Scientific Study of Religion* 25 (1986): 41–55.

31 Beckford, "Accounting for Conversion," 249–62.

32 Ziller, "A Helical Theory of Personal Change," 33–73.

33 For comparative studies of motives for conversion, see G. Jan van Butselaar, "Christian Conversion in Rwanda: The Motivations," *International Bulletin of Missionary Research* 5 (1981): 111–13, and Jarle Simensen, "Religious Change as Transaction," 82–100.

Chapter 10

1 See Ken Wilber, "The Pre/Trans Fallacy," *ReVISION* 3 (1980): 51–72. Wilber focuses on the difficulty in discerning when a religious experience is progressive or regressive. To some observers the behavior manifested and the experiences reported may be very similar. Wilber approaches these issues from a transpersonal psychology perspective. For Christian approaches, see James E. Loder, *The Transforming Moment* (Colorado Springs: Helmers and Howard, 1989), and Conn, *Christian Conversion*.

2 I phrase the nature of Saul/Paul's conversion in this manner quite deliberately. To argue, as some do, that Saul was converting to Christianity is an imposition of our point of view on the relationship of Judaism to what later became Christianity. Saul's conversion—assuming that the New Testament's description is accurate—was not from Judaism to Christianity, but the change of a Jew from one movement within Judaism, in Saul's case the Pharisees, to a group of Jews who were believers in Jesus as the Messiah. For an extensive discussion of these issues, see Segal, *Paul the Convert*.

3 Even though the dramatic changes in Paul's life are affirmed by all, C. H. Dodd argues that while Paul's allegiance shifted from attacking the Jesus sect to advocating it, Paul's personality was not significantly changed in the instant of his conversion. He argues that Paul's epistles demonstrate a developmental process over a long period. See C. H. Dodd, *New Testament Studies* (Manchester: Manchester University Press, 1953): 67–128, originally published as "The Mind of Paul: A Psychological Approach," *John Rylands Library Bulletin* 17 (1933): 91–105, and "The Mind of Paul: Change and Development," *John Rylands Library Bulletin* 18 (1934): 69–110.

4 Donald J. Gelpi has written extensively on the topic of conversion. See the following essays specifically exploring conversion: "Conversion: The Challenge of Contemporary Charismatic Piety," *Theological Studies* 43 (December 1982): 606–28; "The Converting Jesuit," *Studies in the Spirituality of Jesuits* 18 (January 1986): 1–38; "The Converting Catechumen," *Lumen vitae* 42 (1987): 401–15; "Religious Conversion: A New Way of Being," in *The Human Experience of Conversion: Persons and Structures in Transformation*, ed. Francis A. Eigo (Villanova, Pa.: Villanova University Press, 1987), 175–202; and "Conversion: Beyond the Impasses of Individualism," in *Beyond Individualism*, ed. Donald J. Gelpi (Notre Dame, Ind.: University of Notre Dame Press, 1989), 1–30.

5 Gelpi, "The Converting Jesuit," 4–5.

6 See Conn, *Christian Conversion*, and Wallis, *The Call to Conversion*. These books, along with Gelpi's work, are important challenges to the Christian community. Conn's book is a very sophisticated exploration of conversion processes from the perspectives of ethics and developmental psychology. Conn's work explores the same categories as Gelpi (affective, intellectual, ethical, religious, and social), but from the point of view of the psychological processes and capacities of the developing human being. Wallis, on the other hand, focuses primarily upon the sociopolitical dimensions of conversion. His book is provocative and profound. What is interesting here is that there is a confluence of concerns from the perspectives of Roman Catholic theology and Protestant evangelicalism.

7 Paul R. Turner, "Religious Conversion and Community Development," *Journal for the Scientific Study of Religion* 18 (1979): 252–60, and "Religious Conversion and Folk Catholicism," *Missiology* 12 (1984): 111–21.

8 See Paul R. Turner, "Evaluating Religions," *Missiology* 19 (1991): 131–42.

9 J. B. Gokhale, "The Sociopolitical Effects of Ideological Change." For a fine overview of the Ambedkar movement, see her "Castaways of Caste."

10 Gokhale, "Sociopolitical Effects of Ideological Change," 270.

11 Ling, *Buddhist Revival in India*. See also Heinrich Dumoulin, ed., *Buddhism in the Modern World* (New York: Collier Books, 1976), 67–92.

12 MacMullen, *Christianizing the Roman Empire*. See also his "Two Types of Conversion to Early Christianity," *Vigiliae Christianae* 37 (1983): 174–92; "Conversion: A Historian's View," *The Second Century* 5 (1985/1986): 67–96; *Paganism and the Roman Empire* (New Haven: Yale University Press, 1981); and *Constantine* (London: Croom Helm, 1967).

13 Ramsay MacMullen, "What Difference Did Christianity Make?" *Historia* 35 (1986): 322–43.

14 Another reaction, after some reflection, emerged. My "deeper" reaction reflected my fundamentalist past, with all its biases. "Well, of course," I said to myself, "there were no changes because the Roman Catholic Church corrupted Christianity and thus there were few positive consequences because it was a distorted, apostate religion."

15 Alistair Kee, *Constantine versus Christ* (London: SCM Press, 1982).

16 Vicente L. Rafael, "Confession, Conversion, and Reciprocity in Early Tagalog Colonial Society," *Comparative Studies in Society and History* 29 (1987): 320–39, and *Contracting Colonialism*.

17 Kenton J. Clymer, *Protestant Missionaries in the Philippines*.

18 Daniel Doeppers, "The Evolution of the Geography of Religious Adherence in the Philippines before 1898," *Journal of Historical Geography* 2 (1976): 95–110, and "The Philippine Revolution and the Geography of Schism," *Geographical Review* 66 (1976): 158–77.

19 Brendan Carmody, "Conversion and School at Chikuni, 1905–39," *Africa* 58 (1988): 193–209; "Conversion to Roman Catholicism in Zambia: Shifting Pedagogies," *African Christian Studies* 4 (1988): 5–24; and "Mission Primary Schools and Conversion: Help or Hindrance to Church Growth?" *Missiology* 17 (1989): 177–92. For a complete discussion

of these issues, see Carmody's "Nature and Consequences of Conversion in Jesuit Education at Chikuni: 1905–1978," unpub. diss., Graduate Theological Union, Berkeley, 1986.

20 Norman Etherington, "Social Theory and the Study of Christian Missions in Africa: A South African Case Study," *Africa* 47 (1977): 31–40; "Mission Station Melting Pot as a Factor in the Rise of South African Black Nationalism," *International Journal of African Historical Studies* 9 (1976): 592–605; and "An American Errand into the South African Wilderness," *Church History* 39 (1970): 62–71.

21 Lamin Sanneh, *Translating the Message: The Missionary Impact on Culture* (Maryknoll, N.Y.: Orbis Books, 1989). See also his *West African Christianity: The Religious Impact* (Maryknoll, N.Y.: Orbis Books, 1983); "The Horizontal and the Vertical in Mission: An African Perspective," *International Bulletin of Missionary Research* 7 (1983): 165–71; and for the most succinct statement of the issue, "Christian Missions and the Western Guilt Complex," *Christian Century* 104 (8 April 1987): 330–34.

22 Secularization is, of course, an extremely complex topic in and of itself. For example, see Shiner, "Six Meanings of 'Secularization,'" and Martin, *A General Theory of Secularization*, 207–220.

23 Elmer S. Miller, "The Christian Missionary: Agent of Secularization," *Anthropological Quarterly* 43 (1970): 14–22.

24 Robert B. Simmonds, "Conversion or Addiction: Consequences of Joining a Jesus Movement Group," *American Behavioral Scientist* 20 (July/August 1977): 909–24.

25 David F. Gordon, "Dying to Self: Self-Control through Self-Abandonment," *Sociological Analysis* 45 (1984): 41–56.

26 See Joel Allison, "Adaptive Regression and Intense Religious Experience," *Journal of Nervous and Mental Disease* 145 (1968): 452–63, and "Religious Conversion: Regression and Progression in Adolescent Experience," *Journal for the Scientific Study of Religion* 8 (1969): 23–38.

27 See Chana Ullman, *The Transformed Self* (New York: Plenum Press, 1989), 29–74.

28 James W. Fowler, *Stages of Faith: The Psychology of Human Development and the Quest for Meaning* (San Francisco: Harper and Row, 1981), and *Becoming Adult, Becoming Christian* (San Francisco: Harper and Row, 1984). Also see Romney M. Moseley, *Becoming a Self Before God: Critical Transformations* (Nashville: Abingdon Press, 1991).

29 See the work of Arnold S. Weiss and Richard H. Mendoza, "Effects of Acculturation into the Hare Krishna Movement on Mental Health and Personality," *Journal for the Scientific Study of Religion* 29 (1990): 173–84.

30 For an excellent discussion of this issue, see James T. Richardson, "The Psychology of Induction," 211–38.

31 This point is eloquently made on a personal level by Emilie Griffin in *Turning.* An excellent scholarly approach to this issue is presented by Anne Hunsaker Hawkins in *Archetypes of Conversion.*

32 For a recent study of Augustine's *Confessions,* see Donald Capps and James E. Dittes, eds., *The Hunger of the Heart: Reflections on the Confessions of Augustine* (West Lafayette, Ind.: Society for the Scientific Study of Religion, 1990).

33 Lichtenstein, "On Conversion," 1–18.

34 James Axtell astutely explores this issue in "Were Indian Conversions *Bona Fide?*" in his *After Columbus: Essays in the Ethnohistory of Colonial North America* (New York: Oxford University Press, 1988), 100–21. Directly challenging scholars who have recently denigrated the missionary enterprise of conversion among Native Americans, Axtell persuasively argues that, given their theological perspective, the missionaries applied rigorous standards to the new converts. In fact, Axtell asserts that the standards were even more stringent than those in the Puritan churches among the English settlers.

35 For an excellent discussion of guilt, see Edward V. Stein, *Guilt: Theory and Therapy* (Philadelphia: Westminster Press, 1968).

36 For a discussion of this topic, see Robert O. Ferm with Caroline M. Whiting, *Billy Graham: Do the Conversions Last?* (Minneapolis: World Wide Publications, 1988).

Conclusion

1 Eugene V. Gallagher, *Expectation and Experience: Explaining Religious Conversion* (Atlanta: Scholars Press, 1990).

2 Wayne Proudfoot, *Religious Experience* (Berkeley: University of California Press, 1985).

3 I want to note some very important recent trends in an emerging theology of conversion. It is important to highlight the attention being given to the ongoing quality of the conversion process for people who were "born Christians"—that is, those who were

reared in a Christian church. Jim Wallis, *The Call to Conversion* (San Francisco: Harper and Row, 1981) depicts an evangelical Christian seeking to reach beyond the individual's initial conversion to faith in Jesus Christ as Lord and Savior. Wallis introduces the more radical notion of conversion being a total transformation of a person's way of life, even to the extent of radical challenging of political, economic, and religious traditions—in this case, the conservative stance of the United States. Needless to say, Wallis's book has sparked extensive discussion among evangelical leaders.

Bernard Lonergan, a Roman Catholic theologian, has stimulated a number of extremely provocative works on conversion. (For a survey of Lonergan's work and a complete bibliography, see Vernon Gregson, ed., *The Desires of the Human Heart: An Introduction to the Theology of Bernard Lonergan* [New York: Paulist Press, 1988].) Responses to Lonergan include works by Walter Conn, Robert M. Doran, and Donald Gelpi. (See Walter Conn, *Christian Conversion: A Developmental Interpretation of Autonomy and Surrender* [New York: Paulist Press, 1986]; Robert M. Doran, *Psychic Conversion and Theological Foundations: Toward a Reorientation of the Human Sciences* [Chico, Calif.: Scholars Press, 1981]; and Donald L. Gelpi, *Inculturating North American Theology: An Experiment in Foundational Method* [Atlanta: Scholars Press, 1988].) Building upon Lonergan's notion that conversion encompasses religious, moral, and intellectual factors, they have added affective (emotional and psychological) and social (political and so forth) factors to the list of changes and effects of conversion. These theologians are primarily concerned about the ongoing, deepening process of total transformation experienced by the person who is already a Christian. They manifest little, if any, interest in conversion in the missionary setting or in large-scale conversion to Catholicism. They are concerned about the radical changes mediated by obedience to the call of Jesus Christ and the Reign of God. Conn approaches the issue from the point of view of developmental psychology, and Gelpi examines them from the American philosophical/theological tradition.

4 Susan Juster, " 'In a Different Voice': Male and Female Narratives of Religious Conversion in Post-Revolutionary America," *American Quarterly* 41 (1989): 34–62. Since completing this book I have found two new books on the topic of women's conversions: Lynn Davidman, *Tradition in a Rootless World: Women Turn to Orthodox Judaism* (Berkeley: University of California Press, 1991), and Virginia Lieson Brereton, *From Sin to Salvation: Stories of Women's Conversions, 1800 to the Present* (Bloomington: University of Indiana Press, 1991). Brereton mentions another article: Debra Renee Kaufman, "Patriarchal Women: A Case Study of Newly Orthodox Jewish Women," *Symbolic Interaction* 12 (1989): 299–315.

5 Juster, "'In a Different Voice,'" 36.

6 See Norman K. Gottwald, *Tribes of Yahweh* (Maryknoll, N.Y.: Orbis, 1979), and "Religious Conversion," *Perspectives in Religious Studies* 15 (1988): 49–66; Jacob Milgrom, "Religious Conversion and the Revolt Model for the Formation of Israel," *Journal of Biblical Literature* 101 (1982): 169–76; Donald P. Gray, "Was Jesus a Convert?" *Religion in Life* 43 (1974): 445–55; and M. Montgomery Watt, "Conversion in Islam at the Time of the Prophet," *Journal of the American Academy of Religion* 47 (1979): 721–32.

7 An example of what I am advocating is found in the work of Karl F. Morrison, *Understanding Conversion* (Charlottesville: University Press of Virginia, 1992), and *Conversion and Text: The Cases of Augustine of Hippo, Herman-Judah, and Constantine Tsatsos* (Charlottesville: University Press of Virginia, 1992).

8 Edward E. Sampson, "The Challenge of Social Change for Psychology: Globalization and Psychology's Theory of the Person," *American Psychologist* 44 (1989): 914–21. See also Philip Cushman, "Why the Self Is Empty: Toward a Historically Situated Psychology," *American Psychologist* 45 (1990): 599–611.

Bibliography

Allison, Joel. 1966. "Recent Empirical Studies in Religious Conversion Experiences." *Pastoral Psychology* 17:21–34.

———. 1968. "Adaptive Regression and Intense Religious Experience." *Journal of Nervous and Mental Disease* 145:452–63.

———. 1969. "Religious Conversion: Regression and Progression in an Adolescent Experience." *Journal for the Scientific Study of Religion* 8:23–38.

Ammerman, Nancy Tatom. 1987. *Bible Believers: Fundamentalists in the Modern World.* New Brunswick, N.J.: Rutgers University Press.

An-Na'im, Abdullah Ahmed. 1986. "The Islamic Law of Apostasy and Its Modern Applicability." *Religion* 16:197–224.

Anthony, Dick, Bruce Ecker, and Ken Wilbur, eds. 1987. *Spiritual Choices: The Problem of Recognizing Authentic Paths to Inner Transformation.* New York: Paragon House Publishers.

Antoun, Richard T., and Mary Elain Hegland, eds. 1987. *Religious Resurgence: Contemporary Cases in Islam, Christianity, and Judaism.* Syracuse, N.Y.: Syracuse University Press.

Arens, W. 1975. "Islam and Christianity in Sub-Saharan Africa: Ethnographic Reality or Ideology." *Cahiers d'études africaines* 15:443–56.

Arnold, T. W. 1986. *The Preaching of Islam: A History of the Propagation of the Muslim Faith.* Westminster, U.K.: Archibald Constable.

Aronson, Elliot, and Judson Mills. 1959. "The Effect of Severity of Initiation on Liking for a Group." *Journal of Abnormal and Social Psychology* 59:177–81.

Augustine. 1960. *The Confessions of St. Augustine.* Translated by John K. Ryan. Garden City, N.Y.: Doubleday.

Aviad, Janet. 1983. *Return to Judaism: Religious Renewal in Israel.* Chicago: University of Chicago Press.

Axtell, James. 1985. *The Invasion Within: The Contest of Cultures in Colonial North America.* New York: Oxford University Press.

———. 1988. *After Columbus: Essays in the Ethnohistory of Colonial North America.* New York: Oxford University Press.

Bagnall, Roger S. 1982. "Religious Conversion and Onomastic Change in Early Byzantine Egypt." *Bulletin of the American Society of Papyrologists* 19:105–24.

Baker, Henry, Jr. 1862. *The Hill Arrians.* London: British Book Society.

———. 1862. *The Hill Arrians of Travancore and the Progress of Christianity among Them.* London: British Book Society.

Baker, Irwin R., and Raymond F. Currie. 1985. "Do Converts Always Make the Most Committed Christians?" *Journal for the Scientific Study of Religion* 24:305–13.

Balch, Robert W. 1980. "Looking behind the Scenes in a Religious Cult: Implications for the Study of Conversion." *Sociological Analysis* 41:137–43.

Balch, Robert W., and David Taylor. 1977. "Seekers and Saucers: The Role of the Cultic Milieu in Joining a UFO Cult." *American Behavioral Scientist* 20:839–60.

Bankston, William B., H. Hugh Floyd, Jr., and Craig J. Forsyth. 1981. "Toward a General Model of the Process of Radical Conversion: An Interactionist Perspective on the Transformation of Self-Identity." *Qualitative Sociology* 4:279–97.

Barker, Eileen. 1985. "The Conversion of Conversion: A Sociological Anti-Reductionist Perspective." *Reductionism in Academic Disciplines.* Edited by Arthur Peacocke. London: Society for Research in Higher Education.

Barnhart, Joe Edward, and Mary Ann Barnhart. 1981. *The New Birth: A Naturalistic View of Religious Conversion.* Macon, Ga.: Mercer University Press.

Barrett, David B. 1982. *World Christian Encyclopedia: A Comparative Study of Churches and Religions in the Modern World, 1900–2000.* Nairobi: Oxford University Press.

———. 1984. "Five Statistical Eras of Global Mission." *Missiology* 12:21–37.

———. 1984. "Five Statistical Eras of Global Mission: A Thesis and Discussion." *International Bulletin of Missionary Research* 8:160–69.

———. 1985–1990. "Annual Statistical Table[s] on Global Mission." *International Bulletin of Missionary Research* 9:30–31; 10:22–23; 11:24–25; 12:16–17; 13:20–21; 14:26–27.

————. 1987. "Getting Ready for Mission in the 1990s: What Should We Be Doing to Prepare?" *Missiology* 15:3–14.

————. 1987. "Forecasting the Future in World Mission: Some Future Faces of Missions." *Missiology* 15:433–50.

————. 1987. *Cosmos, Chaos, and Gospel: A Chronology of World Evangelization from Creation to New Creation.* Birmingham, Ala.: New Hope.

————. 1987. *Evangelize! A Historical Survey of the Concept.* Birmingham, Ala.: New Hope.

————. 1988. *Evangelize the World: The Rise of a Global Evangelization Movement.* Birmingham, Ala.: New Hope.

————. 1988. "The Twentieth-Century Pentecostal/Charismatic Renewal in the Holy Spirit, with Its Goal of World Evangelization." *International Bulletin of Missionary Research* 12:119–29.

Barrett, David B., and Todd M. Johnson. 1990. *Our Globe and How to Reach It: Seeing the World Evangelized by A.D. 2000 and Beyond.* Birmingham, Ala.: New Hope.

Barrett, David B., and James W. Reapsome. 1986. *Seven Hundred Plans to World-Class Cities and World Evangelization.* Birmingham, Ala.: New Hope.

Battin, Margaret P. 1990. *Ethics in the Sanctuary: Examining the Practices of Organized Religion.* New Haven: Yale University Press.

Beaver, R. Pierce. 1962. "American Missionary Motivation before the Revolution." *Church History* 31:216–26.

Beckford, James A. 1978. "Accounting for Conversion." *British Journal of Sociology* 29:249–62.

————. 1983. "The Restoration of 'Power' to the Sociology of Religion." *Sociological Analysis* 44:11–33.

Beidelman, Thomas O. 1974. "Social Theory and the Study of Christian Missions in Africa." *Africa* 44:235–49.

————. 1981. "Contradictions between the Sacred and Secular Life: The Church Missionary Society in Ukaguru, Tanzania, West Africa, 1876–1914." *Comparative Studies in Society and History* 23:73–95.

————. 1982. *Colonial Evangelism.* Bloomington: Indiana University Press.

Beit-Hallahmi, Benjamin. 1989. *Prolegomena to the Psychological Study of Religion.* Lewisburg, Pa.: Bucknell University Press.

——. 1992. *Despair and Deliverance: Private Salvation in Contemporary Israel.* Albany, N.Y.: State University of New York Press.

Berger, Peter L. 1969. *The Sacred Canopy.* Garden City, N.Y.: Doubleday.

——. 1974. "Some Second Thoughts on Substantive versus Functional Definitions of Religion." *Journal for the Scientific Study of Religion* 13:125–34.

——. 1977. *Facing Up to Modernity.* New York: Basic Books.

——. 1979. *The Heretical Imperative.* Garden City, N.Y.: Doubleday.

Berger, Peter L., and Thomas Luckmann. 1967. *The Social Construction of Reality.* Garden City, N.Y.: Doubleday.

Berkhofer, Robert F., Jr. 1963. "Protestants, Pagans, and Sequences among the North American Indians, 1760–1860." *Ethnohistory* 10:201–32.

Bond, George D. 1980. "Theravada Buddhism's Meditations on Death and the Symbolism of Initiatory Death." *History of Religions* 19:237–58.

Bopegamage, A. 1979. "Status Seekers in India: A Sociological Study of the Neo-Buddhist Movement." *Archives européennes de sociologie* 20:19–39.

Boyack, Kenneth, ed. 1987. *Catholic Evangelization Today.* New York: Paulist Press.

Brauer, Jerald C. 1978. "Conversion: From Puritanism to Revivalism." *Journal of Religion* 58:227–48.

Bregman, Lucy. 1987. "Baptism as Death and Birth: A Psychological Interpretation of Its Imagery." *Journal of Ritual Studies* 1:27–42.

Brereton, Virginia Lieson. 1991. *From Sin to Salvation: Stories of Women's Conversions, 1800 to the Present.* Bloomington: University of Indiana Press.

Britsch, R. Lanier. 1977. "Mormon Missions: An Introduction to the Latter-Day Saints Missionary System." *Occasional Bulletin of Missionary Research* 3:22–27.

Bromley, David G., ed. 1988. *Falling from the Faith: Causes and Consequences of Religious Apostasy.* Beverly Hills: Sage Publications.

Bromley, David G., and Anson Shupe. 1986. "Affiliation and Disaffiliation: A Role-

Theory Interpretation of Joining and Leaving New Religious Movements." *Thought* 61:197–211.

Brown, G. Thompson. 1986. *Christianity in the People's Republic of China*. Atlanta: John Knox Press.

Brown, Peter. 1967. *Augustine of Hippo: A Biography.* Berkeley: University of California Press.

Bulliet, Richard W. 1979. *Conversion to Islam in the Medieval Period: An Essay in Quantitative History.* Cambridge, Mass.: Harvard University Press.

Burke, Kathryn L., and Merlin B. Brinkerhoff. 1981. "Capturing Charisma: Notes on an Elusive Concept." *Journal for the Scientific Study of Religion* 20:274–84.

Burridge, Kenelm. 1991. *In the Way: A Study of Christian Missionary Endeavours.* Vancouver: University of British Columbia Press.

Caldwell, Patricia. 1983. *The Puritan Conversion Narrative.* New York: Cambridge University Press.

Camic, Charles. 1980. "Charisma: Its Varieties, Preconditions, and Consequences." *Sociological Inquiry* 50:5–23.

Capps, Donald. 1990. "Sin, Narcissism, and the Changing Face of Conversion." *Journal of Religion and Health* 29:233–51.

Capps, Donald, and James E. Dittes, eds. 1990. *The Hunger of the Heart: Reflections on the Confessions of Augustine.* West Lafayette, Ind.: Society for the Scientific Study of Religion.

Carmen, C. Tineke. 1987. "Conversion and the Missionary Vocation: American Board of Missionaries in South Africa." *Mission Studies: Journal of the IAMS* 4:27–38.

Carmody, Brendan Patrick. 1986. "The Nature and Consequences of Conversion in Jesuit Education at Chikuni, 1905–1978." Unpub. diss., Graduate Theological Union, Berkeley.

——. 1988. "Conversion and School at Chikuni, 1905–39." *Africa* 58:193–209.

——. 1988. "Conversion to Roman Catholicism in Zambia: Shifting Pedagogies." *African Christian Studies* 4:5–24.

——. 1989. "Mission Primary Schools and Conversion: Help or Hindrance to Church Growth?" *Missiology* 17:177–92.

———. 1992. *Conversion and Jesuit Schooling in Zambia*. New York: E. J. Brill.

Charney, Linda Ann. 1986. "Religious Conversion: A Longitudinal Study." Ph.D. diss., University of Utah, Salt Lake City.

Churchill, Winston. 1956–1958. *A History of the English-Speaking Peoples*. New York: Dodd and Mead.

Cleaver, Eldridge. 1968. *Soul on Ice*. New York: McGraw-Hill.

———. 1978. *Soul on Fire*. Waco, Tex.: Word Books.

Clymer, Kenton J. 1986. *Protestant Missionaries in the Philippines, 1898–1916: An Inquiry into the American Colonial Mentality*. Urbana: University of Illinois Press.

Cohen, Charles Lloyd. 1986. *God's Caress: The Psychology of Puritan Religious Experience*. New York: Oxford University Press.

Cohen, Erik. 1990. "The Missionary as Stranger: A Phenomenological Analysis of Christian Missionaries' Encounter with the Folk Religions of Thailand." *Review of Religious Research* 31:337–50.

———. 1991. "Christianity and Buddhism in Thailand: The 'Battle of the Axes' and the 'Contest of Power.'" *Social Compass* 38:115–40.

Colpe, Carsten. 1987. "Syncretism." *Encyclopedia of Religion*. Edited by Mircea Eliade. New York: Macmillan.

Colson, Charles W. 1976. *Born Again*. New York: Bantam Books.

Conn, Walter. 1986. *Christian Conversion: A Developmental Interpretation of Autonomy and Surrender*. New York: Paulist Press.

———. 1986. "Adult Conversions." *Pastoral Psychology* 34:225–36.

———. 1987. "Pastoral Counseling for Self-Transcendence: The Integration of Psychology and Theology." *Pastoral Psychology* 36:29–48.

Conway, Flo, and Jim Siegelman. 1978. *Snapping: America's Epidemic of Sudden Personality Change*. Philadelphia: J. B. Lippincott.

Cronin, Brian. 1989. "Missionary Motivation." *Milltown Studies* 23:89–107.

Cushman, Philip. 1986. "The Self Besieged: Recruitment-Indoctrination Processes in Restrictive Groups." *Journal for the Theory of Social Behavior* 16:1–32.

Daniel, K. G. 1989. "The Conversion of the 'Hill Arrians' of Kerala State in India from

1848 to 1878: The Implications for Twentieth-Century Evangelism in India." D. Min. diss., San Francisco Theological Seminary, San Anselmo.

Danzger, M. Herbert. 1989. *Returning to Tradition: The Contemporary Revival of Orthodox Judaism*. New Haven: Yale University Press.

Davidman, Lynn. 1991. *Tradition in a Rootless World: Women Turn to Orthodox Judaism*. Berkeley: University of California Press.

Dawson, Lorne. 1990. "Self-Affirmation, Freedom, and Rationality: Theoretically Elaborating 'Active' Conversions." *Journal for the Scientific Study of Religion* 29:141–63.

Deikman, Arthur J. 1985. *The Observing Self: Mysticism and Psychotherapy*. Boston: Beacon Press.

———. 1990. *The Wrong Way Home: Uncovering the Patterns of Cult Behavior in American Society*. Boston: Beacon Press.

Dodd, C. H. 1953. *New Testament Studies*. Manchester, U.K.: Manchester University Press.

Doeppers, Daniel. 1976. "The Evolution of the Geography of Religious Adherence in the Philippines before 1898." *Journal of Historical Geography* 2:95–110.

———. 1976. "The Philippine Revolution and the Geography of Schism." *Geographical Review* 66:158–77.

Donahue, Michael J. 1985. "Intrinsic and Extrinsic Religiousness: Review and Meta-Analysis." *Journal of Personality and Social Psychology* 48:400–19.

Donovan, Vincent J. 1978. *Christianity Rediscovered: An Epistle from the Masai*. Maryknoll, N.Y.: Orbis Books.

Dow, James. 1986. "Universal Aspects of Symbolic Healing: A Theoretical Synthesis." *American Anthropologist* 88:56–69.

Downton, James V., Jr. 1979. *Sacred Journeys: The Conversion of Young Americans to Divine Light Mission*. New York: Columbia University Press.

———. 1980. "An Evolutionary Theory of Spiritual Conversion and Commitment: The Case of Divine Light Mission." *Journal for the Scientific Study of Religion* 19:381–86.

Drummond, Richard H. 1971. *A History of Christianity in Japan*. Grand Rapids, Mich.: Eerdmans Publishing Company.

Duggan, Robert, ed. 1984. *Conversion and the Catechumenate*. New York: Paulist Press.

Dumoulin, Heinrich, ed. 1976. *Buddhism in the Modern World*. New York: Collier Books.

Earhart, H. Byron. 1980. "Toward a Theory of the Formation of the Japanese New Religions: A Case Study of Gedatsu-Kai." *History of Religions* 20:175–97.

Eaton, Richard M. 1985. "Approaches to the Study of Conversion to Islam in India." *Approaches to Islam in Religious Studies*. Edited by Richard C. Martin. Tucson: University of Arizona Press.

Ebaugh, Helen R. F. 1988. *Becoming an Ex: The Process of Role Exit*. Chicago: University of Chicago Press.

Eberhard, Ernest. 1974. "How to Share the Gospel: A Step-by-Step Approach for You and Your Neighbors." *Ensign* 4:6–12.

Engel, James F. 1990. "The Road to Conversion: The Latest Research Insights." *Evangelical Missions Quarterly* 26:184–95.

Epstein, Seymour. 1985. "The Implications of Cognitive-Experiential Self-Theory for Research in Social Psychology and Personality." *Journal for the Theory of Social Behavior* 15:283–310.

Epstein, Seymour, and Edward J. Obrien. 1985. "The Person-Situation Debate in Historical and Current Perspective." *Psychological Bulletin* 98:513–37.

Etherington, Norman A. 1970. "An American Errand into the South African Wilderness." *Church History* 39:62–71.

————. 1976. "Mission Station Melting Pot as a Factor in the Rise of South African Black Nationalism." *International Journal of African Historical Studies* 9:592–605.

————. 1977. "Social Theory and the Study of Christian Missions in Africa: A South African Case Study." *Africa* 47:31–40.

Feldman, Emanuel, and Joel B. Wolowelsky, eds. 1990. *The Conversion Crisis: Essays from the Pages of Tradition*. Hoboken, N.J.: Ktav.

Ferm, Robert O. 1959. *The Psychology of Christian Conversion*. Westwood, N.J.: Fleming H. Revell.

Ferm, Robert O., with Caroline M. Whiting. 1988. *Billy Graham: Do the Conversions Last?* Minneapolis: World Wide Publications.

Finn, Thomas M. 1989. "Ritual Processes and the Survival of Early Christianity: A Study of the Apostolic Tradition of Hippolytus." *Journal of Ritual Studies* 3:69–90.

————. 1990. "It Happened One Saturday Night: Ritual and Conversion in Augustine's North Africa." *Journal of the American Academy of Religion* 58:589–616.

Finney, John M. 1978. "A Theory of Religious Commitment." *Sociological Analysis* 39:19–35.

Fisher, Humphrey J. 1973. "Conversion Reconsidered: Some Historical Aspects of Religious Conversion in Black Africa." *Africa* 43:27–40.

————. 1986. "The Juggernaut's Apologia: Conversion to Islam in Black Africa." *Africa* 55:153–73.

Flinn, Frank K. 1987. "Criminalizing Conversion: The Legislative Assault on New Religions et al." *Crime, Values, and Religion.* Edited by James M. Day and William S. Laufer. Norwood, N.J.: Ables.

Forster, Brenda, and Joseph Tabachnik. 1991. *Jews by Choice: A Study of Converts to Reform and Conservative Judaism.* Hoboken, N.J.: Ktav.

Fowler, James W. 1981. *Stages of Faith: The Psychology of Human Development and the Quest for Meaning.* San Francisco: Harper and Row.

————. 1984. *Becoming Adult, Becoming Christian.* San Francisco: Harper and Row.

Frank, Jerome D. 1974. *Persuasion and Healing.* Rev. ed. New York: Schocken Books.

Fried, Morton H. 1987. "Reflections on Christianity in China." *American Ethnologist* 14:94–106.

Galanter, Marc. 1978. "The 'Relief Effect': A Sociobiological Model for Neurotic Distress and Large-Group Therapy." *American Journal of Psychiatry* 135:588–91.

————. 1980. "Psychological Induction into the Large Group: Findings from a Modern Religious Sect." *American Journal of Psychiatry* 137:1574–79.

————. 1989. *Cults, Faith, Healing, and Coercion.* New York: Oxford University Press.

Galanter, Marc, Richard Babkin, Judith Babkin, and Alexander Deutsch. 1979. "The 'Moonies': A Psychological Study of Conversion and Membership in a Contemporary Religious Sect." *American Journal of Psychiatry* 136:165–70.

Gallagher, Eugene V. 1990. *Expectation and Experience: Explaining Religious Experience.* Atlanta: Scholars Press.

————. "Conversion and Salvation in the Apocryphal Acts of the Apostles." *The Second Century* 8:13–30.

Garfunkel, H. 1956. "Conditions of Successful Degradation Ceremonies." *American Journal of Sociology* 6:420–24.

Garrett, William R. 1974. "Troublesome Transcendence: The Supernatural in the Scientific Study of Religion." *Sociological Analysis* 35:167–80.

Gartrell, C. David., and Zane K. Shannon. 1985. "Contacts, Cognitions, and Conversion: A Rational Choice Approach." *Review of Religious Research* 27:32–48.

Gaventa, Beverly Roberts. 1986. *From Darkness to Light*. Philadelphia: Fortress Press.

Geertz, Clifford. 1973. *The Interpretation of Cultures*. New York: Basic Books.

Gelpi, Donald J. 1982. "Conversion: The Challenge of Contemporary Charismatic Piety." *Theological Studies* 43:606–28.

———. 1986. "The Converting Jesuit." *Studies in the Spirituality of Jesuits* 18:1–38.

———. 1987. "The Converting Catechumen." *Lumen vitae* 42:401–15.

———. 1987. "Religious Conversion: A New Way of Being." *The Human Experience of Conversion: Persons and Structures in Transformation*. Edited by Francis A. Eigo. Villanova, Pa.: Villanova University Press.

———. 1989. "Conversion: Beyond the Impasses of Individualism." *Beyond Individualism*. Edited by Donald J. Gelpi. South Bend, Ind.: University of Notre Dame Press.

Gerlach, Luther P., and Virginia H. Hine. 1970. *People, Power, Change: Movements of Social Transformation*. Indianapolis: Bobbs-Merrill.

———. 1968. "Five Factors Crucial to the Growth and Spread of a Modern Religious Movement." *Journal for the Scientific Study of Religion* 7:23–40.

Gernet, Jacques. 1985. *China and the Christian Impact: A Conflict of Cultures*. Translated by Janet Lloyd. New York: Cambridge University Press.

Gibbon, Edward. 1936. *The Decline and Fall of the Roman Empire*. New York: Harper and Brothers.

Gillespie, V. Bailey. 1991. *The Dynamics of Religious Conversion: Identity and Transformation*. Birmingham, Ala.: Religious Education Press.

Gilligan, Carol. 1982. *In a Different Voice: Psychological Theory and Women's Development*. Cambridge, Mass.: Harvard University Press.

Gokhale, B. G. 1976. "Dr. Bhimrao Ramji Ambedkar: Rebel against Hindu Tradition." *Journal of Asian and African Studies* 11:13–23.

Gokhale, J. B. 1986. "Castaways of Caste." *Natural History* 95:31–39.

———. 1986. "The Sociopolitical Effects of Ideological Change: The Buddhist Conversion of Maharashtrian Untouchables." *Journal of Asian Studies* 45:269–82.

Goody, Jack, ed. 1975. *Changing Social Structure in Ghana: Essays in the Comparative Sociology of a New State and an Old Tradition.* London: International African Institute.

Gordon, David F. 1974. "The Jesus People: An Identity Synthesis." *Urban Life and Culture* 3:159–78.

———. 1984. "Dying to Self: Self-Control through Self-Abandonment." *Sociological Analysis* 45:41–56.

Gottwald, Norman K. 1988. "Religious Conversion and the Societal Origins of Ancient Israel." *Perspectives in Religious Studies* 15:49–66.

Gration, John A. 1983. "Conversion in Cultural Context." *International Bulletin of Missionary Research* 7:157–63.

Greeley, Andrew M. 1972. *Unsecular Man: The Persistence of Religion.* New York: Schocken Books.

———. 1989. *Religious Change in America.* Cambridge, Mass.: Harvard University Press.

Greil, Arthur L., and David R. Rudy. 1984. "Social Cocoons: Encapsulation and Identity Transformation Organizations." *Sociological Inquiry* 54:260–78.

Griffin, Emilie. 1980. *Turning: Reflections on the Experience of Conversion.* Garden City, N.Y.: Doubleday.

———. 1984. *Clinging: The Experience of Prayer.* San Francisco: Harper and Row.

Harding, Susan F. 1987. "Convicted by the Holy Spirit: The Rhetoric of Fundamental Baptist Conversion." *American Ethnology* 14:167–81.

Harran, Marilyn J. 1983. *Luther on Conversion: The Early Years.* Ithaca, N.Y.: Cornell University Press.

Hassan, Steve. 1988. *Combatting Cult Mind Control.* Rochester, Vt.: Park Street Press.

Hawkins, Ann Husaker. 1985. *Archetypes of Conversion: The Autobiographies of Augustine, Bunyan, and Merton*. Lewisburg, Pa.: Bucknell University Press.

Heirich, Max. 1977. "Change of Heart: A Test of Some Widely Held Theories about Religious Conversion." *American Journal of Sociology* 83:653–80.

Heise, David R. 1967. "Prefatory Findings in the Sociology of Missions." *Journal for the Scientific Study of Religion* 6:49–58.

Hiebert, Paul G. 1978. "Conversion, Culture, and Cognitive Categories." *Gospel in Context* 1:24–29.

———. 1983. "The Category 'Christian' in the Mission Task." *International Review of Mission* 72:421–27.

Hine, Virginia H. 1970. "Bridge Burners: Commitment and Participation in a Religious Movement." *Sociological Analysis* 31:61–66.

Hofmeyr, J. 1986. "A Catastrophe Model of Conversion." *Religions in Southern Africa* 7:47–58.

Hoge, Dean R. 1981. *Converts, Dropouts, Returnees: A Study of Religious Change among Catholics*. New York: Pilgrim Press.

Holy Bible. 1988. New Revised Standard Version. Grand Rapids, Mich.: Zondervan.

Horsley, G. H. R. 1987. "Name Changes as an Indication of Religious Conversion in Antiquity." *Numen* 34:1–17.

Horton, Robin. 1971. "African Conversion." *Africa* 41:85–108.

———. 1975. "On the Rationality of Conversion, Part I." *Africa* 45:219–35.

———. 1975. "On the Rationality of Conversion, Part II." *Africa* 45:373–99.

Hutchison, William R. 1983. "A Moral Equivalent for Imperialism: Americans and the Promotion of 'Christian Civilization,' 1880–1910." *Indian Journal of American Studies* 13:55–67.

———. 1987. *Errand to the World: American Protestant Thought and Foreign Missions*. Chicago: University of Chicago Press.

Ifeka-Moller, Caroline. 1974. "White Power: Social-Structural Factors in Conversion to Christianity, Eastern Nigeria, 1921–1966." *Canadian Journal of African Studies* 8:55–72.

Ikenga-Metuh, Emefie. 1985. "The Shattered Microcosm: A Critical Survey of Explanations of Conversion in Africa." *Neue Zeitschrift für Missionswissenschaft* 41:241–54.

Isichei, Elizabeth. 1970. "Seven Varieties of Ambiguity: Some Patterns of Igbo Response to Christian Missions." *Journal of Religion in Africa* (3):209–27.

Jacobs, Janet Liebman. 1989. *Divine Disenchantment: Deconverting from New Religions.* Bloomington: Indiana University Press.

James, William. 1929. *The Varieties of Religious Experience: A Study in Human Nature.* New York: Modern Library.

Jennings, Francis. 1971. "Goals and Functions of Puritan Missions to the Indians." *Ethnohistory* 18:197–212.

Jennings, Theodore W. 1982. "On Ritual Knowledge." *Journal of Religion* 62:113–27.

Johnson, Cedric B., and H. Newton Malony. 1982. *Christian Conversion: Biblical and Psychological Perspectives.* Grand Rapids, Mich.: Zondervan.

Johnson, Weldon T. 1971. "The Religious Crusade: Revival or Ritual?" *American Journal of Sociology* 76:873–90.

Jones, James W. 1991. *Contemporary Psychoanalysis and Religion: Transference and Transcendence.* New Haven: Yale University Press.

Jules-Rosette, Benneta. 1976. "The Conversion Experience: The Apostles of John Maranke." *Journal of Religion in Africa* 7:132–64.

Juster, Susan. 1989. "'In a Different Voice': Male and Female Narratives of Religious Conversion in Post-Revolutionary America." *American Quarterly* 41:34–62.

Kanter, Rosabeth Moss. 1968. "Commitment and Social Organization: A Study of Commitment Mechanisms in Utopian Communities." *American Sociological Review* 33:499–517.

Kaplan, Steven. 1985. "Rejection of Conversion." Unpub. paper, Hebrew University of Jerusalem.

———. 1986. "The Africanization of Missionary Christianity: History and Typology." *Journal of Religion in Africa* 16:166–86.

Karras, Ruth Mazo. 1986. "Pagan Survivals and Syncretism in the Conversion of Saxony." *The Catholic Historical Review* 72:553–72.

Kasdorf, Hans. 1980. *Christian Conversion in Context.* Scottsdale, Pa.: Herald Press.

Kaufman, Debra Renee. 1989. "Patriarchal Women: A Case Study of Newly Orthodox Jewish Women." *Symbolic Interaction* 12:299–315.

Kee, Alistair. 1982. *Constantine versus Christ*. London: SCM Press.

Kelly, Henry Ansgar. 1985. *The Devil at Baptism: Ritual, Theology, and Drama*. Ithaca, N.Y.: Cornell University Press.

Kilbourne, Brock K., and James T. Richardson. 1988. "A Social Psychological Analysis of Healing." *Journal of Integrative and Eclectic Psychotherapy* 7:20–34.

King, John Owen. 1983. *The Iron of Melancholy*. Middletown, Conn.: Wesleyan University Press.

Kirkpatrick, Lee A. 1992. "An Attachment Theory Approach to the Psychology of Religion." *The International Journal for the Psychology of Religion* 2:3–28.

Kirkpatrick, Lee A., and Phillip R. Shaver. 1990. "Attachment Theory and Religion: Childhood Attachments, Religious Beliefs, and Conversion." *Journal for the Scientific Study of Religion* 29:315–35.

Kobrin, David. 1967. "The Expansion of the Visible Church in New England, 1629–1650." *Church History* 36:189–209.

Kox, Willem, Wim Meeus, and Harm't Hart. 1991. "Religious Conversion of Adolescents: Testing the Lofland and Stark Model of Religious Conversion." *Sociological Analysis* 52:227–40.

Kraft, Charles H. 1976. "Cultural Concomitant of Higi Conversion: Early Period." *Missiology* 4:431–42.

———. 1979. *Christianity in Culture*. Maryknoll, N.Y.: Orbis Books.

Kroll-Smith, J. Stephen. 1980. "The Testimony as Performance: The Relationship of an Expressive Event to the Belief System of a Holiness Sect." *Journal for the Scientific Study of Religion* 19:16–25.

Lawless, Elaine J. 1988. " 'The Night I Got the Holy Ghost': Holy Ghost Narratives and the Pentecostal Conversion Process." *Western Folklore* 47:1–19.

———. 1988. *God's Peculiar People*. Lexington: University Press of Kentucky.

Lawrence, Bruce B. 1989. *Defenders of God*. San Francisco: Harper and Row.

Leonard, Bill J. 1985. "Getting Saved in America: Conversion Event in a Pluralistic Culture." *Review and Expositor* 82:111–27.

Levtzion, Nehemia, ed. 1979. *Conversion to Islam.* New York: Holmes and Meier.

Lewis, C. S. 1955. *Surprised by Joy.* New York: Harcourt, Brace and World.

Lex, Barbara. 1978. "Neurological Bases of Revitalization Movements." *Zygon* 13:276–312.

Lichtenstein, Aharon. 1988. "On Conversion." Translated by Michael Berger. *Tradition* 23:1–18.

Lifton, Robert Jay. 1968. "Protean Man." *Partisan Review* 35:13–27.

Ling, Trevor. 1980. *Buddhist Revival in India: Aspects of the Sociology of Buddhism.* New York: St. Martin's Press.

Liu, Christine. 1991. "Becoming a Christian Consciously versus Nonconsciously." *Journal of Psychology and Theology* 19:364–75.

Loder, James E. 1989. *The Transforming Moment.* Colorado Springs: Helmers and Howard.

Lofland, John. 1977. "'Becoming a World-Saver' Revisited." *American Behavioral Scientist* 20:805–18.

Lofland, John, and Norman Skonovd. 1981. "Conversion Motifs." *Journal for the Scientific Study of Religion* 20:373–85.

Lofland, John, and Rodney Stark. 1965. "Becoming a World-Saver: A Theory of Conversion to a Deviant Perspective." *American Sociological Review* 30:862–75.

Luzbetak, Louis J. 1988. *The Church and Cultures.* Maryknoll, N.Y.: Orbis Books.

MacMullen, Ramsay. 1967. *Constantine.* London: Croom Helm.

———. 1981. *Paganism and the Roman Empire.* New Haven: Yale University Press.

———. 1983. "Two Types of Conversion to Early Christianity." *Vigiliae Christianae* 37:174–92.

———. 1984. *Christianizing the Roman Empire, A.D. 100–400.* New Haven: Yale University Press.

———. 1985–86. "Conversion: A Historian's View." *The Second Century* 5:67–96.

———. 1986. "What Difference Did Christianity Make?" *Historia* 35:322–43.

———. 1988. *Corruption and the Decline of Rome.* New Haven: Yale University Press.

Martin, David. 1978. *A General Theory of Secularization*. New York: Harper and Row.

McFague, Sallie. 1978. "Conversion: Life on the Edge of the Raft." *Interpretation* 32:255–68.

McGuire, Meredith B. 1977. "Testimony as a Commitment Mechanism in Catholic Pentecostal Prayer Groups." *Journal for the Scientific Study of Religion* 16:165–68.

_____. 1983. "Discovering Religious Power." *Sociological Analysis* 44:1–10.

McLoughlin, William G. 1978. *Revivals, Awakenings, and Reform*. Chicago: University of Chicago Press.

Meeks, Wayne A. 1983. *The First Urban Christians: The Social World of the Apostle Paul*. New Haven: Yale University Press.

Metzner, Ralph. 1980. "Ten Classical Metaphors of Self-Transformation." *Journal of Transpersonal Psychology* 12:47–62.

_____. 1986. *Opening to Inner Light: The Transformation of Human Nature and Consciousness*. Los Angeles: Jeremy P. Tarcher.

Migdal, Joel S. 1974. "Why Change? Toward a New Theory of Change among Individuals in the Process of Modernization." *World Politics* 26:189–206.

Milgrom, Jacob. 1982. "Religious Conversion and the Revolt Model for the Formation of Israel." *Journal of Biblical Literature* 101:169–76.

Miller, Elmer S. 1970. "The Christian Missionary: Agent of Secularization." *Anthropological Quarterly* 43:14–22.

Montgomery, Robert L. 1991. "The Spread of Religions and Macrosocial Relations." *Sociological Analysis* 52:37–53.

Morinis, Alan. 1985. "The Ritual Experience: Pain and the Transformation of Consciousness in Ordeals of Initiation." *Ethos* 13:150–74.

Morris, Thomas H. 1989. *The RCIA: Transforming the Church*. New York: Paulist Press.

Morrison, Karl F. 1992. *Conversion and Text: The Cases of Augustine of Hippo. Herman-Judah, and Constantine Tsatsos*. Charlottesville: University Press of Virginia.

_____. 1992. *Understanding Conversion*. Charlottesville: University Press of Virginia.

Moseley, Romney M. 1991. *Becoming a Self before God: Critical Transformation*. Nashville: Abingdon Press.

————. 1991. "Forms of Logic in Faith Development Theory." *Pastoral Psychology* 39:143–52.

Murphey, Murray G. 1979. "The Psychodynamics of Puritan Conversion." *American Quarterly* 31:135–47.

Needleman, Jacob. 1970. *The New Religions*. Garden City, N.Y.: Doubleday.

Neill, Stephen. 1986. *A History of Christian Missions*. 2d ed. Revised by Owen Chadwick. Harmondsworth, U.K.: Penguin Books.

Newport, Frank. 1979. "The Religious Switcher in the United States." *American Journal of Sociology* 44:528–52.

Nock, A. D. 1933. *Conversion*. New York: Oxford University Press.

Notehelfer, F. G. 1985. *American Samurai: Captain L. L. Janes and Japan*. Princeton: Princeton University Press.

Ofshe, Richard, and Margaret T. Singer. 1986. "Attacks on Peripheral versus Central Elements of Self and the Impact of Thought-Reforming Techniques." *Cultic Studies Journal* 3:3–24.

Okorocha, Cyril C. 1987. *The Meaning of Religious Conversion in Africa*. Aldershot, U.K.: Avebury.

Ownby, Ted. 1990. *Subduing Satan: Religion, Recreation, and Manhood in the Rural South, 1865–1920*. Chapel Hill: University of North Carolina Press.

Peel, J. D. Y. 1977. "Conversion and Tradition in Two African Societies: Ijebu and Buganda." *Past and Present: A Journal of Historical Studies* 77:108–41.

Perry, John Weir. 1976. *Roots of Renewal in Myth and Madness*. San Francisco: Jossey-Bass.

Pettifer, Julian, and Richard Bradley. 1990. *Missionaries*. London: BBC Books.

Pettit, Norman. 1989. *The Heart Prepared: Grace and Conversion in Puritan Spiritual Life*. 2d ed. Middletown, Conn.: Wesleyan University Press.

Pitt, John E. 1991. "Why People Convert: A Balanced Theoretical Approach to Religious Conversion." *Pastoral Psychology* 39:171–83.

Post, Stephen G. 1991. "Psychiatry, Religious Conversion, and Medical Ethics." *Kennedy Institute of Ethics Journal* 1:207–23.

Poston, Larry. 1992. *Islamic Da'wah in the West: Muslim Missionary Activity and the Dynamics of Conversion to Islam.* New York: Oxford University Press.

Preston, David L. 1981. "Becoming a Zen Practitioner." *Sociological Analysis* 42:47–55.

––––––. 1982. "Meditative Ritual Practice and Spiritual Conversion-Commitment: Theoretical Implications Based on the Case of Zen." *Sociological Analysis* 43:257–70.

Proudfoot, Wayne, and Phillip Shaver. 1975. "Attribution Theory and the Psychology of Religion." *Journal for the Scientific Study of Religion* 14:317–30.

Pruyser, Paul W. 1974. *Between Belief and Unbelief.* New York: Harper and Row.

Rafael, Vicente L. 1987. "Confession, Conversion, and Reciprocity in Early Tagalog Colonial Society." *Comparative Studies in Society and History* 29:320–39.

––––––. 1988. *Contracting Colonialism: Translation and Christian Conversion in Tagalog Society under Early Spanish Rule.* Ithaca, N.Y.: Cornell University Press.

Rambo, Lewis R. 1981. "Education and Conversion." *Christian Teaching.* Edited by Everet Ferguson. Abilene, Tex.: Abilene Christian University Press.

––––––. 1982. "Current Research on Religious Conversion." *Religious Studies Review* 13:146–59.

––––––. 1982. "Charisma and Conversion." *Pastoral Psychology* 31:96–108.

––––––. 1983. *The Divorcing Christian.* Nashville: Abingdon Press.

––––––. 1987. "Conversion." *Encyclopedia of Religion.* Edited by Mircea Eliade. New York: Macmillan. Pages 72–79.

––––––. 1987. "Reflections on Conflict in Israel and the West Bank." *Pacific Theological Review* 21:48–56.

––––––. 1989. "Conversion: Toward a Holistic Model of Religious Change." *Pastoral Psychology* 38:47–63.

––––––. 1990. "Congregational Care and Discipline in the San Francisco Church of Christ: A Case Study." Unpub. paper, Christian Theological Seminary, Indianapolis, 3 March 1990.

––––––. 1992. "Psychology of Conversion." *Handbook on Conversion.* Edited by H. Newton Malony and Samuel Southard. Birmingham, Ala.: Religious Education Press.

Rambo, Lewis R., with Lawrence A. Reh. 1992. "Phenomenology of Conversion."

Handbook on Conversion. Edited by H. Newton Malony and Samuel Southard. Birmingham, Ala.: Religious Education Press.

Reese, Jack Roger. 1988. "Routes of Conversion: A Sociopsychological Study of the Varieties of Individual Religious Change." Ph.D. diss., University of Iowa, Iowa City.

Richardson, Don. 1974. *Peace Child.* Glendale, Calif.: Regal Books.

Richardson, James T. 1985. "The Active vs. Passive Convert: Paradigm Conflict in Conversion/Recruitment Research." *Journal for the Scientific Study of Religion* 24:163–79.

―――. 1989. "The Psychology of Induction: A Review and Interpretation." *Cults and New Religious Movements.* Edited by Marc Galanter. Washington, D.C.: American Psychiatric Association. Pages 211–38.

Ring, Kenneth. 1984. *Heading toward Omega.* New York: William Morrow.

Robbins, Thomas. 1984. "Constructing Cultist 'Mind Control.'" *Sociological Analysis* 45:241–56.

Robertson, Roland. 1978. *Meaning and Change: Explorations in the Cultural Sociology of Modern Societies.* New York: New York University Press.

Rochford, E. Burke, Jr. 1982. "Recruitment Strategies, Ideology, and Organization in the Hare Krishna Movement." *Social Problems* 4:399–410.

―――. 1985. *Hare Krishna in America.* New Brunswick, N.J.: Rutgers University Press.

Rogers, Everett M. 1983. *Diffusion of Innovations.* 3d ed. New York: The Free Press.

Roof, Wade Clark, and William McKinney. 1987. *American Mainline Religion.* New Brunswick, N.J.: Rutgers University Press.

Rotenberg, Mordechai. 1986. "The 'Midrash' and Biographic Rehabilitation." *Journal for the Scientific Study of Religion* 25:41–55.

Rounds, John C. 1982. "Curing What Ails Them: Individual Circumstances and Religious Change among Zulu-Speakers in Durban, South Africa." *Africa* 52:77–89.

Rouse, Ruth. 1936. "The Missionary Motive." *International Review of Missions* 25:250–58.

Rubenstein, Richard L., ed. 1987. *Spirit Matters: The Worldwide Impact of Religion on Contemporary Politics.* New York: Paragon House.

Ruthven, Malise. 1984. *Islam in the World*. New York: Oxford University Press.

Sahay, Keshari N. 1968. "The Impact of Christianity on the Uraon of the Chainpur Belt in Chotanagpur: An Analysis of Its Cultural Processes." *American Anthropologist* 70:923–42.

———. 1986. *Christianity and Culture Change in India*. New Delhi: Inter-India Publications.

Sales, Stephen M. 1972. "Economic Threat as a Determinant of Conversion Rates in Authoritarian and Nonauthoritarian Churches." *Journal of Personality and Social Psychology* 23:420–28.

Sanneh, Lamin. 1983. *West African Christianity: The Religious Impact*. Maryknoll, N.Y.: Orbis Books.

———. 1989. *Translating the Message: The Missionary Impact on Culture*. Maryknoll, N.Y.: Orbis Books.

———. 1983. "The Horizontal and the Vertical in Mission: An African Perspective." *International Bulletin of Missionary Research* 7:165–71.

———. 1987. "Christian Missions and the Western Guilt Complex." *The Christian Century* 104:330–34.

Sarbin, Theodore R., and Nathan Adler. 1970. "Self-Reconstitution Processes: A Preliminary Report." *The Psychoanalytic Review* 57:599–616.

Scheiner, Irwin. 1970. *Christian Converts and Social Protest in Meiji Japan*. Berkeley: University of California Press.

Scroggs, James R., and William G. T. Douglas. 1967. "Issues in the Psychology of Religious Conversion." *Journal of Religion and Health* 6:204–16.

Segal, Alan F. 1990. *Paul the Convert*. New Haven: Yale University Press.

Selengut, Charles. 1988. "American Jewish Converts to New Religious Movements." *The Jewish Journal of Sociology* 30:95–110.

Shiner, Larry. 1968. "Six Meanings of 'Secularization.'" *Journal for the Scientific Study of Religion* 6:207–20.

Shirer, William L. 1960. *The Rise and Fall of the Third Reich*. New York: Simon and Schuster.

Silverstein, Steven M. 1988. "A Study of Religious Conversion in North America." *Genetic, Social, and General Psychology Monographs* 114:261–305.

Simensen, Jarle. 1986. "Religious Change as Transaction: The Norwegian Mission to Zululand, South Africa, 1850–1906." *Journal of Religion in Africa* 16:82–100.

Simmonds, Robert B. 1977. "Conversion or Addiction: Consequences of Joining a Jesus Movement Group." *American Behavioral Scientist* 20:909–24.

Singer, Margaret T. Interview with author. Berkeley, 19 November 1989.

Singer, Merrill. 1978. "Chassidic Recruitment and the Local Context." *Urban Anthropology* 7:373–83.

———. 1980. "The Use of Folklore in Religious Conversion: The Chassidic Case." *Review of Religious Research* 22:170–85.

Snow, David A., and Richard Machalek. 1983. "The Convert as a Social Type." *Sociological Theory 1983.* Edited by Randall Collins. San Francisco: Jossey-Bass.

———. 1984. "The Sociology of Conversion." *Annual Review of Sociology* 10:167–90.

Snow, David A., and Cynthia L. Phillips. 1980. "The Lofland-Stark Conversion Model: A Critical Reassessment." *Social Problems* 27:430–47.

Snow, David A., Louis A. Zurcher, Jr., and Sheldon Ekland-Olson. 1980. "Social Networks and Social Movements: A Microstructural Approach to Differential Recruitment. *American Sociological Review* 45:787–801.

———. 1983. "Further Thoughts on Social Networks and Movement Recruitment." *Sociology* 17:112–20.

Spilka, Bernard, Phillip Shaver, and Lee A. Kirkpatrick. 1985. "A General Attribution Theory for the Psychology of Religion." *Journal for the Scientific Study of Religion* 24:1–20.

Staples, Clifford L., and Armand L. Mauss. 1987. "Conversion or Commitment? A Reassessment of the Snow and Machalek Approach to the Study of Conversion." *Journal for the Scientific Study of Religion* 26:133–47.

Stark, Rodney, and William Sims Bainbridge. 1980. "Networks of Faith: Interpersonal Bonds and Recruitment to Cults and Sects." *American Journal of Sociology* 85:1376–95.

"Statistical Report 1988." *The Ensign* 18 (May 1988):20.

Stein, Edward V. 1968. *Guilt: Theory and Therapy.* Philadelphia: Westminster Press.

Stone, Olive M. 1962. "Cultural Uses of Religious Visions: A Case Study." *Ethnology* 1:329–48.

Straus, Roger A. 1976. "Changing Oneself: Seekers and the Creative Transformation of Life Experience." *Doing Social Life.* Edited by John Lofland. New York: John Wiley and Sons.

———. 1979. "Religious Conversion as a Personal and Collective Accomplishment." *Sociological Analysis* 40:158–65.

———. 1981. "The Social Psychology of Religious Experience: A Naturalistic Approach." *Sociological Analysis* 41:57–67.

Stromberg, Peter G. 1985. "The Impression Point: Synthesis of Symbol and Self." *Ethos: Journal of the Society for Psychological Anthropology* 13:56–74.

———. 1981. "Consensus and Variation in the Interpretation of Religious Symbolism: A Swedish Example." *American Ethnologist* 8:544–59.

———. 1986. *Symbols of Community: The Cultural System of a Swedish Church.* Tucson: University of Arizona Press.

———. 1990. "Ideological Language in the Transformation of Identity." *American Anthropologist* 92:42–56.

Susumu, Shimazono. 1986. "Conversion Stories and Their Popularization in Japan's New Religions." *Japanese Journal of Religious Studies* 13:157–75.

Taylor, Brian. 1976. "Conversion and Cognition: An Area for Empirical Study in the Microsociology of Religious Knowledge." *Social Compass* 23:5–22.

———. 1978. "Recollection and Membership: Converts' Talk and the Ratiocination of Commonality." *Sociology* 12:316–24.

Taylor, John V. 1963. *The Primal Vision: Christian Presence amid African Religion.* London: SCM Press.

Thumma, Scott. 1991. "Seeking to be Converted: An Examination of Recent Conversion Studies and Theories." *Pastoral Psychology* 39:185–94.

Tiebout, Harry M. 1944. *Conversion as a Psychological Phenomenon.* New York: National Council on Alcoholism.

————. 1944. "Therapeutic Mechanisms of Alcoholics Anonymous." *American Journal of Psychiatry* 100:468–73.

————. 1946. "Psychological Factors Operating in Alcoholics Anonymous." *Current Therapies of Personality Disorders.* Edited by Bernard Glueck. New York: Grune and Stratton.

————. 1949. "The Act of Surrender in the Therapeutic Process, with Special Reference to Alcoholism." *Quarterly Journal of Studies on Alcohol* 10:48–58.

————. 1953. *Surrender versus Compliance in Therapy.* Center City, Minn.: Hazelden.

————. 1961. "Alcoholics Anonymous—An Experiment of Nature." *Quarterly Journal of Studies on Alcohol* 22:52–68.

————. 1963. "What Does 'Surrender' Mean?" *Grapevine* April: 19–23.

Tippett, Alan R. 1977. "Conversion as a Dynamic Process in Christian Mission." *Missiology* 2:203–21.

Tipton, Steven M. 1982. *Getting Saved from the Sixties: Moral Meaning in Conversion and Cultural Change.* Berkeley: University of California Press.

Travisano, Richard V. 1970. "Alternation and Conversion as Fundamentally Different Transformations." *Social Psychology through Symbolic Interaction.* Edited by Gregory P. Stone and Harvey A. Farberman. Waltham, Mass.: Ginn-Blaisdell.

Tremmel, William C. 1971. "The Converting Choice." *Journal for the Scientific Study of Religion* 10:17–25.

Turner, Harold W. 1978. "The Hidden Power of the Whites." *Archives de sciences sociales de religions* 46:41–55.

Turner, Paul R. 1979. "Religious Conversion and Community Development." *Journal for the Scientific Study of Religion* 18:252–60.

————. 1984. "Religious Conversion and Folk Catholicism." *Missiology* 12:111–21.

————. 1991. "Evaluating Religions." *Missiology* 19:131–42.

Turner, Victor W. 1969. *The Ritual Process: Structure and Anti-Structure.* Chicago: Aldine.

Ullman, Chana. 1982. "Cognitive and Emotional Antecedents of Religious Conversion." *Journal of Personality and Social Psychology* 43:183–92.

_____. 1988. "Psychological Well-Being among Converts in Traditional and Nontraditional Religious Groups." *Psychiatry* 51:312–22.

_____. 1989. *The Transformed Self: The Psychology of Religious Conversion.* New York: Plenum Press.

Vanauken, Sheldon. 1977. *A Severe Mercy.* San Francisco: Harper and Row.

Van Butselaar, G. Jan. 1981. "Christian Conversion in Rwanda: The Motivations." *International Bulletin of Missionary Research* 5:111–13.

Van Gennep, Arnold. 1960. *The Rites of Passage.* Translated by Monika B. Vizedom and Gabrielle L. Caffee. Chicago: University of Chicago Press.

Verhoeven, F. R. J. 1962. *Islam: Its Origins and Spread in Words, Maps, and Pictures.* New York: St. Martin's Press.

Von Laue, Theodore H. 1987. *The World Revolution of Westernization: The Twentieth Century in Global Perspective.* New York: Oxford University Press.

Wach, Joachim. 1962. "Master and Disciple." *Journal of Religion* 42:1–21.

Wallace, Anthony F. C. 1956. "Mazeway Resynthesis: A Biocultural Theory of Religious Inspiration." *Transactions of the New York Academy of Sciences,* 2d series, 18:626–38.

_____. 1956. "Revitalization Movements." *American Anthropologist* 58:264–81.

_____. 1957. "Mazeway Disintegration: The Individual's Perception of Socio-Cultural Disorganization." *Human Organization* 16:23–27.

Wallace, Ruth A. 1975. "A Model of Change of Religious Affiliation." *Journal for the Social Scientific Study of Religion* 14: 345–55.

Wallis, Jim. 1981. *The Call to Conversion.* San Francisco: Harper and Row.

Watt, W. Montgomery. 1979. "Conversion in Islam at the Time of the Prophet." *Journal of the American Academy of Religion Thematic Issue* 47:721–32.

Weininger, Benjamin. 1955. "The Interpersonal Factor in the Religious Experience." *Psychoanalysis* 3:27–44.

Weiss, Arnold S., and Richard H. Mendoza. 1990. "Effects of Acculturation into the Hare Krishna Movement on Mental Health and Personality." *Journal for the Scientific Study of Religion* 29:173–84.

Weiss, Robert F. "Defection from Social Movements and Subsequent Recruitment to New Movements." *Sociometry* 26:1–20.

Whaling, Frank. 1981. "A Comparative Religious Study of Missionary Transplantation in Buddhism, Christianity, and Islam." *International Review of Mission* 70:314–33.

————, ed. 1984. *The World's Religious Traditions: Current Perspectives in Religious Studies.* New York: Crossroad.

————, ed. 1987. *Religion in Today's World: The Religious Situation of the World from 1945 to the Present Day.* Edinburgh: T. and T. Clark.

Whitehead, Harriet. 1987. *Renunciation and Reform: A Study of Conversion in an American Sect.* Ithaca, N.Y.: Cornell University Press.

Wilber, Ken. 1980. "The Pre/Trans Fallacy." *ReVISION* 3:51–72.

Wilson, Bryan. 1966. *Religion and Secular Society.* Harmondsworth, U.K.: Penguin Books.

————. 1976. *Contemporary Transformations of Religion.* London: Oxford University Press.

Wilson, Stephen R. 1982. "In Pursuit of Energy: Spiritual Growth in a Yoga Ashram." *Journal of Humanistic Psychology* 22:43–55.

————. 1984. "Becoming a Yogi: Resocialization and Deconditioning as Conversion Processes." *Sociological Analysis* 45:301–14.

Wimberly, Edward P., and Anne Streaty Wimberly. 1986. *Liberation and Human Wholeness: The Conversion Experiences of Black People in Slavery and Freedom.* Nashville: Abingdon Press.

Wimberley, Ronald C., et al. 1975. "Conversion in a Billy Graham Crusade: Spontaneous Event or Ritual Performance?" *The Sociological Quarterly* 16:162–70.

Wolf, Eric R. 1982. *Europe and the People without History.* Berkeley: University of California Press.

Wright, Stuart A. 1987. *Leaving Cults: The Dynamics of Defection.* Washington, D.C.: Society for the Scientific Study of Religion.

Wulff, David M. 1991. *Psychology of Religion: Classic and Contemporary Views.* New York: John Wiley and Sons.

Yamamori, Tetsunao. 1974. *Church Growth in Japan*. South Pasadena, Calif.: William Carey Library.

Yeakley, Flavil Ray, Jr. 1975. "Persuasion in Religious Conversion." Ph.D. diss., University of Illinois, Urbana.

_____. 1979. *Why Churches Grow*. 3d ed. Broken Arrow, Okla.: Christian Communications.

Yearley, Lee. 1985. "Teachers and Saviors." *Journal of Religion* 65:225–43.

Zaleski, Carol. 1987. *Otherworld Journeys: Accounts of Near-Death Experience in Medieval and Modern Times*. New York: Oxford University Press.

Zelliot, Eleanor. 1966. "Background on the Mahar Buddhist Conversion." *Studies on Asia 1966*. Edited by Robert K. Sakai. Lincoln: University of Nebraska Press.

_____. 1966. "Buddhism and Politics in Maharashtra." *South Asian Politics and Religion*. Edited by Donald E. Smith. Princeton: Princeton University Press.

_____. 1968. "The Revival of Buddhism in India." *Asia* 10:33–45.

Zetterberg, Hans L. 1952. "Religious Conversion and Social Roles." *Sociology and Social Research* 36:159–66.

Ziller, Robert C. 1971. "A Helical Theory of Personal Change." *Journal for the Theory of Social Behavior* 1:33–73.

Zurcher, E. 1962. *Buddhism: Its Origin and Spread in Words, Maps, and Pictures*. London: Routledge and Kegan Paul.

Index